The Arts and Play as Educational Media in the Digital Age

Lance Strate
General Editor
Vol. 5

The Understanding Media Ecology series is part
of the Peter Lang Media and Communication list.
Every volume is peer reviewed and meets
the highest quality standards for content and production.

PETER LANG
New York • Bern • Berlin
Brussels • Vienna • Oxford • Warsaw

Robert Albrecht and Carmine Tabone

The Arts and Play as Educational Media in the Digital Age

PETER LANG
New York • Bern • Berlin
Brussels • Vienna • Oxford • Warsaw

Library of Congress Cataloging-in-Publication Data
Names: Albrecht, Robert, author. | Tabone, Carmine, author.
Title: The arts and play as educational media in the digital age /
Robert Albrecht and Carmine Tabone.
Description: New York: Peter Lang, 2020.
Series: Understanding media ecology; vol. 5
ISSN 2374-7676 (print) | ISSN 2374-7684 (online)
Includes bibliographical references and index.
Identifiers: LCCN 2019046998 (print) | LCCN 2019046999 (ebook)
ISBN 978-1-4331-5425-6 (hardback: alk. paper)
ISBN 978-1-4331-5426-3 (paperback: alk. paper) | ISBN 978-1-4331-5427-0 (ebook pdf)
ISBN 978-1-4331-5428-7 (epub) | ISBN 978-1-4331-5429-4 (mobi)
Subjects: LCSH: Arts—Study and teaching. | Arts—Study and teaching—New
Jersey—Jersey City—Case studies. | Active learning—New Jersey—Jersey
City—Case studies. | Experiential learning—New Jersey—Jersey
City—Case studies. | Arts and children. | Technology and children. |
Digital media—Social aspects.
Classification: LCC NX282.A53 2020 (print) | LCC NX282 (ebook) |
DDC 700.71—dc23
LC record available at https://lccn.loc.gov/2019046998
LC ebook record available at https://lccn.loc.gov/2019046999
DOI 10.3726/b16402

Bibliographic information published by **Die Deutsche Nationalbibliothek**.
Die Deutsche Nationalbibliothek lists this publication in the "Deutsche
Nationalbibliografie"; detailed bibliographic data are available
on the Internet at http://dnb.d-nb.de/.

The paper in this book meets the guidelines for permanence and durability
of the Committee on Production Guidelines for Book Longevity
of the Council of Library Resources.

© 2020 Peter Lang Publishing, Inc., New York
29 Broadway, 18th floor, New York, NY 10006
www.peterlang.com

All rights reserved.
Reprint or reproduction, even partially, in all forms such as microfilm,
xerography, microfiche, microcard, and offset strictly prohibited.

Printed in the United States of America

For teachers in classrooms all around the world
who struggle each day of their lives to create a better future
for their students and their societies

Table of Contents

Prologue ix

Introduction: When Change Changed 1

Part One: The Digital Storm
Chapter One: A Descent into the Maelström: The Digital Environment of Childhood 7
Chapter Two: The Faustian Dilemma: The Unintended Consequences of Digital Media 23
Chapter Three: Building Noah's Arks: Media Environments and Counterenvironments 45
Chapter Four: The Man Who Had No Story: Why the Arts in Education Matter 63

Part Two: Teaching as a Creative Activity
Chapter Five: The Oral Curriculum: A Prelude to Literacy and Learning 85
Chapter Six: Building a Bridge to Literacy: Drama in Education as a Pedagogical Method 115

Chapter Seven: The Seesaw Principle: Summer Camp as
    Counterenvironment   137

Epilogue   161
Index   165

Prologue

This book marks the meeting of two different worlds. One world lives in the academy and conducts scholarship, publishes articles and presents papers at conferences. Its ranks include luminaries such as Elizabeth Eisenstein, Walter Ong, Lewis Mumford, Eric Havelock, Neil Postman and Marshall McLuhan. The other world lives in the primary school classroom and uses the arts and play as a way of transforming the educational environment of children. This world is populated with anonymous teachers who go to work each morning and attempt to guide young people in the difficult processes of learning. One world represents a field of inquiry that demands we ask the big questions; the other is a method of teaching that uses the arts to inspire children to write well and read closely. One of these worlds is called "media ecology"; the other is called "the educational arts." Both are deeply concerned with the dramatic consequences of the electronic media revolution. They need to talk to each other. That's what this book is about.

For those unfamiliar with the term, media ecology is an approach to the study of human communication that aims to make us more aware and more critical of the technologies that form our environment and socialize our patterns of thought, feeling and interaction. These techniques and technologies—the human tool kit—mediate not only our relationships with the natural world that surrounds us but also transform how we think, feel, perceive and interact with others. A person growing up in the days of the horse and buggy would necessarily experience and conceptualize home, work, distance, time, family, community, nature and leisure much differently than someone growing up in the days of the automobile and jet air travel. As the technological environment that envelopes our lives changes, everything we assume, experience and think is also transformed. The point stressed by media ecology is that technologies are never neutral: they are active and transforming experiences.

In this book, we will be combining the insights uncovered by media ecology with an approach to teaching known as the "educational arts." For those unacquainted with the term, the educational arts build upon a child's natural tendency to sing, dance, draw, paint, imagine and play. From a pedagogical perspective, these modalities of expression can be transformed into opportunities for social, emotional and academic learning. At a time when children are increasingly exposed to electronic forms of media, changes in the technological environment have had profound consequences on the ways in which children are socialized and educated. As educators, we need to ask how this has impacted our pedagogical mission and how we should respond in a way that affirms our humanity and that of our pupils.

Prominent media ecologists such as Marshall McLuhan and Neil Postman were well aware of this problem and urged the creation of spaces—psychological as well as physical and social—they called "counterenvironments." Counterenvironments would include exposure to the arts, literature and the processes of critical questioning. Through the cultivation of counterenvironments, people are able to stand outside the dominant environment and, from this vantage point, examine more critically the nature of electronic technology, its biases and its societal consequences. It is our contention that tactile activities in the arts and play generate interpersonal experiences, forming counterenvironments that can help to balance and recalibrate the overwhelming influence of digital media in the lives of children.

The digital revolution we are now entering is an unchartered terrain pregnant with wondrous prospects but laden with a minefield of unforeseen consequences and dangers. A pedagogy that overlooks the disruptive and often negative influence of digital media on childhood development is necessarily a very shortsighted one. It is not fully responding in critical and creative ways to the new and powerful reality that is rapidly restructuring childhood socialization and education. It sees the possibilities but not the pitfalls. We also hold that a media ecology confined only to academic discourse does not fully serve its purpose or its promise. It has, in effect, reached a dead end. By combining the educational arts with media ecology, we hope to show that an exciting counterenvironment in the classroom is both effective and desirable. Media ecology and the educational arts are, in effect, different sides of the same coin.

***

Although our intent in writing this book is serious and scholarly, we wish to address the general reader more so than the academic. Parents, civic leaders, and citizens of all shapes and stripes need to articulate, debate and rationally analyze the emerging technological environment that surrounds and socializes us and our children. "Great events," observed the historian Samuel Hand (1984), "are great events because they deeply influence the lives of countless persons" (p. 53). This is certainly true of the digital revolution into which we have all been swept. The discussion needs to be wider than an academic dispute and deeper than a school-board squabble. We all have a stake in the outcome and we all need to be a part of the conversation.

Most especially, however, this book is directed to teachers and teachers-to-be. These are the ones who will spend a substantial part of their lives engaged with children and who must struggle on a daily basis with the fallout that we are all experiencing as a result of digital disruption. Rather than speak to teachers through the tired metaphors of war that are commonly invoked—"in the trenches," "on the frontline," "above and beyond the call of duty"—we wish to address them as artists and creative innovators. Being a teacher is like no other job. It is a calling, an inclination, a vocation. In countless situations, filled with frustrating setbacks, moments of self-doubt, and flashes of grand elation, teachers are routinely called on to reach down into their souls in search of ingenious means to open the hearts and minds of children. In the end, more than anything else, teaching is a creative activity.

We do not come to this assessment of childhood education lightly but only after 40 years of work with young people in classrooms, day camps, housing projects, libraries, church basements and community centers. Our work is also informed by years of study, both in education and in the field of media ecology. Carmine Tabone, who holds advanced degrees in education from New York University and Seton Hall, first discovered the pedagogical power of the arts in his early work with inner city children on the Lower East Side of Manhattan. He reasoned if children are instinctively drawn to the arts, why not develop a pedagogy that builds upon this attraction rather than ignore or downplay it? Seizing an opportunity for innovation, Tabone founded the Educational Arts Team in Jersey City in 1974 as a vehicle to teach various subjects through the arts. From the very outset, Carmine conceptualized his work with children as a team effort, that is, as a collaboration of artists and educators working together that would experiment, reflect and make adjustments based on their successes and failures.

Robert Albrecht became a part of the organization in 1982 while he was still working on his doctoral degree in the Media Ecology program at NYU under the tutelage of Neil Postman. In his research and in his publications, Albrecht has consistently focused on the relationship of the arts and play to everyday life and the ways in which technologies have altered the nature of that relationship. As a musician, Albrecht became acutely aware of how active participation in music through singing, movement and dance changed the moods, attitudes and social interactions of children. A song is not merely a sonic object or a collection of notes and lyrics but an environment that in all cultures and in all historical periods is, at once, profoundly social, psychological and physiological. Commenting upon his fieldwork among the Venda people in South Africa, the eminent ethnomusicologist John Blacking (1973) quite accurately describes music as "an intricate part of the development of mind, body, and harmonious social relationships" (pp. xi–xii). In short, music, quite literally, *moves* people.

The ideas and experiences of both authors are intertwined throughout this book just as they have been in their four decades of work together with children in Jersey City. The resulting collaboration should be understood as part of a much wider group effort that includes contributions by current and past team members: Roxanne Arrojo, Danny Bacher, Josh Bacher, Dina Bruno Ciborowski, Dominick Buccafusco, Alex Cassaro, Charlie Edmundson, Mary Graham Aiken, Sobha Kavanakudiyil, Dani Kopoulos, Peter LaBrusciano, Samantha Llanes, Teresa Lyon, Abbey Weathers, Lorenzo Veguilla and many others too numerous to mention. Each person brings something unique to the environment of learning; each one is part of a collaboration that transforms what a child experiences. Bob would also like to acknowledge his colleagues and students at New Jersey City University whose comments and criticisms have helped develop and fine tune the argument outlined in these pages.

This educational arts-media ecology approach has been stitched together from a variety of influences. From the world of educational drama, we would like to acknowledge the work of Gavin Bolton, Cecily O'Neill, Brian Edmiston, Gus Weltsek, Lowell and Nancy Swortzell, and Nellie McCaslin. In particular, we wish to thank Dorothy Heathcote, the founder of educational drama, whose pioneering work with children in England is of particular importance in our work with children.

From the world of media ecology, we are grateful to teachers such as Christine Nystrom, Terence Moran and Henry Perkinson whose ideas, generosity and clarity helped to form a whole generation of scholars now known as the New York School of Media Ecology. Most especially, we must acknowledge the inspirational role played by Neil Postman whose influence can be felt throughout this book. In fact, much of what we have to say can best be understood as an extension of his ideas into the digital age. Postman was that unusual scholar who was "bilingual," that is, fluent in both the language of education and the language of media criticism. He spoke with an eloquence, lucidity and a sense of conviction that is far too often absent in academic writing. Our special thanks as well to Lance Strate, a longtime colleague and the editor of this series, who has taken up the torch of media ecology after the untimely death of Neil in 2003.

Finally, we wish to acknowledge the contributions of our wives Patricia Charnay and Laura Blauvelt. Living with an accomplished artist for nearly half a century has helped Bob to understand the world in aesthetic terms and experience ways of being that are "outside the box," that is, within a counterenvironment that continually questions, evaluates and responds critically to cultural change. Laura, with advanced degrees in public administration and social work, has helped Carmine sharpen his insights into social development and group dynamics. Without a heightened appreciation of aesthetics and the never-ending challenge of group dynamics, our work with children would have suffered enormously and this book would not have been possible.

References

Blacking, J. (1973). *How musical is man?* Seattle: University of Washington Press.
Hand, S. (1984). Some words on oral histories. In D. Dunaway & W. Baum (Eds.), *Oral history: An interdisciplinary anthology* (pp. 51–63). Nashville: American Association for State and Local History.

Introduction

When Change Changed

> Change isn't new; what is new is the degree of change ...
>
> Change changed.
>
> Neil Postman and Charles Weingartner[1]

STOP! GO NO FURTHER!

If you are at home, look around the room where you are sitting. How far are you from your cellphone, your laptop, your desktop, your television? How long will it be before this moment is interrupted by one of these digital technologies? Can you make it through a week, or a day, or even the next minute, without using a digital device?

Oops ... Someone is text messaging you now.

If you are not at home but in a public space, put the book down. Once again, look around. To your left, there is a couple walking by, staring intently at screens that they hold in their hands. To your right, someone is pushing a stroller and talking on a cellphone. Sitting on the bench next to yours, a small boy is playing a video game while his sister is listening to music through her ear pods. Mom is scrolling through posts on her Facebook page, the baby in the carriage is playing with a digital screen it grasps clumsily in its hands. Across the way, a young man is gesturing animatedly and appears to be talking to himself. Who is he yelling at?

Oops ... Someone is calling you now.

This is not a dream, nor a fantasy, nor a lost episode of the *Twilight Zone*. It is real, you are here, and we are all very much a part of it. In fact, no one can leave. We have just crossed over into a new dimension. With a speed that astounds, digital media have taken center stage in our lives. Never in human history have we experienced anything of this same reach, magnitude or proportion. Speech took millennia to evolve, writing centuries, print decades, but the digital revolution—the most powerful and fullest extension of electronic media—is growing by leaps and bounds that can be measured in hours and minutes. Wherever we look, it is there staring us in the face. Wherever we go, it is there waiting for us. The future is here and it is changing us on a daily basis. Who in their right mind can keep up with this pace? Who in their right mind would want to?

The results of these changes are most disturbingly evident in the lives of children. Having had little time or opportunity to absorb the complexities of oral and literate forms of communication, children are easily fascinated and even mesmerized by the hyperkinetic speed, convenience and amusements of the digital novelties which have surrounded them since birth. There is little in their daily lives that balances the relentless intrusion of the digital into their processes of socialization. No doubt, there are multiple benefits to be had from the digital deluge but it is also difficult to deny that such a powerful and transformative force doesn't call out for more attention, reflection and debate. It is the point of view of this book that we should be taking these environmental transformations more seriously than we have. Not to do so is to vacate our obligations as teachers, parents and responsible adults.

More than just highlight our misgivings about digital media, however, this book has a purpose far more ambitious and infinitely more useful. In the pages that follow, we will be proposing a pedagogical strategy that seeks to offset and counterbalance the dominance of digital media in the lives of children. Rather than call for the elimination of such media—clearly an impossibility even if it were desirable—we will be maintaining that children need to be exposed to non-digital, non-electronic experiences that cultivate alternative ways of thinking, feeling, and being in the world. In the pages that follow, we ask the reader to keep an open mind. We are not calling for an end to the digital, but we are only asking readers to consider the urgent need to establish a balance.

An Overview of the Book

The Arts and Play as Educational Media in the Digital Age is divided into two parts. Part One outlines the theoretical and intellectual underpinnings of a pedagogical strategy that is arts focused and biased towards social forms of interaction.

In Chapter One, "A Descent into the Maelström: The Digital Environment of Childhood," we will survey the influence of digital technologies in the lives of children. In Chapter Two, "The Faustian Dilemma: The Unintended Consequences of Digital Media," we review some of the alarming effects that digital technologies are having upon the socialization and education of children. In Chapter Three, "Building Noah's Arks: Media Environments and Counterenvironments," we explore the often ignored significance of what Marshall McLuhan described as "counterenvironments" or "anti-environments." In Chapter Four, "The Man Who Had No Story: Why the Arts in Education Matter," we explain why hands-on experiences in the arts are essential to the academic, social and psychological development of children.

In Part Two, we turn to more practical considerations and describe some of the activities and programs we have cultivated over the years in our work with children in low performing schools in Jersey City. In Chapter Five, "The Oral Curriculum: A Prelude to Literacy and Learning," we make the case for the inclusion of pedagogical practices that value and actively promote interpersonal experiences as the basic foundation for the education and socialization of children. In Chapter Six, "Drama in Education as a Pedagogical Method," we outline in detail how drama can be used in the classroom as a highly effective way of teaching literacy. In Chapter Seven, "The Seesaw Principle: Summer Camp as Counterenvironment," we reflect on the changing role of play within the lives of children and advocate for the establishment of spaces—counterenvironments—during the summer months where children can run, garden, play games, spontaneously associate with others, and have ample exposure to the full range of recreation and the arts.

Conclusion

We must acknowledge that we have crossed into a new age of awesome potential and unprecedented dangers. The challenges before us are larger than any one teacher can possibly solve, greater than any one parent can conceivably handle. It will be the thesis of this book that the educational arts, combined with the insights and understandings uncovered by media ecology, provides a powerful tool that can help to reshape and rebalance the communication environment in which children are socialized, educated and brought to maturity. In the pages and chapters that follow, we will attempt to demonstrate why this is so and describe some of the strategies we have developed in our own work with children.

A digital future is perhaps inevitable, but our response to it is not. Human beings do not need to be helpless captives of the tools they create. We can, in the words of Danilo Dolci (1968), "*inventare il futuro*," that is, "invent the future."

The "change changed" warning pronounced by Postman and Weingartner some 50 years ago demands a contemporary and efficacious response. The next few years will require clear thinking and imaginative responses from the best minds and hearts in our society. Hopefully, this book will be a small part of that conversation.

***

Sit down. Turn off your cellphone. We need to talk.

Note

1. Neil Postman and Charles Weingartner (1969), *Teaching as a Subversive Activity*, pp. 10–11. New York: Delta.

Reference

Dolci, D. (1968). *Inventare il futuro*. Bari, Italy: Laterza.

PART ONE

The Digital Storm

CHAPTER ONE

A Descent into the Maelström

The Digital Environment of Childhood

Suddenly—very suddenly—this assumed a distinct and definite existence,
in a circle more than a mile in diameter.

Edgar Allan Poe[1]

In Edgar Allan Poe's tale "A Descent into the Maelström," a weary old fisherman recounts the terrifying day that he and his brothers were trapped in an enormous whirlpool. "It was a smooth, shining, and jet-black wall of water ... speeding dizzily round and round with a swaying and sweltering motion, and sending forth to the winds an appalling voice, half shriek, half roar, such as not even the mighty cataract of Niagara ever lifts up in its agony to Heaven." While the wailing maelström sent forth its "appalling voice," the fisherman's schooner and both his brothers were swallowed by the swirling sea. The fisherman who survived to tell the tale was only able to do so by carefully observing the movement of other objects—"fragments of vessels, large masses of building-timber and trunks of trees, with many smaller articles"—similarly pinned to the centrifugal walls of the watery abyss.

In this monstrous maelström imagined by Edgar Allan Poe, Marshall McLuhan (1951) found a metaphor for the technological environment in which we currently find ourselves. Like the old fisherman in the story, we are trapped in a perilous situation that spins at an "amazing velocity." And yet, McLuhan suggests, we may devise an escape if we carefully observe the movement of the objects and events that swirl around us. Strate (2014) draws out the analogy noted by McLuhan:

> In confronting the whirlpool, we find ourselves facing an overwhelming force of nature, and this is how our media and technology appear to us at first glance, as an irresistible force that is beyond our control, that leaves us helpless to do anything except surrender to its imperatives. But McLuhan argued that there is a way out, and that begins with objective observation of the phenomenon and pattern recognition, with the application of a media ecology approach to develop strategies for survival. (p. 136)

Neil Postman was also acutely aware of the enormous pull of the electronic revolution that was rapidly growing in size and strength. Without more attention, our culture and all its institutions may well be amusing itself to death, distracted by an endless stream of entertainments. Postman (1985) compares our present situation to Las Vegas "as a metaphor of our national character and aspiration, its symbol a thirty-foot-high cardboard picture of a slot machine and a chorus girl. For Las Vegas is a city entirely devoted to the idea of entertainment, and as such proclaims the spirit of a culture in which all public discourse increasingly takes the form of entertainment" (p. 3).

Lance Strate (2014), a scholar of McLuhan and a student of Postman, proposes yet another metaphor that parallels the alarm of his predecessors:

> I want to suggest that the *tempest* serves as apt metaphor for our present situation. Insofar as *tempest* denotes a violent windstorm or rainstorm, it seems especially appropriate for the 21st century, as it relates to some of the most noticeable effects of the climate change brought on by our technology. More generally, being synonymous with disturbance, commotion, uproar, and tumult, *tempest* represents the turbulent nature of the electronic media environment as it has evolved via digital technologies, the Internet, the web, social media, and mobile devices. Wave after wave of changes to our modes of communication and interaction, our tools for thought and social action, have altered and continue to alter our societies and our cultures, as well as our psyches and our selves. As human beings, we are certainly well equipped to survive a passing storm, but it is far from clear whether we can build a sustainable way of life in the midst of permanent upheaval, be it natural or cultural. How are we to survive while keeping our humanity intact? That is the fundamental question raised by Postman, and by the field of inquiry he called media ecology. (p. 136)

In this chapter, we will begin by sketching out the magnitude of the digital maelström in which we find ourselves. It is important to know something of the dimensions of this revolution in order to better appreciate its transformative presence.

As our interest in this book is the education and socialization of children, we will give particular attention in describing the ways in which electronic media have entered and modified the environment of childhood. We will then proceed to contrast three pedagogical proposals that attempt to respond to the digital revolution which include those who embrace it (*technophiles*), those who see digital media as generally empowering but in need of critical reflection and intervention (*media literacy*), and those who advocate an approach that runs counter to the biases of digital media and seeks to balance its dominance through the cultivation of other forms of communication (*media ecology/educational arts*). Each one of these approaches is very much aware of the power and place of digital media in the lives of children. They sharply disagree, however, as to how to incorporate them into the curriculum and into the lives of children.

Measuring the Maelström

We live in a most peculiar time. In a matter of a few decades, the digital revolution has seized control of virtually every institution of modern life, fundamentally altering the ways in which we work, play, study, eat, shop, exercise and even sleep. Media ecologists from Mumford to McLuhan to Postman saw something like this coming, but one has to wonder, if even these visionaries would not have been shocked at the radical transformation we see all around us.

The first thing we need to acknowledge is the accelerating rate of change that has become commonplace. In an interview quoted by Sanderson and Macdonald (1989), Marshall McLuhan stated, "Today each of us lives several hundred years in a decade. How can people like us have something in common with their institutions?" (p. 138). Eric McLuhan (1998) later updated his father's concern by adding "innovations of incredible transforming power appear not every generation but every three or four years" (p. 186). How are we as a species to adjust to such continual disruptions in our patterns of thought, feeling and interaction and still remain sane?

Neil Postman, as well, repeatedly cautioned that the ascendancy of electronic media is currently overwhelming and displacing older forms of communication. Before we integrate digital technologies irreversibly into the education of young people and throughout the play world of childhood, Postman advised we should first examine the nature of these powerful media and weigh their consequences on society. If ever there was a time when we should "look before we leap," it is now.

A recent report published by the research group Nielsen (2019) reveals that American adults spend "10-and-a-half hours per day" with various forms of electronic media and that "increases in Internet connected devices and app/web smartphone usage that are gradually replacing time spent on other sources." This is a staggering statistic. The Nielsen findings suggest that our interactions with media now exceed the time most of us spend at work, play, with family, or even in sleep. This is really quite amazing. At the very least, we must come to understand that digital media are not just gadgets we've added to our pastime routines but events that have fundamentally transformed our lives.

The Nielsen findings are not alone. In a report prepared for the Pew Research Center, Andrew Perrin (2015) writes that "Nearly two-thirds of American adults (65%) use social networking sites, up from 7% when Pew Research Center began systematically tracking social media usage in 2005" (p. 2). Once again, we should note the speed and the size of this increase which represents an almost tenfold jump within a short span of just ten years.

These figures pale, however, in comparison to those of youth who are even more connected to social media. "Today," Perrin (2015) continues, "90% of young adults [18–29 years old] use social media, compared with 12% in 2005, a 78-percentage point increase" (p. 4). From a global perspective, Zephoria (2019), a digital marketing firm, published that "Worldwide, there are over 2.38 billion monthly active uses of Facebook," representing an eight percent increase in just one year from 2018. The proliferation of media quite clearly effects not only the United States but just as rapidly has become ubiquitous throughout the social milieu of the entire planet.

But social media are just a part of the online media experience. Statista (2019), a marketing firm, reports that "In 2018, the United States had close to 275 million internet users" and that "this figure is projected to grow to 310.1 million internet users in 2022." In other words, in a nation of 327 million, over 80% are connected via the internet. As was the case with social media, this rise in online use isn't limited to the United States. The United Nations (2018) recently announced that "for the first time, more than half of the world's population of nearly 8 billion will be using the internet by the end of 2018." Ofcom (2018), a British marketing research organization, adds that "Nearly nine in ten (88%) UK adults are online, and this is almost universal among those under 55 … Adult internet users spend a day a week online" (p. 5). While the consequences of this shift in the communication environment are far from clear, it is certain that the "global village," first imagined and announced by Marshall McLuhan more than a half century ago, is now up and running via the electronic web.

Children, sitting in the front seat on this digital roller coaster ride, are in a particularly vulnerable position. They are new to the world and have not yet developed literate habits of mind nor have they fully absorbed the interpersonal skills that might compete with or oppose the powerful pull of electronic amusements. Their world, since the day they were born, has largely been an electronic one. Today, the 800-pound gorilla sitting in a child's playpen may well be a handheld digital device placed there by a parent or a babysitter. Lapierre, Piotrowski, and Linebarger (2012) found that children under two are exposed to television for approximately 5.5 hours a day while Linebarger (2013) points out that "babies' exposure to screen media has intensified considerably since 1997" (p. 175). Earlier research by Rideout and Hamel (2006) pointed out that media corporations were actively targeting children under two who watch media specifically put on for them for about an hour and a half a day. As younger children are increasingly exposed to screen time through the use of parental cellphones, researchers are beginning to evaluate the impact of this on the preschooler. One such report cited by the American College of Pediatricians (2016) noted that in a study of "2200 mothers from 10 developed nations, including the United States and Canada, who had children between two and five years of age ... more of these preschool children could use technology than could demonstrate 'life skills' such as tying their shoes, riding a bike, or swimming. For example, 58 percent of the preschool children knew how to play a computer game versus only 9 percent who could tie their shoes" (p. 2).

More recently, Vega (2017) noted that Facebook has introduced an app specifically designed for children under six called "Messenger Kids" that "will allow children to exchange messages and photos with friends and family, as well as engage in video chats" (p. 7).

As children grow, their contact with media increases radically. In their study of media use among children in the United States, Roberts and Foehr (2004) noted that "over a quarter of 2- through 4-year olds have televisions" and that among 5- through 7-year olds, close to 40% have TV sets in their rooms (p. 192). "Media exposure," the authors continue, "begins quite early—average daily media exposure among 2- through 4-years old is well over 4 hours—and increases rapidly from the preschool years onward" (p. 193). As might be expected, these already high numbers have been escalating dramatically. In a 2013 study conducted by Common Sense Media, it was determined that "Seventy-two percent of children age 8 and under have used a mobile device for some type of media activity such as playing games, watching videos, or using apps ... In fact, today, 38 percent of children *under two* have used a mobile device for media" (p. 9). It would seem safe to assume that these percentages will only increase in the years to come as marketers and engineers devise more digital toys for tots and as parents and teachers become more deeply socialized and accommodating to the rhythms and patterns of the digital environment.

By the time children enter school, they have already become habitual users of digital technologies. Rideout, Foehr and Roberts (2010), in their survey of media use by young people from eight to 18, found that children were much more attached to electronic media in 2009 than they were just a decade earlier. In 1999, TV/video viewing measured 3:47 hours per day; in 2009, it registered 4:29 hours per day. Music listening went from 1:48 hours per day in 1999 to 2:31 hours per day in 2009. Computer use more than tripled from 27 minutes a day in 1999 to 1:48 hours per day in 2009. The use of video games more than quadrupled, multitasking nearly doubled and overall media use increased from 6:19 hours per day in 1999 to 7:38 hours per day in 2009. They also noted that text messaging, which was not counted in their study as media, registered an hour and a half per day. As a result, the total time that children are engaged in some form of electronic media is nearly nine hours per day, that is, more time than is spent in any other activity including sleep. Moreover, since many young people now sleep with their phones tucked under their pillows and their laptops on all night, even sleep is subject to frequent digital interruptions.

In a recent update "based on a national sample of more than 2,600 young people" (p. 5), Common Sense Media (2015) found that "American teenagers (13-to 18-year olds) now average about nine hours (8:56) of entertainment use, excluding time spent at school or for homework. Tweens (8-to 12-years old) use an average of about six hours' (5:55) worth of entertainment media daily" (p. 13). It would seem reasonable to assume that this increase in media use will continue into the foreseeable future not only here in the United States but elsewhere around the globe. Moreover, we can also safely assume that media will continue to grow in sophistication, availability, and variety of use.

Three Pedagogical Perspectives Responding to the Digital Revolution

Given the enormous exposure of young people to a rapidly changing media environment, it would seem prudent for us all to pause and consider how digital technologies are altering the socialization and education of children. At the moment, broadly speaking, there are three general positions that have evolved commenting upon the consequences of digital media in the education and socialization of children. The first position, the one that currently dominates the debate, argues that the benefits of digital media far outweigh the deficits. Because of their passionate advocacy for digital media, we shall call this group the "*technophiles*." From this point of view, digital technologies are creating new opportunities for learning that need to be explored, cultivated and expanded. Will there be setbacks and problems? Of course. But the potential gains of digitalia far exceed some inevitable losses.

A second position has evolved that is much more cautious in its approach to digital media use. While acknowledging both the pros and cons of media usage, they argue that children need to be taught how to use media much more critically and creatively. This group has come to be known as "*media literacy*" and it urges that children, teachers, parents, and citizens in general learn how to become less passive and more "proactive" in their use of media.

Yet a third position, the one that we will be advocating in this book, parallels much of the point of view of media literacy but takes a step further by proposing the construction of something it calls "counterenvironments." These counterenvironments consist of psychological, physical and/or social spaces *outside* the purview of digital media from which children and their teachers are more able to question and contest their dominance and reach. The perspective that we will be proposing, "*media ecology/educational arts*," represents a hybrid of the ideas of Marshall McLuhan and Neil Postman with pedagogical practices that cultivate the arts as educational tools rather than as content areas.

Technophiles. For those who are enamored of digital technologies and captivated by their amazing possibilities, the response is as easy as it is obvious. Go with it. Their argument is based on three assertions: (1) digital instruction is superior to traditional and outdated ways of learning which are bland, boring and ineffective by comparison; (2) since students are already accustomed and comfortable with digital media, the curriculum should seek to accommodate and cultivate their preferred mode of communicating; and (3) the job market demands digital competency and it is the responsibility of schools to prepare children for gainful employment in the future.

Books promoting variations of this point of view currently line the shelves of our libraries and dominate the discussion on school boards all across America. In reviewing the literature, one is immediately struck by the repeated use of the word "integration" in the titles of their books (Cennamo, Ross, & Ertmer, 2010; Mouza & Lavigne, 2013; Roblyer & Doering, 2013; Shelly, Cashman, Gunter, & Gunter, 2006) and the common desire for "full technology integration in the future" (Lavigne & Mouza, 2013, p. 285). For them, it's a foregone conclusion. If students prefer digital media and electronic screens to books, pens, and paper, then that's the way they should be taught. Roblyer and Doering (2013) write that their book *Integrating Technology into Teaching*, "offers a total technology integration package across all content areas that gives students practice with technology tools as they learn how to incorporate technology into the curriculum to support and shape learning" (p. xviii). Shelly et al. (2006) agree and urge teachers to discover ways of "integrating technology and digital media in your instructional strategies, lessons, student-based projects, and student assessments ... throughout the curriculum" (p. 2). Mouza and Lavigne (2013) add that "rapid advances in technology have revolutionized the way in which children learn, play, communicate, and socialize ... [Educators] can create effective learning environments that support student agency and serve as a bridge between learning in school and out-of-school settings" (pp. 1–2).

Technophiles also argue that with the use of digital technologies, teachers are able to meet students "where they live," that is, with technologies and modes of interaction with which they are comfortably acquainted. Cennamo et al. (2010), for example, direct their appeal to undergraduate students preparing to teach:

> Imagine yourself teaching a lesson to a classroom of students ... Would you use technology? ... If you are like many college students, computers, cellphones, and other digital tools are interfaces to your life. You communicate there. You think there. You create there. You take care of the day-to-day events of your life there. You are entertained, informed, stimulated, and soothed ... How will you integrate technology into your teaching practice? (p. 3)

Technophiles commonly argue that instruction in the multiple uses of digital technology will insure that students develop the competencies today that will be required in tomorrow's job market. Apparently, most parents agree with this assessment. A study by Lenhart, Rainie, and Lewis (2001) of 754 teenagers and their parents found that "most parents believe mastery of the Internet is important for their children's success and 55 percent say that the Internet has been a good thing for their children, especially when it comes to schoolwork. A scant six percent say it is a bad thing" (p. 3). Shelly et al. (2006) caution teachers that "traditional twentieth-century educational practices will no longer provide you with the necessary skills you need to teach your students effectively how to become productive citizens in today's high-tech, global workplace" (p. 2). Bitter and Legacy (2008) warn that educational institutions need to get onboard with the program or be left behind at the station:

> Many U.S. corporations have undergone a transformation to respond to the changes in the world marketplace and have installed state-of-the-art technology to make the workplace more efficient, economical and safe ... The enormous retraining costs cannot be incurred indefinitely solely by industry. Education must share the responsibility of developing technologically literate people, not only to help people maintain a standard of living but also to help people create a balanced life style. (p. 4)

What we find most disturbing about the position of the technophiles is its unreflective assurance. Technophiles are not just suggesting that digital media be used in the classroom but that it be integrated throughout the curriculum and beyond. There is a singularity of focus here that ignores problems, concerns, and even dangers, with an over-reliance on digital technology in the education and socialization of children. In our rush to adapt and adjust to the digital revolution, we may find that we are losing much more in the process than we realize or want to acknowledge. There are already multiple indications of behaviors that suggest we take a bit more caution before we proceed any further. We know, for example, that digital technology frequently becomes addictive, that it stimulates constant distraction, inhibits the ability to concentrate, and promotes a perpetual desire for immediate and easily attained gratification. We know as well that the digital often reduces the time spent in robust physical activity, erodes the reflective and focused state of mind necessary for the cultivation of literacy, and restructures and redefines the nature of social relationships. Even our very concept of self is being radically transformed.

Media Literacy. A more measured response to the rapid proliferation of electronic media is advocated by a second group loosely described as "*media literacy.*" Media literacy maintains that it is the responsibility of teachers and thinking adults to work with and adapt to electronic media but in a way fosters a greater social awareness. Hobbs (2013) comments on the dual mission of media literacy:

> Empowerment and protection have long been identified as the two overarching themes in the media literacy education community, reflecting a dynamic and generally productive tension between those who see media literacy education as a means to address the complexities and challenges of growing up in a media- and technology-saturated cultural environment and those who see media literacy as a tool for personal, social, cultural and political empowerment. (p. 417)

Media literacy, then, seeks to empower parents, teachers and children by advocating a greater awareness of some of the pitfalls of electronic media while finding uses that are safe, creative and beneficial. Scholars and educators such as Buckingham (2007), Burn and Duran (2007), Hobbs (2006), Jenkins (2009), Lemish, Liebes, and Seidmann (2001), Livingstone, Kjartan, Helsper, Lupianez-Villanueva, and Folkvord (2017), Livingstone and Bovill (1999), and many others argue that rather than condemn new technologies, we should carefully explore methods to use new media in positive ways. While acknowledging that internet use among young people presents substantial risks that "do warrant serious attention and intervention by government, educators, industry and parents," Livingstone and Bober (2005) conclude that "the risks do not merit a moral panic, and nor do they warrant seriously restricting children's internet use because this would be to deny them the many benefits of the internet" (p. 4). Kirkorian, Wartella, and Anderson (2008) agree, adding that although "electronic media, particularly television, have long been criticized for their potential impact on children," there are effective ways "for maximizing the positive effects of media and minimizing the negative effects" (p. 39).

Those sympathetic to media literacy emphasize that along with problems associated with electronic media, there are also many advantages. Lemish (2007) notes that although "there is a body of research that points out the possibility that there is a negative relationship between the amount of viewing television, combined with specific kind of television genres, and performance in schools, including literacy skills," there is also sufficient evidence to suggest that educational TV does have a positive effect (pp. 155, 179). Studies by Bogatz and Ball (1972) and by Rice, Huston, Truglio, and Wright (1990), for example, have demonstrated that regular exposure to the popular children's show *Sesame Street* "is associated with impressive gains in preschoolers' vocabularies and prereading skills as well" (Shaffer, 2000, p. 412). Educational gains have also been attributed to other educational TV programs such as *The Electric Company* (Ball & Bogatz, 1973), as well as *Science Court* and *Popular Mechanics for Kids* (Farhl, 1998).

Far from inhibiting creativity, they argue, electronic media may even be nourishing it. Paralleling findings of several other researchers (Anderson, Huston, Schmidt, Linebarger, & Wright, 2001; Calvert, Strong, Jacobs, & Conger, 2007; Valkenburg, 1999; Valkenburg & van der Voort, 1994; van der Voort & Valkenburg, 1994), Getz, Lemish, Aidman, and Moon (2005) argue that the make-believe worlds that children encounter in the media inspire the imagination. "In some instances a media setting serves as a springboard for a child's fantasy-world, providing space for his or her own drama to evolve" (p. 199). Drawing on the work of Lenhart and Madden (2007), Peppler (2013) points out that "longitudinal trends indicate that production practices are steadily on the rise" and that "39 percent of online teens electronically share original artist creations (such as artwork, photos, stories or videos) up from 33 percent in 2004, and one in four teens also report remixing content they found online into their own creations, up from 19 percent in 2004" (p. 193).

Even online gaming, the digital form that critics love to assail, may be having significant beneficial advantages. Griffiths (2010) notes that "in over two decades of examining both the possible dangers and the potential benefits of video game playing, evidence suggests that in the right context playing video games can have positive health and educational benefits for a large range of different sub-groups, such as those with autism and impulsive disorders" (p. 38). Like other advocates of media literacy, Griffiths advocates for more parental involvement and monitoring.

Those generally critical also point to some of the advantages of the new forms of media. A recent policy statement published by The American College of Pediatricians (2016) noted that:

While the limited use of high-quality and developmentally appropriate media may have a positive influence, excessive or developmentally inappropriate use carries grave health risks for children and their families. Excessive exposure to screens (television, tablets, smartphones, computers, and video game consoles), especially at early ages, has been associated with lower academic performance, increased sleep problems, obesity, behavior problems, increased aggression, lower self-esteem. depression, and increased high risk behaviors, including sexual activity at an earlier age. The American College of Pediatricians encourages parents to become media literate and limit all screen time for their children.(p. 1)

In sum, according to media literacy, while we should be attentive to some of the negative consequences of electronic forms of media, we should not be afraid to work with these technologies and make use of their multiple benefits.

Media literacy represents an important perspective in the digital age for it advocates a more cautious and critical use of media. But it is not sufficient for it underestimates the tremendous transformative powers of electronic media. Children not only need to learn how to use media but, more importantly, they need to learn how *not* to use them. By this we mean, children need to learn to be comfortable and conversant with forms of media that do not depend upon digital media and the kinds of experiences, behaviors and habits they cultivate. It's not only the abuses of electronic media that need to be addressed but the myriad of ways in which these technologies restructure society and redefine who we are.

Media Ecology/Educational Arts. In this book, we wish to address the "what do we do about it" question in yet a third way that combines media ecology with the educational arts. We agree with the technophile that digital media are amazingly useful and inevitable but we do not share their same unrestrained euphoria. Love is blind and the technophile's fascination with things digital leads him to see the beauty of his bride but not her blemishes. The dominant culture assumes, and expects us to assume, that the shift to digital technology is all for the best or, at least, inevitable. Any "glitches" in the dominant system will soon be addressed and offset by new technological advances. But there is a real problem here. If the dominant perspective is the only one we ever experience, it becomes extremely difficult to imagine other possibilities or to see the problem in a new light. How can we ever learn to think outside the box when all we've ever experienced was inside the box?

Media literacy is much more alert to the serious dangers we face but their response, like an umbrella in a hurricane, isn't sufficient. More needs to be done. We agree that digital media can empower young people and that children should learn to use them creatively, appropriately and competently. But a child who has not been sufficiently exposed to orality or to literacy is too easily overcome by the speed and the sparkle of the digital. It is dauntingly difficult to slow down and read effectively or interact with others in an attentive way when a child's primary form of socialization has been a hyperkinetic and an impersonal one.

In the maelström that engulfs us, a media ecology/educational arts approach proposes something very different. This perspective advocates the cultivation of counterenvironments not to eliminate electronic media but to provide alternative experiences that balance and moderate their influence. Given an environment dominated by digital interactions and experiences, media ecology/educational arts features interpersonal interactions and tactile experiences. This is not a radical proposal but common sense. Whereas digital media accelerate the movement of information, the media ecology/educational arts approach slows it down where it can be more carefully articulated, processed and discussed. Whereas digital media are screen biased experiences, media ecology/educational arts are characteristically conducted face-to-face. Whereas digital media are useful in finding answers, media ecology/educational arts are useful in generating questions. Whereas digital media work with screens, keyboards and apps, media ecology/educational arts work with pen and paper, paint brushes and crayons, drama and role play. It is our contention that by joining a media ecological approach with the educational arts, we can begin to create the necessary counterenvironments that embody and reinforce non-electronic ways of being. Barring these counterenvironments, we abandon our children to an unstable environment dominated by digital technologies.

In the second part of the book, we will elaborate in much more detail how these counterenvironments are organized in the classroom and in play spaces. By having the opportunity to stand outside of the digital mainstream and experience life on a regular basis through a different lens and mediated by a different set of relationships, children are exposed to alternative experiences that add a much needed equilibrium to their lives.

Conclusion

We live in a truly revolutionary time. Pick a metaphor—maelström, vaudeville show, tempest or something else—but the changes we are currently experiencing are perhaps as transformative and unsettling as was the invention of the alphabet, printing press, or even speech itself. The pivotal question for pedagogues becomes, "what do we do about it?" How do we respond? The technophile embraces it and casts caution to the wind. Media literacy suggests we learn to question and use media more creatively and intelligently. Media ecology/educational arts fashions a new pedagogy that seeks to balance the prodigious power of the digital with the use of the arts as a method of teaching.

Note

1. Edgar Allan Poe (1951), *A Descent into the Maelstrom*, p. 279. New York: Pocket Library.

References

American College of Pediatricians. (September 22, 2016). The impact of media use and screen time on children, adolescents, and families. November, 1–20. Retrieved from- https://www.acpeds.org/the-college-speaks/position-statements/parenting-issues/the-impact-of-media-use-and-screen-time-on-children-adolescents-and-families

Anderson, D. R., Huston, A. C., Schmidt, K., Linebarger, D., & Wright, J. C. (2001). Early childhood television viewing and adolescent behavior. *Monographs of the Society for Research in Child Development, 68* (1, Serial No. 264), 1–143.

Ball, S., & Bogatz, C. (1973). *Reading with television: An evaluation of The Electric Company*. Princeton, NJ: Educational Testing Service.

Bitter, G. G., & Legacy, J. M. (2008). *Using technology in the classroom*. New York: Pearson.

Bogatz, G. A., & Ball, S. (1972). *The second year of Sesame Street: A continuing evaluation*. Princeton, NJ: Educational Testing Service.

Buckingham, D. (2007). *Media education: Literacy, learning and contemporary culture*. Cambridge: Polity Press.

Burn, A., & Duran, J. (2007). *Media literacy in schools*. London: Sage.

Calvert, S. L., Strong, B. L., Jacobs, E. L., & Conger, E. E. (2007). Interaction and participation for young Hispanic and Caucasian children's learning of media content. *Media Psychology, 9*(2), 431–445.

Cennamo, K. S., Ross, J. D., & Ertmer, P. A. (2010). *Technology integration for meaningful classroom use: A standards-based approach*. Belmont, CA: Wadsworth.

Common Sense Media. (2013). *Zero to eight: Children's media use in America 2013*. New York: Common Sense Media.

Common Sense Media. (2015). *The common sense census: Media use by tweens and teens*. Retrieved from https://www.commonsensemedia.org/sites/default/files/uploads/research/census_researchreport.pdf

Farhl, P. (1998). "Educational" TV programs are flunking in viewership. *Athens Banner-Herald*, January 10, pp. A1, QA14.

Getz, M., Lemish, D., Aidman, A., & Moon, H. (2005). *Media and the make believe worlds of children: When Harry Potter meets Pokémon in Disneyland*. Kentucky: Lawrence Erlbaum Associates.

Griffiths, M. (2010). Online video gaming: What should educational psychologists know? *Educational Psychology in Practice, 26*(1), 35–40.

Hobbs, R. (2006). Multiple visions of multimedia literacy: Emerging areas of synthesis. In M. McKenna, L. Labbo, R. Kieffer, & D. Reinking (Eds.), *Handbook of literacy and technology*

(Vol. II, pp. 15–28). International Reading Association. Mahwah, NJ: Lawrence Erlbaum Associates

Hobbs, R. (2013). Media literacy. In D. Lemish (Ed.), *The Routledge international handbook of children, adolescents and media* (pp. 417–424). New York: Routledge.

Jenkins, H. (2009). *Confronting the challenges of participatory culture: Media education for the 21st century*. Cambridge, MA: The MIT Press.

Kirkorian, H. L., Wartella, E. A., & Anderson, D. R. (2008). Media and young children's learning. *The Future of Children, 18*(1), Spring, 39–61.

Lapierre, M., Piotrowski, J. T., & Linebarger, D. L. (2012, October). Background television in the homes of US children. *Pediatrics, 130*(5). doi: 10.1542/peds.2011-2581

Lavigne, N. C., & Mouza, C. (2013). Epilogue: Designing and integrating emerging technologies for learning, collaboration, reflection, and creativity. In C. Mouza & N.C. Lavigne (Eds.), *Emerging technologies for the classroom* (pp. 269–288). New York: Springer.

Lemish, D. (2007). *Children and television*. Malden, MA: Blackwell.

Lemish, D., Liebes, T., & Seidmann, V. (2001). Gendered media meanings and uses. In , S. Livingstone & M. Bovill (Eds.), *Children and their changing media environment: A European comparative study* (pp. 263–282). Mahwah, NJ: Lawrence Erlbaum.

Lenhart, A., & Madden, M. (2007). *Social networking websites and teens: An overview*. Washington, DC: Pew Internet and American Life Project.

Lenhart, A., Rainie, L., & Lewis, O. (2001). *Teenage life online: The rise of the instant message generation and the internet's impact on friendships and family relationships*. Washington, DC: Pew Internet and American Life Project.

Linebarger, D. L. (2013). Screen media, early cognitive development, and language: Babies learning from screens. In D. Lemish (Ed.), *The Routledge international handbook of children, adolescents and media* (pp. 171–178). New York: Routledge.

Livingstone, S., & Bober, M. (2005). *UK children go online: Final report of key project findings*. London: London School of Economics and Political Science.

Livingstone, S., & Bovill, M. (1999). *Children young people and the changing media environment*. London: Department of Media and Communications, London School of Economics and Political Science.

Livingstone, S., Kjartan, O., Helsper, E. J., Lupianez-Villanueva, F., & Folkvord, F. (2017). Maximizing opportunities and minimizing risks for children online: The role of digital skills in emerging strategies of parental mediation. *Journal of Communication, 67*(1), 82–105.

McLuhan, E. (1998). *Electric language: Understanding the present*. Toronto: Stoddart.

McLuhan, M. (1951). *The mechanical bride: Folklore of industrial man*. New York: Vintage.

Mouza, C., & Lavigne, N. C. (2013). Introduction to emerging technologies for the classroom: A learning sciences perspective. In C. Mouza & N.C. Lavigne (Eds.), *Emerging technologies for the classroom* (pp. 1–14). New York: Springer.

Nielsen. (2019). The Nielsen total audience report: Q3 2018. Retrieved from https://www.nielsen.com/us/en/insights/reports/2019/q3-2018-total-audience-report.html

Ofcom. (2018, April 25). *Adults media use and attitudes report*. Retrieved from https://www.ofcom.org.uk/__data/assets/pdf_file/0011/113222/Adults-Media-Use-and-Attitudes-Report-2018.pdf

Peppler, K. (2013). Social media and creativity. In D. Lemish (Ed.), *The Routledge international handbook of children, adolescents and media* (pp. 193–200). New York: Routledge.

Perrin, A. (2015, October 8). *Social media usage: 2005–2015.*. Retrieved from https://www.secretintelligenceservice.org/wp-content/uploads/2016/02/PI_2015-10-08_Social-Networking-Usage-2005-2015_FINAL.pdf

Postman, N. (1985). *Amusing ourselves to death*. New York: Penguin Books.

Rice, M. L., Huston, A. C., Truglio, R., & Wright, J. (1990). Words from "Sesame Street": Learning vocabulary while viewing. *Developmental Psychology, 26,* 421–428.

Rideout, V. J., Foehr, U. G., & Roberts, D. F. (2010). *Generation M2: Media in the lives of 8-18 year-olds*. Menlo Park, CA: The Henry J. Kaiser Family Foundation.

Rideout, V. J., & Hamel, E. (2006). *The media family: Electronic media in the lives of infants, toddlers, preschoolers and their parents*. Menlo Park, CA: Kaiser Family Foundation.

Roberts, D. F., & Foehr, U. G. (2004). *Kid and media in America*. NY: Cambridge University Press.

Roblyer, M. D., & Doering, A. H. (2013). *Integrating educational technology into teaching*. Boston, MA: Pearson.

Sanderson, G., & Macdonald, F. (1989). *Marshall McLuhan: The man and his message*. Golden, CO: Fulcrum.

Shaffer, D. (2000). *Social and personality development*. Belmont, CA: Wadsworth/Thompson Learning.

Shelly, G. B., Cashman, T. J., Gunter, G. A., & Gunter, R. E. (2006). *Integrating technology and digital media in the classroom*. Boston, MA: Thomsen.

Statista. (2019). *Number of internet users in the United States from 2017 to 2023 (in millions)*. Retrieved from https://www.statista.com/statistics/325645/usa-number-of-internet-users/

Strate, L. (2014). *Amazing ourselves to death: Neil Postman's brave new world revisited*. New York: Peter Lang.

United Nations. (2018, December 8). Internet milestone reached, as more than 50 per cent go online: UN telecoms agency. *UN News*. Retrieved from https://news.un.org/en/story/2018/12/1027991

Valkenburg, P. M. (1999). Television and creative imagination. In M. Runco & S. Pritzker (Eds.), *Encyclopedia of creativity* (Vol. 1, pp. 651–658). San Diego: Academic Press.

Valkenburg, P. M., & van der Voort, T. H. A. (1994). Influence of TV on daydreaming and creative imagination: A review of research. *Psychological Bulletin, 116,* 316–339.

van der Voort, T. H. A., & Valkenburg, P. M. (1994). Television's impact on fantasy play: A review of research. *Developmental Review, 14,* 27–51.

Vega, N. (2017, December 15). Look, ma! Now kids can text: Facebook's chat app for children. *New York Post*, p. 7.

Zephoria. (2019, April 2019). *The top 20 valuable Facebook statistics—Updated*. Retrieved from https://zephoria.com/top-15-valuable-facebook-statistics/

CHAPTER TWO

The Faustian Dilemma

The Unintended Consequences of Digital Media

About the time that Columbus was first stepping foot in the Americas, people in Germany were telling a strange tale about a disgruntled scholar who had sold his soul to the devil in exchange for bodily pleasures and boundless knowledge. As part of the oral culture of the time, there were multiple versions of the Faust story. In some accounts, the repentant scholar was able to redeem his soul and save himself from eternal damnation. In others, he could not and is promptly dragged into hell at the end of the time agreed to (usually twenty-four years) in the ill-fated bargain.

Within a few decades of the invention of the printing press, several chapbook versions were circulated on the streets of Frankfurt and in other German towns. Soon Christopher Marlowe (c. 1604) and then Goethe (1808) reimagined the story as theater, Berlioz (1846) made into an opera, Wagner (1840s) an overture, Perrot (1848) a ballet, Liszt (1857) a symphony, Murnau (1926) a movie, Benet (1937) a short story, Mann (1947) a novel, and Chespirito (1994) a television comedy. In the 1960s, Rod Serling often presented Faust-like characters in his *Twilight Zone* series and, in 2004, David Mamet put Faust back on stage. We are even told that there are multiple online video games based on some version of the Faust character.

Media critic and educator Neil Postman employed the story as a metaphor to question the power and presence of electronic media—most especially television—in modern life. "All technological change," Postman (1995) wrote, "is a Faustian bargain. For every advantage a new technology offers, there is always a corresponding disadvantage" (p. 192). This may seem to be a rather obvious point but, if followed through to its logical conclusion, the observation leads to some provocative discoveries. Technology, Postman constantly reminded his readers, not only giveth; it also taketh. Certainly electronic media have bestowed enormous gifts upon humankind, but we must also ask "at what price?"

Digital media, the most recent extension of the electronic revolution, has greatly expanded the reach of television and other technologies while filling our lives with new wonders never dreamed of just a few years before. Postman prods us to ask, therefore, what parts of our humanity and our culture are we exchanging for the advantages of digital technology? Postman pushes us to examine not only "what does a technology do?" but more importantly, "what will it undo?" All technologies come to us as double-edged swords. "The greater the wonders of a technology, the greater will be its negative consequences. You need only think of the automobile, which for all its obvious advantages, has poisoned our air, choked our cities and degraded the beauty of our natural landscape" (Postman, 1992, p. 8).

It is difficult for many us to fathom or see clearly the scope of this dramatic change. McLuhan (1967) maintained that we view the present through a "rear-view mirror," that is, we continue to see the present as if it were still the past. "When faced with a totally new situation, we tend always to attach ourselves to the objects, to the flavor of the most recent past. We look at the present through a rear-view mirror. We march backwards into the future" (pp. 74–75).

Adults, sometimes referred to as "digital immigrants," grew up within a mixed media environment where electronic media were meshed in with powerful oral and literate institutions and forms of communication. Electronic media were not the core of their reality, only a component of it. Young people, however, are different. They are "digital natives" currently maturing within a world where digital media dominates their lives and both oral and literate forms of communication are on the wane. Because of the digital environment that has surrounded them since birth, children have had less of an opportunity to engage in spontaneous face-to-face interactions, continuous physical movement and the negotiation of rules and procedures that are not organized, supervised or regulated by adult intervention. More and more, the interactions of childhood have become disembodied, stationary and mediated by screens. To be sure, a video game is still a form of play and Facebook chat is still a form of social interaction, but these experiences are of an entirely different order and character than were traditional oral forms of socializing.

In this chapter, we will be pushing the pause button for just a moment and making an effort to outline some of the problems engendered by this sudden leap to the digital. It would seem prudent at this time to stop, think and ponder before racing blindly into a future where the digital environment has become the single most powerful influence in the education and socialization of our children. Unquestionably, there are enormous benefits to the digital but, in the end, like the mythical Dr. Faust that Postman cautioned us about, we may be giving up more than what we thought we bargained for.

Although we are still in the incunabula of the digital age, a whole host of problems are already quite apparent:

(1) *Digital Addiction*. Clinicians, scholars, and the layperson have arrived at a general consensus that dependence upon digital media is a serious concern. But is it accurate to describe this dependence as an "addiction" or is it only a question of technology overuse? Certainly the word "addiction" is commonly used when lay people are asked about the issue. A recent survey sponsored by Common Sense Media (2018) found that nearly half of the parents polled believe their children were "addicted" to their mobile devices. In her ethnography of teenage girls and their use of social media, Nancy Sales (2016) writes that "the words 'addicted' and 'addiction,' and 'obsessed' and 'obsessing,' came up again and again in my interviews with more than 200 teenage girls as they talked about their use of their smartphones and consuming media and using social media" (p. 10).

But are digital media actually addictive or are we speaking in metaphors and hyperbole that exaggerate their dangers? "Among researchers," Sales (2016) continues, "the jury's still out on whether social media addiction is truly an addiction in the way of dependence on drugs and other substances, although it's becoming increasingly well established that social media use lights up the reward centers in our brains, causing our hormones to dance" (p. 10). Nevertheless, The World Health Organization (2018) recently classified gaming disorder "as a pattern of gaming behavior ('digital-gaming' or 'video-gaming') characterized by impaired control over gaming, increasing priority given to gaming over other activities to the extent that gaming takes precedence over other interests and daily activities, and continuation or escalation of gaming despite the occurrence of negative consequences."

While scientists in the United States have been cautious in labeling digital dependence as an actual addiction, Ladika (2019) notes "concerns about tech addiction are a global phenomenon ... At least seven countries—Australia, China, India, Italy, Japan, South Korea and Taiwan—consider addiction to technology a disorder" (p. 92). Thai researchers Boonvisudhi and Kuladee (2017) describe "Internet addiction as a loss of control over Internet use that impacts daily life functions, relationship and emotional stability, [which] is an emerging issue with growing interest nowadays" (p. 2). "Behavioural addiction," add Tao et al. (2010) "affects a vast number of individuals and occurs when people find themselves unable to control the frequency or amount of a previously harmless behavior such as love, sex, gambling, work, internet and chatroom usage, shopping or exercise" (p. 556).

Addiction or behavioral dependency takes on many forms: online gaming, constant checking of emails, visits to porn sites, chatrooms, texting, Facebook, and so on. Since this form of compulsive behavior is unprecedented, little is known about its exact nature, the extent of the dependency or its treatment. "The age of behavioral addiction is still young," writes Adam Alter (2017), "but early signs point to a crisis" (p. 10). Children (and increasingly adults) seem to be developing an irresistible compulsion to stare at screens no matter where they are or what the context is. This should not be taken lightly for, in all probability, it will only get worse.

Online gaming is an area receiving quite a bit of attention both by researchers interested in studying addiction and by marketers interested in exploiting the financial advantages of such practices. The growing sophistication of online gaming has made it extremely attractive to millions and increasingly difficult to resist. According to *Report Linker* (2017), "the gaming industry has achieved immense success world-wide, evolving from board and video games to games that incorporate the most advanced technologies including 3D simulations, virtual reality, and augmented reality." PC Gaming Alliance (2014), a non-profit organization of hardware manufacturers, game developers, game publishers and others, reported a market of over $23.5 billion in software sales in 2013, while *Newzoo* (2017), a marketing research company, estimated that "2.2 billion gamers across the globe are expected to generate $108.9 billion in game revenues. This represents an increase of $7.8 billion, or 7.8 percent, from the year before" with mobile technology being "the most lucrative segment."

Boys and young men, traditionally the target group, seem especially attracted to internet gaming. Entering vicarious worlds for hours on end in the role of avatars, players confront "life and death" situations where they combat dragons, orcs and demons and their superpowers. At the same time that online games are entertaining, they have been deliberately designed to be seductive environments that will hold a gamer's attention not only for several hours every day, but for several years. Like slot machines or any other arcade game, online games use bells, whistles, music, images and prizes to stimulate the senses and lure the user into repeated use. "Product designers," writes Alter (2017), "are smarter than ever. They know how to push our buttons and how to encourage us to use their product not just once but over and over" (p. 67).

While not everyone agrees that digital gaming constitutes an actual addiction, the American Psychiatric Association in 2013 noted that Internet Gaming Addiction (IGA) was a condition that warranted more scholarship. A study by Kim, Hughes, Park, Quinn, and Kong (2016) concluded "that excessive Internet gaming was related to alterations in autonomic functions and distressed personality traits in male adolescents" (p. 667). So enticing in fact are these online games that several leading technophiles, such as Steve Jobs (founder of Apple), Chris Anderson (a former editor of a popular technophile magazine *Wired*) and Evan Williams (a founder of Blogger, Twitter, and Medium) did not allow their children to play them (Bilton, 2014). Edwards (2018) reports that "former Google employee Tristan Harris and early Facebook investor Roger McNamee have accused the tech giants of deliberately creating addictive products, without regard for human or social health" (p. 33).

The obsession with the digital, of course, doesn't begin or end with online gaming. Ramsey Brown, a co-founder of a tech company called Boundless Mind, states that "your kid is not weak-willed because he can't get off the phone … Your kid's brain is being engineered to get him to stay on his phone" (Edwards, 2018, p. 33). The portability and omnipresence of smartphones make them a convenient contributor to addictive behavior. Robert Lustig (2017), professor of pediatrics at the University of California-San Francisco, likens the cellphone to a slot machine. "With every ding, a variable reward, either good or bad, is in store for the user—the ultimate dopamine rush" (p. 192).

"In 2015," Sales (2016) reports, "Facebook, Instagram, Snapchat, Twitter, and online pinboards such as Pinterest were the most popular sites for girls. Girls in 2015 were exchanging anywhere from 30 to more than 100 texts per day" (p. 10). This obsession with social media, moreover, is not limited to adolescent girls any more than online gaming is strictly a purview of adolescent boys. Old and young alike stare at their handheld devices as they walk through the streets and instinctively grab them every time they sit down regardless where they are or who they are with. It was amazing to us, for example, during last year's (2017) World Series of baseball, how many fans sitting in prime seats spent a good portion of their time romancing their cellphones. This compulsion to be online even in the most inappropriate situations was driven home during a performance by Broadway legend Patti LuPone. The actress was forced to step out of character and off stage to snatch the cellphone of a young woman who had been texting throughout the entire first act of the play. "She was oblivious to everybody," exclaimed LuPone in an interview with Cecilia Vega (2015) on ABC's *Good Morning America*, "except for herself and her phone."

"Addictions are damaging," Alter writes, "because they crowd out other essential pursuits, from work and play to basic hygiene and social interaction" (p. 10).

Werner Herzog in his documentary *Lo and Behold: Reveries of the Connected World* (2016) notes that gamers in South Korea sometimes wear diapers so as not to interrupt online gaming marathons. Sean Elder (2014) reports a case of an infant dying from neglect while her parents were involved in compulsive online gaming.

Whether such behavior surrounding digital media—online gaming, Facebook, tweeting, texting and so on—is actually addictive or "merely" a behavioral obsession, it is certainly something we need to take into account before we advocate for an expanded use of computers in the education and socialization of children.

(2) *The Young and the Restless.* Television was a game changer. From the habit of reading a daily newspaper or following the audio narrative of a radio drama, the public was enamored by a device that brought sound, moving images and a cavalcade of celebrities, right there in every living room in America. We loved Lucy but we loved television even more. As the medium developed, the programming choices expanded, the movement of the images accelerated, and the places we watched TV steadily grew. In many homes, the TV was on all day, sometimes in multiple rooms. It became the background, and often the foreground, to dinner, to conversation, to parties, housework, homework, and whatever. The introduction of the remote and cable TV meant even more acceleration, more channel hopping, more disjointed viewing. TV is no longer just in our homes, cars, diners and schools: it is in us as well.

Media ecologists often talk of technologies as having an inherent "bias," that is, a tendency to be used in particular ways and not in others. Television, for example, has the bias of presenting information in the form of entertaining images to audiences that are typically indoors, sedentary, and passively involved. Television could conceivably be used for other purposes such as it is in airports where it lists the arrival and departures of flights, but this isn't the favored use of television technology. We expect television to be stimulating with entertaining moving images, not a static presentation of words and numbers.

At the same time, television teaches us to accept continuous commercial interruptions as normal. Besides the obsessive focusing of our attention on material goods, this unending parade of advertisements creates a pattern of discourse that is constantly redirecting the attention of the viewer to unconnected events. We learn by doing and by doing TV we learn distraction. One may be watching a serious drama or documentary which is fragmented by a string of soap, soup and shampoo commercials before returning to the movie. Television teaches us to jump from thing to thing, to seek constant stimulation, and to space out for hours on end.

But what of digital technologies? What kinds of biases do they seem to cultivate? Taken as a group, digital media clearly have a bias towards multitasking, that is, doing many things simultaneously. The computer, by its nature, is a multitasking technology which, when combined with the internet, allows us to send and receive emails, watch TV, stream movies, take photographs, send and receive text messages, tweet, word process, call an Uber, order a pizza, use maps, skype, check out a YouTube video, post to Facebook, surf the Web for a series of disconnected tidbits, and so on. One could narrow his or her focus to just one of these functions, but the tendency is to use more, sometimes several, at the same time. It is the rare person who does but one thing at a time when online. Most typically, it is a multi-mediated experience punctuated with various forms of multitasking.

Foehr (2006) writes that "the computer is the most multitasked medium because it offers many opportunities for media multitasking, both within itself as well as across other platforms" (p. 25). An extensive survey conducted by Rideout, Foehr, and Roberts (2010) found that more than half (58%) of 7th-12th graders say "they multitask 'most' of the time when using media" and that "nearly one in three (31 percent) 8- to 18-years old say that 'most' of the time they are doing homework, they are also using one medium or another—watching TV, texting, listening to music, and so on" (pp. 33, 34).

How might this pattern of behavior effect the intellectual development of a child? One consequence that several scholars have found is called the "bottle neck effect." This hypothesis suggests that when there is an information overload it tends to clog the ability to think clearly and reasonably. Ophir, Nass, and Wagner (2009), for example, conducted a series of experiments with college students demonstrating that heavy multitaskers performed poorly on the execution of tests measuring cognitive control. Results of a study by Junco and Cotton (2011) revealed that college students in general exhibit high rates of multitasking and that "over half report that instant messaging has had a detrimental effect on their schoolwork" (p. 370). Bickham, Schmidt, and Huston (2012) add that "Studies examining efforts to use media and simultaneously perform a cognitively demanding task (e.g., a reading comprehension task) have found support for a limit capacity model; when the media and the task compete for similar cognitive resources, the completion of the task is more difficult" (p. 120). Citing work by Hembrooke and Gay (2003), Bergen, Grimes, and Potter (2005), Foerde, Knowlton, and Poldrack (2006), Rockwell and Singleton (2007), and Trafton and Monk (2008), Carr (2011) concludes that "the division of attention demanded by multimedia further strains our cognitive abilities, diminishing our learning and weakening our understanding" (p. 129).

Mark Bauerlein (2009) quotes one of his students as complaining, "I can't concentrate on my homework without the TV on. The silence drives me crazy" (p. 80). What is remarkable about this comment is how unremarkable it is. Young people are being socialized in a 3-ring media circus in which the ability to focus on one thing and one thing only is becoming more and more difficult. This generation, the young and the restless, is always craving more stimulus, more distraction. This is not to blame them but only to highlight the all-consuming media environment that surrounds and devours them.

In sum, although the computer is quite obviously a powerful tool for learning, it is also one that encourages the formation of habits for a generation that is increasingly "young and restless," that is, unable to concentrate for extended periods of time on a single task. To suggest, as technophiles often do, that a computer-centric education will enhance learning while ignoring its bias towards distraction is misguided. We have all been in this environment and we know very well how seductive it is to multitask and be continually diverted by the screen before us. At issue here is the loss of the ability to focus on one thing and one thing only for an extended period of time.

(3) *The Atrophy of Literacy*. Writing on the eve of the computer age when television was still the dominant medium, Neil Postman foresaw that advances in new electronic technologies were competing for prominence and replacing an earlier one: literacy. One of the casualties of this competition was the ability to concentrate. Postman (1985) argued that literacy had trained the mind to increase its attention span in a way that is unimaginable in the present day. The bias of television, because it communicates through rapidly moving images, undermines and overpowers the habits of mind and body cultivated by literacy:

> We face the rapid dissolution of the assumptions of an education organized around the slow-moving printed word, and the equally rapid emergence of a new education based on the speed-of-light electronic image. The classroom is, at the moment, still tied to the printed word, although that connection is rapidly weakening. Meanwhile, television forges ahead, making no concessions to its great technological predecessor, creating new conceptions of knowledge and how it is acquired … (T)elevision has by its power to control the time, attention and cognitive habits of our youth gained the power to control their education. (p. 145)

Postman, who died in 2003, never had the opportunity to say much about the digital revolution. One of his former students, however, became the driving force in the formation of the Media Ecology Association and has shepherded Postman's ideas into the digital age. Lance Strate's book, *Amazing Ourselves to Death* (2014), is an excellent summary of Postman's ideas that extends his former mentor's work into the contemporary media environment. Like his professor at NYU, Strate states that our uncritical fascination with "media and technology … are the cause of considerable concern" (xii). In extending Postman, Strate urges:

> (L)iteracy desperately needs to be encouraged. Reading rewires the brain, and the wiring is not a permanent fixture, but needs to be continually renewed. And as tempting

as ebooks and ereaders may be, resist the temptation to use them, because more and more they include digital distractions that break the concentration of reading, not to mention the fact that you lose the sensual quality of holding a book in your hand. Reading out loud as a form of entertainment also needs to be encouraged, especially reading to children, but also in adult settings. Handwriting is becoming a lost art, but there is value in putting pen to paper, in the art of calligraphy, and in the simple act of copying passages out by hand. And by whatever means necessary, write a letter to a loved one or friend, a real letter to be sent by the postal service. (p. 139)

The dangers of digital reading often alarm the most literate among us. Our minds tend to wander, our eyes scan text not read, our attention becomes shallow and moves in spurts. Like Lance Strate, Nicholas Carr (2011) is alarmed that we no longer read with the same degree of concentration as before:

> Over the last few years I've had the uncomfortable sense that someone, or something, has been tinkering with my brain, remapping the neural circuitry, reprogramming the memory ... I'm not thinking the way I used to think. I feel it most strongly when I'm reading ... Now my concentration starts to drift after a page or two. I get fidgety, lose the thread, begin looking for something else to do ... The deep reading that used to come naturally has become a struggle. (pp. 5–6)

The observations of Strate and Carr reflect what many of us have also experienced: our reading is becoming rushed and superficial; we scan a text rather than engage it slowly and in depth. We are, in Carr's words, entering "the shallows." Carr, who graduated from Dartmouth with a degree in literature, goes on to quote a conversation with a faculty member from the University of Michigan Medical School who observed that his reading had taken on a "staccato" rhythm. "I now have almost totally lost the ability to read and absorb a longish article on the web … I can't read *War and Peace* anymore. I've lost the ability to do that. Even a blog post of more than three or four paragraphs is too much to absorb. I skim it" (Carr, 2011, p. 7).

Along with this lament recorded by Carr, it's fair to say that many of us do not read quite as well or as extensively as we used to. Personal emails are not attended to with the same focus as we once did handwritten "snail" mail. Facebook encourages scanning disparate communiques and, if it is much longer than a meme, there is less likelihood that it will be read at all. *Cliff Notes*, once a popular rescue for the less than ambitious student in the Age of Television, provided summaries of texts that were assigned reading. *Cliff Notes*, which ran in the neighborhood of a hundred pages or more, have been replaced in the digital age by *SparkNotes* consisting of just a few pages. "I never read a book, I'll be honest," boasts a student interviewed by Rachel Dretzin (2010), "I can't remember the last time I read a book. Nowadays, people are so busy that they need to get summaries of it like *SparkNotes*.

You can read the whole book in a matter of pages. So I read all online. I actually never read *Romeo and Juliet* until I read it yesterday in five minutes."

In many instances reading has become such a tortuous experience for young people that professors, even at elite universities, are being forced to adapt how they teach. Carr quotes an English professor from Duke University who confessed that she "can't get students to read whole books anymore" (Carr, 2011, p. 9). While there are students who enjoy reading, the trend appears to be just as she describes it. Media ecologist Ray Guzzi of Ithaca College confided to colleagues at a conference that he could no longer lecture for more than fifteen or twenty minutes. "Their eyes gloss over and they just shut down."

Using a term first introduced by historian Daniel Boorstin (1984) when he was the Librarian of Congress, Mark Bauerlein (2009) describes the growing decline of both literacy and habitual reading among young people as "a-literacy." In making his argument, the former director of Research and Analysis at the National Endowment for the Arts quotes study after study (*National Survey of Statistical Engagement, American Freshman Survey, National Freshman Attitudes Report, High Survey of Student Engagement, Changing Times of American Youth: 1981–2003, National Assessment of Educational Progress, American Time Use Survey, Reading at Risk: A Survey of Literary Reading in America*) to demonstrate a growing decline in literacy and a loss of interest in the practice of reading among youthful populations. After reviewing the importance of literature in the intellectual and social development of Frederick Douglass, John Stuart Mill, Walt Whitman, and W.E.B. DuBois, Bauerlein (2009) concludes that "books afford young readers a place to slow down and reflect, to find role models, to observe their own turbulent feelings well expressed, or to discover moral convictions missing from their real situations" (p. 58).

Bauerlein is reminding us that not only is the ability to read and write in decline, but much more profoundly, so is the cultivation of habits of mind and body peculiar to the medium of literacy. The mind formed by literacy, for example, is much more capable of extended periods of attention than the mind socialized in an environment dominated by electronic media. Illustrating this phenomenon, Neil Postman (1985) recalls the famous Lincoln-Douglas debates of 1859 in which the two statesmen tangled for as long as four, five and even seven hours before patient and engaged audiences. "What kind of audience was this?" Postman (1985) asks. "Who were these people who could so cheerfully accommodate seven hours of oratory?" (p. 44). Certainly not us. At this point in American history, when debates are reduced to soundbites and insulting one liners, citizens have no patience for extended discussions with well elaborated arguments. Compare the seriousness of the Lincoln-Douglas debates about the future of slavery in the

United States to the skimpy "debates" and unchallenged assertions that were presented to the public before the military invasion of Iraq and the overthrow of Sadam Hussein. A review of those televised discussions in the weeks leading up to war will reveal all the biases of television: attractive on-air personalities, exciting music, stimulating images, short unsubstantiated statements and, of course, a line of argument punctuated by continuous commercial interruptions. What is missing are coherent and well-defined arguments and rebuttals.

And today as we write, an a-literate president of the United States communicates to the citizenry through 280 characters on his twitter account. We can only wonder what Lincoln (and Postman) would have thought. #Sad.

(4) *Instant Gratification*. As electronic forms of communication evolved over the course of the twentieth century, they increasingly became instruments of instant gratification. Hollywood, the "Entertainment Capital of the World," led the way with a body of work that successfully cultivated their audiences with a steady stream of glamour, gossip and easy to digest content. Radio, once it discovered that it was a mass medium that could be commercialized, did exactly the same with audio. Television brought Hollywood into the living room and transformed radio into a visual medium. The marketing strategy of this new American media triumvirate of movies, radio and television was as simple as it was effective: give the audience what it wants.

In the emerging digital environment that we are now experiencing in its infancy, the instant gratification of earlier forms of electronic media seems almost quaint in contrast. The demand for instant gratification now is not only common, it is constant and uninterrupted by context or circumstance no matter how serious or solemn. The advance of "smart" phones assures that there is never a moment of the day—not at work, dinner, school, or sleep—that cannot be disturbed to gratify a whim. We expect to be gratified every moment of our waking lives, 24/7, and one wonders how long it will be before even our sleep becomes another space to be colonized and conquered by media that aim to instantly gratify.

Perhaps the greatest beneficiary of this emergent set of circumstances has been the porn industry. Following Cooper (1998) and Hald, Kuyper, Adam, and DeWit (2013), Klaasen and Peter (2015) point out that "as Internet pornography is easily accessible, affordable and anonymous, the Internet has become the main source of pornography consumption" (p. 721). Fall and Howard (2015), after describing online pornography as being a "Triple A-engine" of "accessibility, affordability and anonymity," note that Internet pornography is a 13 billion dollar industry and the United States is its leading producer and fourth largest consumer (p. 273). Belinda Luscombe (2016) adds that "One of the world's largest adult sites, Pornhub, an explicit-video-sharing site … gets 2.4 million visitors per hour and that in 2015 alone, people around the globe watched 4,392,486,580 hours of its content." Webroot (ND), an internet security company, states that every second over "$3,075 is being spent on pornography on the internet." Amazingly, Webroot continues, "25 percent of all search engine queries are related to pornography, or about 68 million queries a day." Obviously, there's quite a bit of instant gratifying going on here.

A prominent bias of internet technology, then, is to gratify the user. The problem with using this technology in the classroom is that those who have become accustomed to continuous gratification will expect more of the same in its educational uses. Teachers everywhere are finding it difficult to hold the attention of students who have been socialized with the expectation that everything must be instantly gratifying. Attention spans are shorter and teachers feel compelled to add more bells and whistles to their lessons in order to get even a simple point across. There is little patience for sustained thought that may require some solitude, study and prolonged discussion. Teachers who try to engage the class in reflection often find themselves stymied by students rushing through complicated issues. With instant gratification driving the rhythms of thought, how does one teach philosophy, literature, or history? Because of the need for instant gratification, what remains is a very shallow version of education.

(5) *The Atrophy of Physical Activity*. It is important to keep in mind that the time doing digital media often translates as the undoing of the time allotted to traditional forms of physical activity. Electronic technology is biased toward stationary postures in front of screens, particularly indoors, while traditional children's games are biased towards movement, particularly outdoors. Bodies that are sedentary for long periods of time before screens or with electronic devices cradled in their hands are physically less active beings. It is not at all incidental, then, that the rise of electronic technology is frequently associated with the tremendous growth of childhood obesity (P.M. Anderson & Butcher, 2006). Studies by R.E. Anderson, Crespo, Bartlett, Cheskin, and Pratt (1998), Faith et al. (2001), Jason, Danielewicz, and Mesina (2005) and van den Bulck (2000) also found similar correlations between elevated levels of time spent on computers and watching TV with the lack of physical activity, poor diets, and childhood obesity.

There is also an ample body of research that associates excessive use of electronic technology with diabetes (Jason, Danielewicz, & Mesina, 2005), brain tumors (Hardell et al., 2002; House, 1999), eye strain (Bonilla-Warford, 2010; Ophthalmology Times, 2002), carpel tunnel syndrome and musculoskeletal pain (Intolo & Baxter, 2010; Kozak et al., 2015), hearing loss (Le Prell, Hensley, Campbell, Hall, & Guire, 2011; Ragg, 1994), hyperactivity (M. Huizinga, Nikkelen, & Valkenburg, 2013; Swing, Gentile, Anderson, & Walsh, 2010), depression and addiction (Ha et al., 2007; Thomée, Härenstam, & Hagberg, 2012), aggressive behavior (Bushman, Gollewitzer, & Cruz, 2015; Greitemeyer & Mügge, 2014) and a number of other maladies.

The main take away is that when children spend massive amounts time with electronic media, they are also undoing the time that they used to spend in vigorous physical activity. At just the point in their lives when they should be most physically active and in perpetual motion, children find themselves in front of a screen that inhibits vigorous exercise. Tag, jump rope, hide-and-go-seek, hopscotch, and any sport you can name are games that characteristically encourage movement, speed, endurance, and bodily coordination. Computers don't do that. The on-screen avatar we adopt can fly across mountains, swim oceans, and fight demons with his superhuman powers, but the child sitting in front of the screen remains stationary and still.

(6) *Social Isolation*. Tess and Don invited all their children and grandchildren to spend Thanksgiving. Having a large family, it was quite an undertaking that required a great deal of planning. In the weeks leading up to the event, Don researched a place to host the dinner (their home was too small to accommodate such a large gathering) while Tess made preparations, bought food, researched recipes, borrowed cooking utensils and chairs, and began baking and cooking some things ahead of time. When I ran into them a week later, I asked "how did it go?" "Never again," Don grumbled. "They spent the entire meal looking at their cellphones."

In their enthusiasm to integrate digital technology across the curriculum, technophiles will often point out that it is a medium that promotes social interaction. This assertion, of course, borders on the silly. In actuality, the tendency of digital technology is to atomize groups—each person with their own screen, keyboard, content—not to socialize them. Online "communities" are not communities. As described in the scene above, every family and every group of friends has experienced the individualization promoted by cellphones at what should be social gatherings. True, children can, and sometimes do, gather around a classmate's cellphone or computer, but that is the exception, not the rule. If one pages through the handsomely designed textbooks advocating a digital-centric curriculum, one will immediately note the abundance of color photographs of solitary children staring at a screen. This is not an oversight of the photographer but an accurate depiction of the nature of the technology we are discussing.

Reading and writing, of course, are also isolating activities, but literacy is not so all-consuming. We read, we write, but then we put the book down and the pen away. The cellphone, however, is always at hand and in hand. Moreover, literacy has co-existed with orality—face-to-face, interpersonal forms of communication—for centuries and our culture has had the time to evolve a kind of homeostasis that leaves a time and place for both. Not so for digital media. Digital media, arriving with the force of a hurricane, rout everything in their path. They have not given us enough time to establish a balance.

Digital media accentuate two forms of isolation both of which are reflected in the Thanksgiving story mentioned above. On the one hand, digital media work to reduce the opportunities for open and spontaneous face-to-face communication with our peers. When those opportunities do appear, there is a marked tendency to retreat to an isolated and protected space that allows each person to remain perched in their own individualized comfort zone. In her ethnography of teenage girls, Sales (2016) quotes a 16-year-old girl who complains, "I find most of the time I'm with my friends I feel so disconnected with them because of technology. They're always on their phones to play a game or see what someone is doing somewhere else" (p. 222). Tethered to our digital devices, therefore, we are often alone even when in characteristically social environments. Similarly, the children sitting around the Thanksgiving table with Don and Tess stared blankly into their own individual cellphones rather than reach out to converse and play with their siblings and cousins. With the ability to text message, the social disconnect has become more complete. "Many teens," writes Alter (2017), "refuse to communicate on the phone or face-to-face, and they conduct their fights by text" (p. 41).

At the same time, family gatherings such as Thanksgiving should be a grand opportunity for intergenerational communication. But when the digital devices are added to the environmental mix, the special occasion squanders the possibility of different ages bonding. MIT professor Sherry Turkle observes that digital technology is playing an important role in the undoing of the social rituals that were once inherent in prolonged, interpersonal, face-to-face experiences of an environment structured by oral communication. In an interview with Mark Fischetti (2014), Turkle states that "when boring Auntie starts to talk at the family dinner table, her little niece pulls out her phone and goes on Facebook … Dinner used to be the utopian ideal of the American family having a canonical three-generation gathering. Facebook is what's utopian now" (p. 84).

In Turkle's tale, the child with the cellphone is unaware that she is in a social situation, that there is a hierarchy and social structure within a family, that there are other people in the room that need to be acknowledged and their presence respected, that dinner is a social ritual with a history extending back to our primordial roots. This same loss of sociality, of course, is extended from the dinner table to elsewhere in the home, to the school, to the workplace, to relationships of all descriptions.

We may be cohabiting a shared social space but we act in individualistic, non-social ways. Turkle (2011) recalls a scene familiar to anyone who has ever attended an academic conference:

> I remember my own sense of disorientation the first time I realized that I was "alone together." I had traveled an exhausting thirty-six hours to attend a conference on advanced robotic technology held in central Japan. The packed grand ballroom was Wi-Fi enabled: the speaker was using the Web for his presentation, laptops were open throughout the audience, fingers were flying, and there was a sense of great concentration and intensity. But not many in the audience were attending to the speaker. Most people seemed to be doing their e-mail, downloading files, and surfing the Net. The man next to me was searching for a *New Yorker* cartoon to illustrate his upcoming presentation ... Outside, in the hallways, the people milling around me were looking past me to virtual others. They were on their laptops and their phones, connecting to colleagues at the conference going on around them and to others around the globe. There but not there. (p. 14)

The very growth of digital technologies has given rise to an environment in which children and adolescents live in a world only marginally inhabited by adults. Over the course of the twentieth century, the penetration of pop culture and electronic media into the culture of childhood and adolescence became intensely felt as each new generation celebrated the music, stories, and stars of which the other was unaware and uninterested. By the 1960s, we were speaking of a "generation gap" that separated the generations. The onslaught of digital media has accelerated and extended this gap in ways that challenges the ability of adults to influence and guide the young. Bauerlein (2009) states the situation quite accurately:

> The more kids contact one another [through digital media], the less they heed the tutelage of adults. When peer consciousness grows too fixed and firm, the teacher's voice counts for nothing outside the classroom. When youth identity envelops them, parent talk at the dinner table only distracts them. The lure of school gossip, fear of ridicule, the urge to belong—they swamp the minds of the young and stunt their intellectual growth. (p. ix)

At a time when technologies are steadily pulling us apart, a wiser pedagogy would respond to the social ecology in which students live and respond accordingly. School is not only an intellectual and academic experience but a social one. Schools are traditionally a gathering place for young people to meet, make friends, and learn to interact in appropriate ways. Schools should contribute to that process, not impede or exasperate it. Being more sensitive to changes in the media environment, an enlightened pedagogy would actively find ways of bringing children together in contexts that cultivate face-to-face interaction and encourage a greater sense of the common.

(7) *A Materialistic Conceptualization of Life, Learning and Education.* By digitalizing everything related to education from teacher training to classroom instruction, from homework to testing and administrative services, public education has in effect entered into an intimate partnership with computer corporations. This evolution of an "education-industrial complex" within our institutions of learning is undeniable yet it is seldom commented upon nor are its implications ever debated or even questioned. Buried deep within the technophile's passionate advocacy to integrate digital technology across the curriculum, there are financial interests who know a golden goose when they see one. Quoting a report issued by IDC Government Insights, McCandless (2015) notes, "IT spending in the United States K-12 schools is expected to increase to about $4.7 billion in 2015. Much of that spending is expected to be on general PC upgrades or investments in applications." Schaffhauser (2016), referring to a report compiled by EdNET Insight, states, "the biggest areas of expansion are hardware (46 percent of districts will see more in this category) and teacher training (38 percent). At the same time 28 percent of districts are boosting software budgets and 27 percent are increasing tech support over the previous year."

In prying open this lucrative market, the technophile promotes the assumption that digital technology can solve key educational problems, improve test scores, better prepare students for the future job market, and increase student engagement in the classroom. On one level, this optimism is perfectly understandable. Digital technologies are truly amazing. But it would be wise to keep in mind that all salespeople exaggerate the benefits of the products they peddle while sweeping the deficiencies under the rug. All technologies, however, are a double-edged sword. As we just pointed out, there are emerging consequences associated with the unbridled use of digital media amongst children that need to be taken seriously. It has been established that digital technologies are associated with addictive behavior, loss of attention span, a decline in literacy, the cultivation of immediate gratification, the atrophy of physical health, and social isolation. Are these reasons sufficient to eliminate digital media from the social and academic lives of children? No, of course not. But let the buyer beware. Digital media are commercial products that are being marketed with all the hype and deceptiveness that has characterized marketing since the beginning of advertising. It is worth remembering that the automobile was initially marketed as a technology to protect the environment (Flink, 1972) just as Wonder Bread was advertised as a health food that could "build strong bodies 12 ways."

Conclusion

In closing, we return once again to the legendary Dr. Faust who opened our chapter. Like the overly ambitious German scholar of old, humanity has struck a myopic bargain with destiny. No doubt we have garnered immeasurable wealth, comfort, and knowledge but, if we don't start thinking more critically about the details and make some decisions, there'll be the devil to pay. As we move more deeply into the digital age, technologies are rapidly leading us into an environment that we may no longer be able to control. What will be the social and psychological consequences of artificial intelligence, cloning, drones, genetic engineering, and extensive surveillance? Certainly there were will be amazing benefits to all these technologies, but what will be the unintended results? Does anyone really think that all the effects will be beneficial?

At this point in history, schools have the responsibility to prepare young people to engage the world beyond narrow personal materialistic needs. Educators should be developing students who can access the creative imagination and be willing to confront these pressing issues with humanistic values in responsible and ethical ways. Preparing a child for the future is much more than a jobs development program. It will require the instilling of a deeper sense of purpose, meaning and social awareness.

In the chapters that follow, we will be discussing how the arts, used as pedagogical and epistemological tools, create multiple opportunities to use the imagination, work collectively with others, and explore issues from contrasting perspectives. Rather than just experienced as isolated or marginalized subject matter, the arts can contribute to a child's sense of self and society while engaging more fully their hearts and minds.

References

Alter, A. (2017). *Irresistible: The rise of addictive technology and the business of keeping us hooked*. New York: Penguin.

Anderson, P. M., & Butcher, K. F. (2006). Childhood obesity: Trends and potential causes. *The Future of Children*, *16*(1), 19–45.

Anderson, R. E., Crespo, C. J., Bartlett, S. J., Cheskin, L. J., & Pratt, M. (1998). Relationship of physical activity and television watching with body weight and level of fatness among children: Results from the third national health and nutrition examination survey. *Journal of the American Medical Association*, *279*, 938–942.

Bauerlein, M. (2009). *The dumbest generation: How the digital age stupefies young Americans and jeopardizes our future*. New York: Penguin.

Bergen, L., Grimes, T., & Potter, D. (2005). How attention partitions itself during simultaneous message presentations. *Human Communication Research, 31*(3), 311–336.

Bickham, D. S., Schmidt, M. E., & Huston, A. C. (2012). Attention, comprehension, and the educational influences of television and other electronic media. In D. G. Singer & J. L. Singer (Eds.), *Handbook of children and the media* (pp. 113–137). Los Angeles: Sage.

Bilton, N. (2014). Steve Jobs was a low-tech parent. *New York Times*, September 11. www.nytimes.com/2014/09/11/fashion/steve-jobs-was-a-low-tech-parent.html

Bonilla-Warford, N. (2010, September–October). Computer-related eye strain in children. *Pediatrics for Parents*. Retrieved from https://www.thefreelibrary.com/Computer-related+eye+strain+in+children.-a0245661774

Boonvisudhi, T., & Kuladee, S. (2017). Association between Internet addiction and depression in Thai medical students at Faculty of Medicine, Rmamthibodi Hospital. *Plos One, 12*(3). Retrieved from https://journals.plos.org/plosone/article?id=10.1371/journal.pone.0174209

Boorstin, D. J. (1984). *Books in our future: A report from the Librarian of Congress to the Congress*. Washington, DC: Library of Congress.

Bushman, B. J., Gollwitzer, M., & Cruz, C. (2015). There is broad consensus: Media researchers agree that violent media increase aggression in children, and pediatricians and parents concur. *Psychology of Popular Media Culture, 4*(3), 200–214.

Carr, N. (2011). *The shallows: What the internet is doing to our brains*. New York: W.W. Norton & Company.

Common Sense Media. (2018). Common sense and SurveyMonkey poll parents on YouTube and technology addiction. Retrieved from https://www.commonsensemedia.org/about-us/news/press-releases/common-sense-and-surveymonkey-poll-parents-on-youtube-and-technology

Cooper, A. (1998). Sexuality and the Internet: Surfing into the new millennium. *Cyber Psychology and Behavior, 1*, 181–187.

Dretzin, R. (2010). *Digital nation*. A documentary film.

Edwards, H. S. (2018, April 23). The masters of mind control. *Time, 191*(15), 30–37.

Elder, S. (2014). A Korean couple let a baby die while they played a video game. *Newsweek Magazine*. Retrieved from https://www.newsweek.com/2014/08/15/korean-couple-let-baby-die-while-they-played-video-game-261483.html

Faith, M. S., Berman, N., Heo, M., Pietrobelli, A., Gallagher, D., & Epstein, L. H. (2001). Effects of contingent television on physical activity and television viewing in obese children. *Pediatrics, 107*(5), 1043–1048.

Fall, K. A., & Howard, R. C. (2015). An Adlerian perspective on problematic pornographic use. *Journal of Individual Psychology, 71*(3), 273–289.

Fischetti, M. (2014). The networked primate. *Scientific American, 311*(3), 82–85.

Flink, J. J. (1972, October). Stages of American automobile consciousness. *American Quarterly*, *XXIV*(4), 451–473.

Foerde, K., Knowlton, B. J., & Poldrack, R. A. (2006). Modulation of competing memory systems by distraction. *Proceedings of the National Academy of Sciences*, *103*(31), 11778–11783.

Foehr, U. G. (2006). *Media multitasking among American youth: Prevalence, predictors and pairings*. Menlo Park, CA: Kaiser Family Foundation.

Greitemeyer, T., & Mügge, D. O. (2014). Video games do affect social outcomes: A meta-analytic review of the effects of violent and prosocial video game play. *Personality and Social Psychology Bulletin*, *40*, 578–589.

Ha, J. H., Kim, S. Y., Bae, S. C., Sujin, B., Kim, H., Sim, M., … Cho, S. C. (2007). Depression and internet addiction in adolescents. *Psychopathology*, *40*, 424–430.

Hald, G. M., Kuyper, L., Adam, P. C. G., & DeWit, J. B. F. (2013). Does viewing explain doing? Assessing the association between sexually explicit materials use and sexual behaviors in a large sample of Dutch adolescents and young adults. *Journal of Sexual Medicine*, *10*, 2986–2995.

Hardell, L., Hallquist, A., Mild, K. H., Carlberg, M., Pahlson, A., & Lilja, A. (2002). Cellular and cordless telephones and the risk for brain tumours. *European Journal of Cancer Prevention*, *11*(4), 377–386.

Hembrooke, H., & Gay, G. (2003). The laptop and the lecture: The effects of multitasking in learning environments. *Journal of Computing in Higher Education*, *15*(1), 46–64.

House, R. (1999). Radiofrequency radiation exposure and other environmental concerns. *Canadian Medical Association Journal*, *160*(9), 1318–1319.

Huizinga, M., Nikkelen, S. W. C., & Valkenburg, P. M. (2013). Children's media use and its relation to attention, hyperactivity, and impulsivity. In Lemish (Ed.), *The Routledge international handbook on children, adolescents and media* (pp. 179–185). London: Taylor & Francis Ltd.

Intolo, P., & Baxter, G. D. (2010). Computer use and adverse health problems—are clinicians concerned? *Physical Therapy Reviews*, *10*(6), 427–429.

Jason, L. A., Danielewicz, J., & Mesina, A. (2005). Reducing media viewing: Implications for behaviorists. *Journal of Early and Intensive Behavior Intervention*, *2*(3)., 194–206.

Junco, R., & Cotton, S. (2011). A decade of distraction? How multitasking affects student outcomes. Paper presented at A Decade in Internet Time Symposium on the Dynamics of the Internet and Society.

Kim, N., Hughes, T. L., Park, C. G., Quinn, L., & Kong, D. (2016). Altered autonomic functions and distressed personality: Traits in male adolescents with Internet gaming addiction. *Cyberpsychology, Behavior and Social Networking*, *19*(11), 667–673.

Klaasen, M. J. E., & Peter, J. (2015). Gender (in)equality in Internet pornography: A content analysis of popular pornographic Internet videos. *Journal of Sex Research*, *52*(7), 721–735.

Kozak, A., Schedlbauer, G., Wirth, T., Euler, U., Westermann, C., & Nienhaus, N. (2015). Association between work-related biomechanical risk factors and the occurrence of carpal tunnel syndrome: An overview of systematic reviews and a meta-analysis of current research. *MC Musculoskeletal Disorders*, *16*(231), 1–19.

Ladika, S. (2019). Technology addiction. In CQ Researcher (Ed.), *Issues in media: Selections from CQ researcher* (pp. 79–103). Los Angeles: Sage.

Le Prell, C. G., Hensley, B. N., Campbell, K. C., Hall III, J. W., & Guire, K. (2011). Evidence of hearing loss in a 'normally-hearing' college-student population. *International Journal of Audiology, 50*, S21–S31.

Luscombe, B. (2016). Porn and the threat to virility. *Time, 187*, 40–47.

Lustig, R. (2017). *The hacking of the American mind*. New York: Avery.

McCandless, J. (2015, May 22). U.S. education institutions spend $6.6 billion on IT in 2015. *Center for Digital Education.*. Retrieved from http://www.centerdigitaled.com/higher-ed/US-Education-Institutions-Spend-66-Billion-on-IT-in-2015.html

McLuhan, M., & Fiore, Q. (1967). *The medium is the massage: An inventory of effects*. New York: Random House.

Newzoo. (2017, December 19). The global games market will reach $108.9 billion in 2017 with mobile taking 42%. Retrieved from https://newzoo.com/insights/articles/the-global-games-market-will-reach-108-9-billion-in-2017-with-mobile-taking-42/

Ophir, E., Nass, C., & Wagner, A. D. (2009). Cognitive control in media multitaskers. *Proceedings of the National Academy of Sciences, 106*(37), 15583–15587.

Ophthalmology Times. (2002). Prolonged computer use in children can lead to vision problems due to eye strain study finds. April 15, *27*(8), p. 18.

PC Gaming Alliance. (2014). Annual pinnacle report. Retrieved September 1, 2018, from http://www.pcgamingalliance.org/press/press-releases/

Postman, N. (1985). *Amusing ourselves to death*. New York: Penguin Books.

Postman, N. (1992). Seven ideas about media and culture. *The Speech Communication Annual, 6*, 7–18.

Postman, N. (1995). *The end of education: Redefining the value of school*. New York: Vintage.

Ragg, M. (1994). Epidemic of hearing loss predicted. *Lancet, 344*(8923), 675.

Report Linker. (2017, December, 19). *Gaming sector: Worldwide forecast until 2021*. Retrieved from https://www.reportlinker.com/p04188500/Global-Gaming-Market.html

Rideout, V. J., Foehr, U. G., & Roberts, D. F. (2010). *Generation M2: Media in the lives of 8–18 year-olds*. Menlo Park, CA: The Henry J. Kaiser Family Foundation.

Rockwell, S. C., & Singleton, L. A. (2007). The effect of the modality of presentation of streaming multimedia on information acquisition. *Journal of Computing in Higher Education, 15*(1), 179–191

Sales, N. J. (2016). *American girls: Social media and the secret lives of teenagers*. New York: Knopf.

Schaffhauser, D. (2016, January 19). Report: Education tech spending on the rise. Retrieved from https://THEjournal.com/articles/2016/01/19/report-education-techspending-on-the-rise.aspx

Strate, L. (2014). *Amazing ourselves to death: Neil Postman's brave new world revisited*. New York: Peter Lang.

Swing, E. L., Gentile, D. A., Anderson, C. A., & Walsh, D. A. (2010). Television and video game exposure and the development of attention problems. *Pediatrics, 126*, 214–221.

Tao, R., Huang, X., Wang, J., Zhang, H., Zhang, Y., & Li, M. (2010). Proposed diagnostic criteria for Internet addiction. *Addiction, 105,* 556–564.

Thomée, S., Härenstam, A., & Hagberg, M. (2012). Computer use and stress, sleep disturbances, and symptoms of depression among young adults—A prospective cohort study. *BMC Psychiatry, 12*(176), 1–12.

Trafton, J. G., & Monk, C. A. (2008). Task interruptions. *Reviews of Human Factors and Ergonomics, 3,* 111–126.

Turkle, S. (2011). *Alone together: Why we expect more from technology and less from each other.* New York: Basic Books.

van den Bulck, J. (2000). Is television bad for your health? Behavior and body image of the adolescent "couch potato." *Journal of Youth & Adolescence, 29,* 273–288.

Vega, C. (2015, July 15). Interview recorded for ABC's *Good Morning America.* Original broadcast. Retrieved from https://www.youtube.com/watch?v=43mB4QuXGTE

Webroot. (ND). Internet porn by the numbers: A significant threat to society. Retrieved from https://www.webroot.com/us/en/home/resources/tips/digital-family-life/internet-pornography-by-the-numbers

World Health Organization. (2018, September). Gaming disorder. Retrieved from https://www.who.int/features/qa/gaming-disorder/en/

CHAPTER THREE

Building Noah's Arks

Media Environments and Counterenvironments

> The artist picks up the message of cultural and technological challenge decades before its transforming impact occurs. He, then, builds models or Noah's arks for facing the change that is at hand.
>
> Marshall McLuhan[1]

In assessing the social, physiological and psychological impact of digital technologies, even the most optimistic amongst us must admit that they come to us as something of a mixed blessing. The benefits they bring are indeed amazing but we should not ignore the consequences that may be harmful and even dangerous. But how should we approach this rapidly evolving environment that comes marked with an air of inevitability and irreversibility? How can we sustain our sanity and a sense of balance in a world flooded by constant waves of unremittent change?

In response to questions such as these, Marshall McLuhan and Neil Postman insisted that we begin by paying very close attention to the ways in which changes in technologies alter our individual and collective existence. Observation and reflection are key. But this isn't as easy as it sounds. Technologies, once they are embedded in a society, are experienced as commonplace and take on the cloak of invisibility. They no longer stand out; they seem "natural." Technologies, and the new patterns of thought and interaction they engender, just become part of the new normal.

As a defense against this "naturalizing" or "normalizing" of technologies, media ecologists often suggest the creation of strategies to act as counter measures. Described as counterenvironments, these measures consist of alternative spaces and perspectives that allow us to distance ourselves from the sway of the dominant technologies in order to ponder, question and study their consequences. It is only by being on the outside of the bubble that we can see the inside of the bubble.

In this chapter, we will begin by elaborating on the idea that technologies are not merely things that are added to our world but are fundamental agents of change. Neil Postman (1985) put it quite bluntly when he said "To be unaware that a technology comes with a program for social change, to maintain that technology is neutral, to make the assumption that technology is always a friend to culture is, at this late hour, stupidity plain and simple" (p. 157). By making an effort to explore how technologies intersect our lives, we get a clearer idea how they transform the ways in which we think, feel and interact with the world.

We will also review the significance that media ecologists place on counterenvironments. Marshall McLuhan first coined the term to describe spaces that exist in opposition to the mainstream and help us to maintain a much needed sense of balance. Although McLuhan never clearly defined what he meant by the term that he himself had introduced, we can infer from his "probes" that he was not referring to actual physical spaces but to alternate visions of what is and what could be. McLuhan reasoned that since we are socialized by the environment that surrounds us, it is difficult to see that environment clearly because it constitutes all that we know. Its way of doing things, becomes our way of doing things; its assumptions, become our assumptions; its ideas, values and understandings become the framework and routine through which we live our lives. It becomes, so to speak, the sea in which we swim. Along these lines, McLuhan was fond of saying "I don't know who discovered water, but I'm pretty sure it wasn't a fish."

For Marshall McLuhan, the role of artists was particularly crucial. Artists are the ones who stand outside of normal society and, through their insights and creative work, bring to the level of awareness the nature of the changes we are experiencing. In his landmark work *Understanding Media*, McLuhan (1964) stated that the artist helps to keep humanity afloat in the deluge that has accompanied the electronic revolution. "The artist picks up the message of cultural and technological challenge decades before its transforming impact occurs. He, then, builds models or Noah's arks for facing the change that is at hand" (p. 70). McLuhan was also fond of quoting Ezra Pound's dictum, "the artist is the antennae of the race," for he believed the artist is the one who is most in touch with his or her surroundings and could assist the culture in its understandings of the new environment. Using yet another metaphor, Phil Rose (2014) writes that McLuhan "liken[s] the artist to the 'seer' in primitive societies, whose province it was … to read the language of environments" (p. 2358). In short, artists are those individuals who are capable of feeling the changes, giving them aesthetic form, and willing to swim against the current. They splash cold water on our faces, they implore us to focus, they try to wake us up. Artists, like the legendary Noah, show us ways to survive the storm.

Neil Postman also advocated the cultivation of spaces outside the mainstream that would render the dominant environment more visible and therefore more accessible to critique. But rather than emphasize the role of the artist as did his predecessor, Postman looked to the public school and the classroom teacher as the agents of balance. In *Amusing Ourselves to Death*, Postman (1985) writes that "The only mass medium of communication that, in theory, is capable of addressing the problem [is] our schools" (p. 162). Since educational institutions are tasked with the responsibility of helping young minds learn, schools should be cultivated to act as counterenvironments that teach children how to question the overwhelming and often pernicious influence of the dominant media. "What is the necessary business of schools?" Postman and Weingartner (1969) asked in their manifesto *Teaching as a Subversive Activity*. "To create eager consumers? To transmit the dead ideas, values, metaphors, and information of three minutes ago? To create smoothly functioning bureaucrats?" And the authors respond to their rhetorical question by stating that the purpose of schools at this time and place "is to subvert attitudes, beliefs, and assumptions that foster chaos and uselessness" (p. 15).

In *Teaching as a Conserving Activity*, Postman (1979) refers to his model not specifically as "counterenvironment" but, also based on a metaphor introduced by McLuhan (1967, p. 68), as one of "thermodynamic opposition." Just as a thermostat maintains a healthy temperature within a room by opposing heat and cold, the school system is charged with the responsibility of counterbalancing the prevailing tendency in society so that our information environment doesn't become too narrow and lopsided in favor of electronic media. Children do not need to learn how to use a television, cellphone or a computer: they do that well enough on their own. In fact, they can probably teach you. What is more important is that children learn how to formulate questions and develop a healthy skepticism. "*Once you have learned how to ask questions,*" Postman and Weingartner (1969) continue, "*—relevant and appropriate and substantial questions—you have learned how to learn and no one can keep you from learning whatever you want or need to know*" (p. 23, italics in the original).

Media Ecology: Media as Environments

Unlike earlier approaches to communication studies that focused strictly on the content of media or on the movement of information between "senders" and "receivers," media ecology is more broadly concerned with understanding how technological changes reshape the social environment in which we live our lives. To emphasize this environmental view, Neil Postman (1970) aptly named this emerging field of study as "media ecology." By "media," Postman means the ways in which a technology is customarily employed within a given culture. A particular technology can be used in a variety of ways but a media ecologist would argue that each technology has an inherent bias to be used in certain ways and not in others. A refrigerator, for example, could hypothetically be used to hide money, store shoes or act as a room divider. But for almost everyone, it is used as a place to protect perishables from spoilage. A frying pan, to take another example, could be worn as a body ornament (as has happened amongst natives in the Amazon) but most typically it is employed as instrument used in cooking. If frying pans were promoted strictly as jewelry or refrigerators as storage bins, it is doubtful they would have had the impact they did. The way in which a technology is customarily used defines its social mission. "A technology," Postman (1985) writes, "becomes a medium as it employs a particular symbolic code, as it finds its place in a particular social setting, as it insinuates itself into economic and political contexts. A technology, in other words, is merely a machine. A medium is the social and intellectual environment a machine creates" (p. 84).

By inserting the word "ecology" in his designation, Postman was directing our attention away from the usual concern with media as "things" to a much wider and more nuanced preoccupation with all the changes that accompany technologies as they are integrated into a cultural environment. "A new technology," Postman (1992) writes, "does not add or subtract something. It changes everything. In the year 1500, fifty years after the printing press was invented, we did not have old Europe plus the printing press. We had a different Europe. After television, the United States was not America plus television; television gave a new coloration to every political campaign, to every home, to every school, to every church, to every industry" (p. 18).

Media ecologists don't suggest that there is a simple cause and effect relationship between technology and change, only that once a new technology is introduced it sets in motion a series of consequences that reverberate throughout the society. These ripples often go unnoted and unassessed but can turn into tidal waves. The new medium changes the old environment. We are no longer "there," we are "here." New relationships and new habits are born and additional technologies and patterns begin to manifest themselves. McLuhan sometimes described this distinction between the technology and the environment that surrounds it as the difference between "figure" (the technology itself) and "ground" (the accompanying background changes). In an interview with Willem Oltmans, McLuhan explained:

Look at the ground around the figure of the automobile or the ground around any technology, which necessarily has a large ground of services and disservices associated with it. Now, the ordinary attention is fixed on the figure rather than the ground … They pay only incidental attentions to the huge service environment of roads, oil companies, filing stations, and other allied services of manufacturing that are the ground of the car … By not looking at the ground [context] around the automobile you miss the message of the car. For it is the ground of any technology that is the medium that changes everybody, and it is the medium that is the message of the technology, not the figure [object]. (quoted in Benedetti & DeHart, 1996, p. 153)

The key here is to appreciate the degree to which each new technology redefines who we are and what we can do. John Culkin (1967), an early advocate for the views expressed by McLuhan, expressed this idea with the saying "we shape our tools and thereafter they shape us" (p. 52). Had we lived a thousand years ago, or even fifty years ago, our ways of thinking, feeling, perceiving and behaving would have necessarily been totally different. As technologies change, our environment changes; as our environment changes, we change. Over the course of several million years, we have gone from a rather puny species scavenging on the plains of Africa to one that now holds the fate of the world in its hands. From stone tools and sharpened sticks to spaceships and cybernetics, every technological change alters who we are and what we can be. Like the australopithecine in Kubrick's *2001* who tosses the bone into the air that transforms into a spaceship, our technologies lead us far beyond where our biologies have placed us.

Albrecht (2004, p. 59) provides this useful schema to illustrate the multiple levels at which our technologies and culture interact:

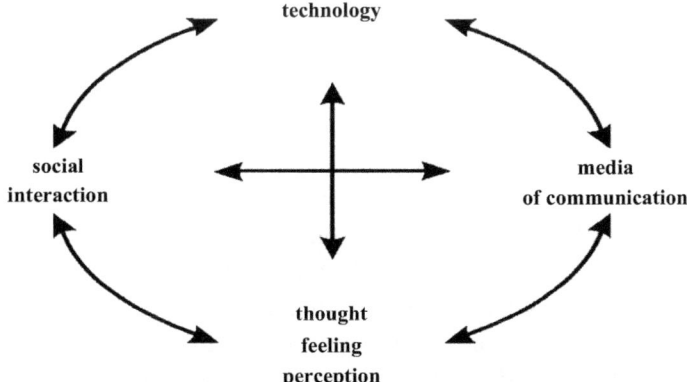

Figure 3.1. Schema of Media Ecology, by Albrecht, R., 2004, retrieved from Mediating the muse: a communications approach to music. New York: Hampton Press.

In the above diagram, we see the interactive nature of technological change. The relationships are not one-directional or a simple case of cause and effect: they are ecological and necessarily interdependent. Everything effects everything else. When cars, cellphones, computers or other technologies are introduced into a culture, they will begin to be used in a variety of ways that reshape how we think, feel, perceive, and socially interact. We alter our habits of mind and behaviors as we adapt to the new set of conditions that surround us. What we did yesterday, we no longer do today; what we do today, we will no longer do tomorrow. Marshall McLuhan famously summarized this interrelationship of technology and cultural change as "the medium is the message." The medium, that is, the manner in which a technology is put to use, leads us to adopt particular habits of mind, body and social interaction. We can never go home again because that once upon a time environment has been torn down and replaced.

Media as Counterenvironments

On a dark, stormy night in June of 1816, a group of young British writers gathered in an old mansion on the banks of Lake Geneva in Switzerland. It was the "Summer of Darkness." Volcanic eruptions in the Pacific—the worst in nearly two thousand years—had resulted in a series of worldwide climatic abnormalities that included colder temperatures, heavy rains and persistent fogs that didn't lift for days on end. Amid crashes of thunder, flashes of lightening, and torrents of falling rain, Lord Byron read aloud a ghost story so chilling that the poet Percy Shelley was forced to flee the room. Upon finishing, Byron dared the others to compose a tale to rival the frightening one he had just read. The eighteen-year-old Mary Shelley tried for several unproductive days but came up with nothing. Finally, after a disturbing dream, she began to draft a story about an ego-driven doctor obsessed with creating a living being from the assembly of stolen body parts.

Frankenstein was born.

Written at the time when the first experiments with electricity produced rumors that scientists would shortly be able to play God and revivify the dead, Mary Shelley's book took shape as a cautionary tale about blind ambition, the limits of science, and the great peril of technologies unwisely employed. "So much has been done," boasts the determined but reckless Dr. Frankenstein in Chapter Three, "more, far more, will I achieve; treading in the steps already marked, I will pioneer a new way, explore unknown powers, and unfold to the world the deepest mysteries of creation." In the end, however, Dr. Frankenstein's collection of body parts did not result in a glorious new creation but an isolated, lonely, and murderous monster.

Mary Shelley's *Frankenstein* was an early warning about technology gone awry but it certainly wouldn't be the last. Fritz Lang's 1927 masterpiece, *Metropolis*, depicts the oppressive alienation of a futuristic technological environment that has suffocated humanity. Aldous Huxley's *Brave New World* (1932) cautioned about the genetic engineering of new life, George Orwell's *1984* (1949) about technologies of video surveillance and propaganda, and Ray Bradbury's *Fahrenheit 451* (1953) about the power of the state to control knowledge by eliminating literacy. During the 1950s and 1960s, Rod Serling often treated such themes on his anthology program, *The Twilight Zone*, which included parables about the frantic pace of modern life and the threat of a technological totalitarian future. *Black Mirror*, a contemporary anthology program that follows in the footsteps of *The Twilight Zone*, consistently questions the blessings promised by technology. Also recently, the Wachowskis's *The Matrix* (1999), Spike Jonze's *Her* (2013), Alex Garland's *Ex-Machina* (2014) and multiple other films too numerous to mention bring us into dystopian worlds and foretell the perils engendered by the advent of advanced technologies. Phil Rose's book length treatments of Pink Floyd (2015) and Radiohead (2016) analyze the attempts of these musicians to expose some of the threats of the modern world.

What's going on here? Our technologies, artists seem to be telling us, are rapidly outrunning our abilities to control them. Are they here to liberate us or to enslave us? Deep in our slumber, artists act as modern day Paul Reveres who alert us to that which we can't see, won't see, or haven't yet noticed. Because they pull our coattails and give us a wakeup call, Marshall McLuhan gave precedence to the work of artists. In his controversial book, *The Medium is the Massage*, through the use of imaginative photographs and poetic statements, McLuhan (1967) asserts the importance of artists in the construction of counterenvironments. "Environments are not passive wrappings, but are, rather, active processes which are invisible. The groundrules, pervasive structure, and over-all patterns of environments elude easy perception. Antienvironments, or countersituations made by artists, provide means of direct attention and enable us to see and understand more clearly" (p. 68).

Postman's conceptualization of counterenvironment was somewhat different. For Postman, the locus of the counterenvironment was not so much the arts but the processes and purposes of education. Schools should not be institutions that merely teach students to adapt to the emergent technological environment but vibrant places where the young learn to think, ask questions and interact critically with their surroundings. "Only through a deep and unfailing awareness of the structure and effects of information," Postman (1985) wrote, "through a demystification of media, is there any hope of our gaining some measure of control over television, or the computer, or any other medium" (p. 161). Postman's idea of a counterenvironment, therefore, was not just a psychological or aesthetic one but involved the cultivation of actual physical spaces. The technological swirl brought on by the digital revolution demands a thoughtful and critical response. Not to do so would be suicidal to our culture and perhaps even destroy our species' chances of survival.

McLuhan and the Arts as Counterenvironments. In the 1950s sci-fi classic *The Incredible Shrinking Man*, a young man is exposed to a radioactive vapor while boating with his wife on a tranquil sea. Soon he realizes that he is growing smaller and smaller until finally he is no bigger than the insects that crawl in the basement of his home. As children, we thought it was pretty "cool" when the guy had to hide inside a miniature dollhouse to escape a housecat, use a straight pin as a sword to fight off a spider, and then disappear into nothingness as he desperately tried to hide in the towering blades of grass on his front lawn. More deeply, however, the movie is a metaphor of the unforeseen consequences of technological—in this case a form of radiation—manipulations of the natural world. It can be read as a warning—one of many that appeared on the screen during the post-World War II era—that there was an underside to the technological miracles of the 1950s not being discussed.

This is why the work of artists is so crucial. In the age of electronic media, McLuhan maintained that artists act as critical voices who draw our attention to the fundamental changes we are experiencing but which we routinely fail to see or understand. Art critic John David Ebert (2005) wrote of Stanley Kubrick's cinematic space odyssey, *2001*, that it "was the first major presentation of a theme that would come to be reiterated in film over and over again, namely that of a battle of an individual human being against an impersonal system that is threatening to dehumanize him, whether that system is defined as megalopolitan city, the meta-national corporation, or technology in general" (p. 37).

Ebert's words echo sentiments found in McLuhan and remind us that the art world has been alerting us to the need to be more vigilant of the technological environment evolving all around us. McLuhan (1962) once asked his readers "Is not the essence of education civil defense against media fallout?" (p. 294). It is not at all insignificant that the metaphor McLuhan chose to describe the essence of education in the electronic age likens it to the need to prepare and protect ourselves against the consequences of atomic warfare. Just as the horrors of a nuclear war only begin with the detonation of an actual bomb but then reverberate throughout all that is life-giving in the environment, our education should be preparing us for the series of events that inevitably follows our exposure to electronic media. By employing the word "fallout," McLuhan is moving our attention away from the immediate effects of a technological device to the multiple repercussions for the environment that surrounds it.

The essence of the education that McLuhan advocates as a form of civil defense against media fallout centers on the willingness of individuals to observe and thoughtfully consider the changes they are experiencing in their environment. For McLuhan, the great teachers who would prepare us for the challenges of media fallout were not those individuals who stand at the front of a classroom and lecture but the artists whose productive work allows us to experience perspectives underrepresented or absent in the dominant environment. Artists are those individuals who are able to see, hear, and feel things generally imperceptible to most others.

In a lecture entitled "Art as Survival in the Electric Age," McLuhan (1973/2003) noted that with the arrival of electric technology the "enormous gap between man's natural equipment and his technology has gotten bigger and bigger. I suggest that the artist's role is to fill that gap by retuning and modifying the perceptual apparatus that enables us to survive in a rapidly developing environment. Art provides the training and perception, the tuning or updating of the senses during technological advance" (p. 208). By putting their feelings into aesthetic and compelling forms, artists help us to experience our environment differently, with a different set of eyes and ears so to speak. Just as we can't see white on white or black on black, artists through their creations reveal counter-perspectives and counter-insights that are obscured by the technological biases of the dominant culture. In such a way, the environment which dominates our way of life can be seen not as *the* environment but as *an* environment.

Artists, however, not only produce *contents* or objects of art that counter or raise questions about technologies and technological change, they may also produce *forms* and *contexts* which counter the biases inherent in the dominant technologies and the environments they create. In a super-kinetic age dominated by flickering images and constant movement, the fine arts train us to slow down and pay close attention. To be able to step away periodically from a laptop, cellphone, or video game and learn to embrace the world of classical art is, in effect, to enter a counterenvironment. In her impassioned defense of art history, Camille Paglia (2012) underscores the significance of this:

> Modern life is a sea of images. Our eyes are flooded by bright pictures and clusters of text flashing at us from every direction. The brain, overstimulated, must rapidly adapt to process this swirling barrage of disconnected data … How to survive is this age of vertigo? We must learn to see … Children above all deserve rescue from the torrential stream of flickering images, which addict them to seductive distractions and make social reality, with its duties and ethical concerns, seem dull and futile. The only way to teach focus is to present the eye with opportunities for steady perception—best supplied by the contemplation of art. (p. vii)

Another counterenvironmental significance of the arts noted by McLuhan is the fact that artists tend to live their lives outside of established norms and are willing to take on and challenge received ways of being. Their role is to uncover this hidden dimension. McLuhan (1967) notes this "anti-social" character of artists:

> The poet, the artist, the sleuth, whoever sharpens our perception tends to be antisocial; rarely "well-adjusted," he cannot go along with currents and trends. A strange bond often exists among anti-social types in their power to see environments as they really are. This need to interface, to confront environments with a certain antisocial power, is manifest in the famous story, "The Emperor's New Clothes." "Well-adjusted" courtiers, having vested interests, saw the Emperor as beautifully appointed. The "anti-social" brat, unaccustomed to the old environment, clearly saw that the Emperor "ain't got nothing' on." The new environment was clearly visible to him. (p. 88)

Because they stand outside the mainstream and have dedicated their energies and talents to giving aesthetic form to their feelings, artists help us to become more aware of some of the deficiencies, challenges, and dangers engendered by the rapid advance of new technologies into our cultures. Most tend to see things as if it were still yesterday—through what McLuhan called the "rearview mirror"—not the actual reality that envelops us today. By taking artists more seriously, McLuhan believed we would come to a better understanding of our current situation and be able, therefore, to respond with greater awareness and intelligence. In sum, without paying *attention to the insights of artists, we are ignoring important lessons we need to learn.*

Postman and Literacy as Counterenvironments. Marshall McLuhan is a tough nut to crack. At multiple turns, he seems bafflingly enigmatic, allusive and even contradictory. Was McLuhan's intention to warn us about the dangers of rapid technological change, excite us about the new possibilities, or merely to describe what was going on all around us? One could easily find support for each one of these three conflicting positions within McLuhan's writings and interviews. An anonymous post on a McLuhan website summarized the situation quite accurately:

> One can't judge McLuhan by any particular statement he makes. One will easily find apparently contradictory statements in other communiques performed by him ... One minute McLuhan seemed to be a utopian, the next a neo-Luddite, then a Gnostic, later an agent of the Vatican, or a Zen Buddhist, then a technological determinist, pseudo-scientist, Manhattan project romantic, and on and on, back and forth. (https://www.facebook.com/groups/marshallmcluhan/permalink/1971340279842056/)

In trying to gage his overall intent, however, it would seem that McLuhan's prime purpose was to alert us to the great challenge before us. McLuhan was well aware that we were on the cusp of a new environment and was warning that electronic technologies would lay havoc to all that preceded it. Perhaps McLuhan, like the time traveling astronaut in Kubrick's *2001*, was overwhelmed by the changes that were coming at him at the speed of light.

Neil Postman, however, brings no such ambiguity or confusion to his discussion of the electronic revolution. By the time you finish reading the title of his book, you usually have a pretty good idea where he stands on the issue he'll be discussing: *Teaching as a Subversive Activity* (1969), *The Disappearance of Childhood* (1982), *Amusing Ourselves to Death* (1985), *Technopoly* (1992), *Building a Bridge to the Eighteenth Century* (1999).

At the same time, there is a consistent theme that runs through Postman's books, lectures and interviews. You may agree or disagree with him but his argument is always clearly expressed and coherently presented. From his earliest works to his final words, Postman was resolute in his support for schooling that would act as a counterbalance to the electronic revolution. Schools should see as their primary mission the encouragement of skepticism, the asking of good questions, and the formulation of coherent sentences. Schooling also has the obligation to cultivate in children a reason to learn. Material goals are not sufficient. A child needs to feel a greater purpose before submitting themselves to the rigors that a true education requires. Without such a preparation, children are left unprotected and unguided.

His defense of literacy was unwavering. By literacy, Postman didn't just mean the ability to read, write or take a multiple choice exam but a whole set of abilities, attitudes and habits that are cultivated by a literate education. In *Building a Bridge to the Eighteenth Century*, published just four years before his death, Postman (1999) gives a summary of the significance he attached to literacy:

> From Erasmus in the 16th century to Elizabeth Eisenstein in the 20th, almost every scholar who has grappled with the question of what reading does to one's habits of mind has concluded that the process encourages rationality; that the sequential, propositional character of the printed word fosters what Walter Ong calls the "analytic management of knowledge." To engage the written word means to follow a line of thought, which requires considerable powers of classifying, inference making, and reasoning. It means to uncover lies, confusions, and overgeneralizations, to detect abuses of logic and common sense. It also means to weigh ideas, to compare and contrast assertions, to connect one generalization to another. To accomplish this, one must achieve a certain distance from the words themselves, which is, in fact, encouraged by the isolated and impersonal text. That is why a good reader does not cheer an apt sentence or pause to applaud even an inspired paragraph. Analytic thought is too busy for that, and too detached. (p. 149)

From the very outset of his career, Postman argued for a radical reform of public schools that would replace the traditional curriculum with its emphasis on facts, tests, and endless trivia with a curriculum that would teach children how to ask questions and make coherent statements. In his first major book on the subject, Postman and co-author Charles Weingartner (1969) state as their thesis that in a time of relentless technological change "schools must serve as the principal medium for developing in youth the attitudes and skills of social, political, and cultural criticism" (p. 2). Calling their approach the "inquiry method," schools would function as counterenvironments where students learn how to develop the critical insights that McLuhan attributed to artists.

In *Teaching as a Conserving Activity*, Postman (1979) presents an argument that he was to expand upon throughout his subsequent writings. For Postman, the learning style required and facilitated by literacy and schooling was being challenged and undermined by the learning style required and facilitated by electronic technology, most especially, by television. Defining curriculum "as a specially constructed information system whose purpose, in its totality, is to influence, teach, train, or cultivate the mind and character of our youth" (p. 49), Postman (1979) goes on to conclude:

> By this definition, television and school not only have curriculums but are curriculums; that is, they are total learning systems. Each has a special way of organizing time and space; their messages are encoded in special forms and moved at different rates of speed; each has its special way of defining knowledge, its special assumptions about the learning process, and its own special requirements concerning how one must attend to what is happening. Moreover, each has a characteristic subject matter, ambiance, and style, all of which reflect the unique context within which one experiences what is going on. And, of course, though their effects are strikingly different, each has its purpose the control of our young. Viewed in this way, television is not only a curriculum but constitutes the major educational enterprise now being undertaken in the United States. (pp. 49–50)

Schools and television, then, constitute two competing curricula, each with their own set of internal biases and tendencies. Whereas the school curriculum is "subject-matter centered, word-centered, reason-centered, future-centered, hierarchical, secular, socializing, segmented, and coherent" (p. 86), the electronic curriculum is biased towards speed, shortness of attention span, amusement, vicariousness, fragmentation, immediacy, novelty, non-hierarchical structures, and non-sequential thought. Since electronic media have such an extensive and ascendant position within American society, Postman maintained that it is of utmost importance that schools remain firm in their traditional role as teachers of literacy and not be swayed or pressured into meeting the demands and seductions of electronic technology.

After the publication of *Teaching as a Conserving Activity* in 1979, Postman never said much more about the "Thermostatic View of Education." Perhaps the term was much too clumsy for such an eloquent writer to cling to, but the idea it represents was sound and it was a theme to which he returned repeatedly. Three years later, in *The Disappearance of Childhood*, Postman (1982) boldly ties the invention of the printing press and the rise of mass literacy to the creation of childhood and then goes on to argue that television is responsible for its demise. Postman explains that before the invention and integration of the printing press into the cultures of Western Europe, the lives of children and adults were intertwined and essentially the same. A child was merely a small human being expected to work and look after himself just like any adult would. With the rise of mass schooling in the 16th and 17th centuries, children and adults begin to become separated into different classes with distinct roles and responsibilities. Postman quotes J.H. Plumb (1971) who writes that "Increasingly the child became an object of respect, a special creature with a different nature and different needs, which required separation and protection from the adult world" (p. 9). The nature of television, however, is to violate this "separation and protection" by providing information indiscriminately to whoever is watching. The information environments of child and adult, then, are once again intermeshed as they were before the rise of mass schooling.

In perhaps his most influential book, *Amusing Ourselves to Death*, Postman (1985) allots a full chapter to the subject of education in the television age which he begins with a stinging critique of the poster child of educational TV, *Sesame Street*. At the time, the program was immensely popular with parents, teachers and children and was being held up as a shining example of the benefits TV could bring to early childhood education. Postman, however, dissented vehemently and argued that the show teaches "by a series of commercials" [which] "undermines what the traditional idea of schooling represents" and "encourages children to love school only if school is like *Sesame Street*" (pp. 142–143). As he did in *Teaching as a Conserving Activity*, Postman contrasts the TV environment with the one experienced at school:

> Whereas a classroom is a place of social interaction, the space in front of a television set is a private preserve. Whereas in a classroom, one may ask a teacher questions, one can ask nothing of a television screen. Whereas school is centered on the development of language, television demands attention to images. Whereas attending school is a legal requirement, watching television is an act of choice. Whereas in school, one fails to attend to the teacher at the risk of punishment, no penalties exist for failing to attend to the television screen. Whereas to behave oneself in school means to observe rules of public decorum, television requires no such observances, has no concept of public decorum. Whereas in a classroom, fun is never more than a means to an end, on television it is the end in itself. (p. 143)

As in his previous work, Postman's paramount concern is with the teaching of literacy at a time when television had come to dominate the cultural landscape. He was writing before the digital revolution took hold of American culture but nearly everything he said above could be applied today—only much more so. Digital media are much more seductive, accessible, varied, portable, and omnipresent than television could ever be. In fact, television is now a digital medium which we can experience virtually anywhere and at any time. Moreover, whereas earlier television was mostly done at home and only occasionally in school, digital media are in the process of becoming not only a part of the curriculum but its very core.

As already noted, study after study has demonstrated that the amount of time children spend online is steadily expanding, far surpassing the hours once dedicated to outdoor activities, study, schooling, and even sleep. Like television, digital media are entertainment biased devices as opposed to schooling which is mandatory, disciplined, and demands study. Although it can be used for serious purposes, the online world is filled with amusing and disconnected distractions. We read a book; we surf the web. These online diversions are a guiding force in a child's development: no fun, nothing done. When inclement weather or a holiday cancels school, children celebrate; when a power shortage or a punishment interrupts the use of digital devices, children mourn. Even at the time when Postman was writing, televisions had a reduced presence in schools, confined to a period here, a lesson there. Computers, in contrast, are increasingly present in every classroom, at every desk, and are integrated into every subject across the curriculum.

It would be another ten years before Postman (1995) returned again to the subject of education "not because the education world has suffered from my absence, but because I have" (p. ix). In *The End of Education*, Postman argues that schools have failed in their mission to give children a compelling reason to learn. Because of this, he concludes that it is difficult to imagine how schooling and the cultivation of literacy can effectively continue into the digital age. He urges schools to provide a "transcendent narrative" that would capture the imagination of children and create an organizing principle around which the curriculum is centered. The essence of the narrative approach as outlined by Postman is to provide students with a story "that tells of origins and envisions a future, a story that constructs ideals, prescribes rules of conduct, provides a source of authority, and, above all, gives a sense of continuity and purpose" (pp. 5–6). He suggests several possible narratives with intriguing titles—"The Spaceship Earth," "The Fallen Angel," "The American Experiment," "The Law of Diversity," "The Word Weavers/The World Makers"—that could be developed to provide students with a *reason* and an organizing framework in which to learn. "With such a purpose," he writes, "school becomes the central institution through which the young may find reasons for continuing to educate themselves" (Postman, 1995, xi).

The optimism of his early work with Charlie Weingartner, however, was clearly waning. The hopefulness with which they expressed their ideas in *Teaching as a Subversive Revolution* (1969) and *The Soft Revolution* (1971) was beginning to sour. As the years went by, Postman seemed increasingly frustrated with an educational establishment that seemed incapable of responding critically to changes in our communication environment. How could they not see what was staring them dead in their eyes? How could they not react more thoughtfully?

Nonetheless, Postman never completely gave up on schools. Schools were our last best hope, our "Hail Mary pass" to survival. In the moving epilogue that concludes *The End of Education*, Postman (1995) writes:

> I offer this book in good faith, if not as much confidence as one would wish. My faith is that school will endure since no one has invented a better way to introduce the young to the world of learning; that the public school will endure since no one has invented a better way to create a public; and that childhood will survive because without it we must lose our sense of what it means to be an adult. (pp. 196–197)

Four years later in *Building a Bridge to the Eighteenth Century*, Postman (1999) devotes full chapters to "Education" and "Childhood" in which he reiterates ideas previously introduced and elaborates on their importance in the digital age. Once again, he laments "the disappearance of childhood," this time connecting our modern understanding of childhood as a special time between infancy and adulthood to the great thinkers of the Enlightenment. "(I)t was in the eighteenth century that a new conception of the young flourished. It took the name 'childhood,' a third stage of life, delightful in itself, providing adults with the time and opportunity to create from it a mature and humane person." Postman then finishes his point by asking his reader a rhetorical question: "Do we leave this idea behind in crossing the bridge to the new millennium?" (p. 126).

As in his previous writings, Postman understands school as the one public institution—a "counterenvironment" if you will—capable of protecting children from the chaotic upheavals unleased by electronic technology. For Postman (1999) school:

> is the only public institution left to us based on the assumption that there are important differences between childhood and adulthood. But the declining authority of school has been well documented, and, even worse, there is a widespread acceptance, as mentioned, of school as having only one purpose—to prepare the young for adult work. The question of how to nourish the souls of students—through art, for example—or how to cultivate taste … or how to promote a sense of educated patriotism … or how to think scientifically … these and other concerns are moved to the rear and certainly not regarded as of importance to the education of consumers and job-seekers. (pp. 131–132)

In *Building a Bridge to the Eighteenth Century*, Postman repeats an idea that harkens back to his pioneering work with Charlie Weingartner some thirty years prior and which parallels some of the concerns expressed by those who adhere to a media literacy approach to education. As the electronic age now extends into digitalized forms, the ability to ask meaningful questions is even more urgently required than it was back in 1969. Confronting the emergence of the digital, Postman (1999) writes:

> If we want our students to live intelligently in a technological society, I don't see how this can be done if they are ignorant of the full meaning and context of technological change ... My point is that, if we are going to make technology education part of the curriculum, its goal must be to teach students to use technology rather than be used by it. And that means that they must know how a technology's use affects the society in which they live, as well as their personal lives. This is something we did not do with television, and, I fear, we are not now doing with computer technology. (p. 171)

These two chapters inserted within *Building a Bridge to the Eighteenth Century* were to be Neil Postman's final published words on the subject of education. Four years later he died of cancer without having had the opportunity to say much more about the changes to education engendered by the onslaught of digital media. Postman's legacy, however, is that he was able to seamlessly connect the education and socialization of children with the media environment in which they were born and raised. Media ecologists often think of Neil Postman only as a media theorist, educators often think of him only as an educational philosopher. In reality, he was both. For Postman, you could not understand the challenges of contemporary education without appreciating the cultural upheavals unleashed by the electronic revolution. Nor could you profitably study the electronic media environment without at least considering schooling as an institution that could help balance it. School should function as a counterenvironment, something outside the mainstream, where habits of critical thought and the art of asking questions could be cultivated in a way that other institutions are incapable of doing.

At various points in his career, Postman urged that teachers needed to be "subversive," that schools needed to "conserve" the best of the literate tradition, and that children should learn how to ask questions, formulate coherent sentences and be exposed to "transcendent narratives" that would capture their imaginations and give them reasons to learn. With Aldous Huxley and H.G. Wells in mind, Postman (1985) wrote that "we are in a race between education and disaster" (p. 163). Either we learn, become aware, and make some intelligent choices or our culture—and perhaps even humanity itself—shall shrivel, shrink and disappear into nothingness.

If you have never read Postman, you should. In fact, it wouldn't be a bad idea at all to put down this book and pick up one of his. Your efforts will be richly rewarded.

Conclusion

In this chapter, we have highlighted the importance that media ecologists place upon technologies. Rather than just things that are added to a society, technologies redefine the cultural environment and act as agents that actively restructure our existence and modify our consciousness. The fluctuating nature of the communication environment in the electronic age calls out for counterenvironments that would help us to question, balance and stabilize these relentless changes. McLuhan gave special attention to artists for they are the ones who are most in touch with the contemporary environment—"the antennae of the race"—and most likely to reveal the underlying changes, challenges and opportunities engendered by new media. Postman believed we must refocus the mission and purpose of schools so that children develop a more critical mindset. Children need to learn how to question, use language intelligently, and carefully inspect the nature of technology and its impact on culture.

"There is absolutely no inevitability," wrote McLuhan (1967), "as long as there is a willingness to contemplate what is happening" (p. 25). Postman, for his part, consistently urged his public "to pay attention to some of the negative effects" (quoted by Woo, 2003). The question is do we have the *willingness*? Are we willing to *pay attention* to some of the negative effects? And, if we do have the willingness and are willing to pay attention, how can we go about this in a coherent and effective way? This will be the subject for the second part of the book. Before we go there, however, we need to make one last stop and probe more thoroughly the significance McLuhan assigned to artists. Indeed, why the arts?

Note

1. Marshall McLuhan (1964), *Understanding Media*, p. 70. New York: Mentor.

References

Albrecht, R. (2004). *Mediating the muse: A communications approach to music, media and cultural change*. Cresskill, NJ: Hampton Press.

Benedetti, P., & DeHart, N. (1996). *On McLuhan: Forward through the review mirror*. Scarborough, ON: Prentice-Hall.

Culkin, J. (1967). Each culture develops its own sense ratio to meet the demands of its environment. In G. Stearn (Ed.), *McLuhan: Hot and cool* (pp. 49–57). New York: New Amsterdam Library.

Ebert, J. D. (2005). *Celluloid heroes & mechanical dragons: Film as the mythology of electronic society.* Rochester, MN: Lisa Loucks Christenson Publishing.

McLuhan, H. M. (1973/2003). Art as survival in the electric age, 206–224. In S. McLuhan & D. Staines (Eds.), *Understanding me.* Cambridge, MA: MIT Press.

McLuhan, H. M., & Fiore, Q. (1967). *The medium is the massage: An inventory of effects.* New York: Bantam Books.

McLuhan, M. (1962). *Gutenberg galaxy: The making of typographic man.* Toronto: University of Toronto Press.

McLuhan, M. (1964). *Understanding media: The extensions of man.* New York: McGraw-Hill.

Paglia, C. (2012). *Glittering images.* New York: Pantheon.

Plumb, J. H. (1971). The great change in children. *Horizon, 13*(1), 4–12.

Postman, N. (1970). The reformed English curriculum. In A.C. Eurich (Ed.), *High school 1980: The shape of the future in American secondary education* (pp. 160–168). New York: Pitman.

Postman, N. (1979). *Teaching as a conserving activity.* New York: Delacorte.

Postman, N. (1982). *The disappearance of childhood.* New York: Delacorte.

Postman, N. (1985). *Amusing ourselves to death.* New York: Penguin Books.

Postman, N. (1992). *Technopoly: The surrender of culture to technology.* New York: Alfred A. Knopf.

Postman, N. (1995). *The end of education: Redefining the value of school.* New York: Vintage.

Postman, N. (1999). *Building a bridge to the eighteenth century: How the past can improve our future.* New York: Alfred A. Knopf.

Postman, N., & Weingartner, C. (1969). *Teaching as a subversive activity.* New York: Delta.

Rose, P. (2014). Musical counter-environments: Media ecology as art criticism. *International Journal of Communication, 8,* 2351–2375.

Rose, P. (2015). *Roger Waters and Pink Floyd: The conceptalbums.* Lanham, MD: Rowman Littlefield.

Rose, P. (2016). *Radiohead and the global movement for change.* Lanham, MD: Rowman Littlefield.

Woo, E. (2003). Obituary: Neil Postman, 72; Author warned of technology threats. *Los Angeles Times.* Retrieved from http://articles.latimes.com/2003/oct/12/local/me-postman12

CHAPTER FOUR

The Man Who Had No Story

Why the Arts in Education Matter

> Nations are Destroy'd, or Flourish, in proportion as Their Poetry Painting and Music, are Destroy'd or Flourish!
>
> William Blake[1]

In the old Irish folktale "The Man Who Had No Story" (O'Cathain, 1980; Yolen, 1986), the hard working but rather dull Brian O'Brannigan is taught a life changing lesson by the fairies of the field. So industrious was he that the people in his village would point at him every time he ran past and say, "There goes Brian O'Brannigan, here again, gone again." One day, while hurrying about and gathering bundles of straw for his basket making business, Brian looked over at the forbidden field of the fairies abundant with the finest straw he had ever seen. "If I cut the straw quickly," thought Brian, "no one will ever know." Working in great haste before he could be spotted, Brian soon became exhausted and fell into a deep, deep sleep.

When he awoke, the young man found himself engulfed by darkness. As he anxiously stumbled through this unfamiliar landscape, he spied a light in the distance and began to make his way towards it. "Where there's light," he reasoned, "there must be people." Sure enough, Brian shortly arrived at a small cottage. When he peered through the window, he saw an elderly couple sitting by the fire sipping tea. "Should I knock at their door?" he thought to himself. "Should I go in?" Brian was startled when the cottage door suddenly opened of its own accord and a voice from within beckoned, "Come on in Brian, we've been expecting you."

This was indeed strange. How did they know his name? And how was it that the door opened by itself? The elderly couple offered Brian a seat on their bench in front of the fire. "So Brian," the old woman asked, "now that you're here, how about telling us a good story." Brian was startled by the peculiar request and simply shrugged his shoulders, "I don't know any. I don't have time for nonsense like that. Besides that, I'm a grown man!"

The old woman glanced over at her husband and the husband rolled his eyes in return. "Well then," said the old man, "how about a song? Certainly you can sing us a little tune to liven up the evening?" Once again, Brian squirmed in his seat and shrugged his shoulders. "Don't know any. I never learned to sing an entire song." Disappointed by his responses, the old woman passed Brian a bucket. "Here," she said, "at least make yourself useful. Go outside to the well and fetch us some water."

This Brian could do. But as he approached the well and started to draw water, a powerful gust of wind began to blow all around him. All at once, it lifted him up off his feet and tossed him head over heels, heels over head, into the inky blackness of night.

When at last Brian finally landed on his feet, he found he was lost once again in the middle of an open field surrounded by darkness. As he stumbled about trying to find his way, Brian spied a light in the distance. "Where there's light," he said to himself, "there must be people." Eventually he arrived at a cottage but realized at once it wasn't the same one he had just left. This one was much larger and, when he peeped in the window, he saw a somber scene with several people gathered around a coffin in the middle of the room. "Sweet Jesus, Mary and St. Joseph!" he gasped. "It's a wake!"

Before he could think twice, the door opened of its own accord and from within a voice of a woman summoned, "Come on in Brian. We've been expecting you." Brian thought to himself, "How does she know my name? And how did the door open by itself?" He cautiously entered and, once inside, a beautiful woman sitting next to the coffin invited Brian to sit down next to her. After a moment of silence that seemed like forever, the widow passed Brian a fiddle and a bow and demanded, "Here Brian, my husband used to love music. How about striking up a tune so that people can dance a bit. This wake is much too sad."

Brian was astonished by the strange request. "Surely, she must be joking," he thought. "I've never touched a musical instrument in my entire life." But the widow insisted and would not take no for an answer. "Now Brian, don't make a liar out of me," she said. "I've already told everyone that you're the finest fiddler in all of Ireland."

Brian looked to his left and he looked to his right. Every eye in the room was on him. There was no escape. Picking up the fiddle and placing it beneath his chin, Brian began to slowly scratch the bow across the strings. To his amazement, a melody started to form of a song he once had heard long ago. As he continued with more confidence, the fiddle seemed to take on a life of its own. Soon, the whole room was up on its feet and dancing until they flopped down and couldn't dance no more.

And when Brian finished, everyone in the room agreed they had never heard a finer fiddler in their entire lives.

One of the mourners suggested that they say some prayers in honor of the deceased. A young man stepped forward and volunteered to run down to the village to fetch the local priest to perform the duties. "No!" protested the widow, "no need for that. We have Brian O'Brannigan with us tonight. He says the finest of prayers in all of Ireland."

Brian was aghast. He had always had problems speaking in front of people. Besides, he never went to church and could no longer remember the prayers he had learned as a child. "Now Brian," she said, "don't make a liar out of me. Show the people what you can do. I've already told them that you recite the finest prayers in all of Ireland."

Reluctantly, Brian rose up from his chair and began to awkwardly mumble some words that were barely audible. But as he continued, the words became louder and the sentiment stronger. By the time he had concluded his homily, everyone agreed they had never heard any finer words in their entire lives.

Suddenly, the silence of the room was interrupted by the sound of a rooster crowing. "Ah," said the woman, "now it's time to take my beloved to the graveyard for his burial." And with those words, six of the dead man's best friends stepped forward to act as the pallbearers. Five of the men were extremely short and one was extremely tall so that when they picked up the coffin to carry the body, the casket tilted so much that it almost fell to the ground.

"This will never do," said the widow. "Brian, you will have to operate on the tall man and make him as short as the wee ones." Once again, Brian was startled by the strange request. "How in the world can I do that!" he exclaimed. "Now Brian," the widow insisted, "don't make a liar out of me. Everyone knows you're the finest surgeon in all of Ireland."

And with those words, the widow passed Brian some thread, a package of needles and a saw. "Now get to work Brian. You know what to do." With trembling hands Brian picked up the saw and slowly began to saw the legs of the tall man at a spot just below the knees. After that, Brian sawed off his feet. Taking the needle and thread, he expertly sewed the severed feet onto the knees of what had once been a tall man. And when Brian had completed the operation, the man stood up as good as new. Now that all six of the pallbearers were of the same height, they were quite able to carry the casket to the graveyard.

And everyone agreed it was the finest operation they had ever seen performed.

When the mourners arrived at the graveyard, they were confronted by a huge wall that barred their entrance. Someone suggested that they turn back and return later when the gate was open. The widow, however, ordered Brian to climb to the top of the wall and pull the casket up while the others pushed from below. Brian knew better than resist her request and soon was standing atop of the great stone wall.

As Brian stood there waiting to pull up the coffin, a gigantic wind came out of nowhere and blew him high into the sky where he twirled and whirled, head over heels, heels over head. And when he finally touched down again, Brian was no longer at the cemetery, but back at the well just outside the elderly couple's cottage where he had been sent to fetch some water a few hours before. Bewildered, Brian picked up the filled bucket and cautiously entered the cottage. The old woman, puffing on her pipe, turned to him and asked him with a sly grin, "So Brian, do you have a story to tell us now?"

And with those words, Brian told them the story that we've just told you. Brian O'Brannigan, the man who had no story, finally had a tale to tell.

***

Brian O'Brannigan—the man who had no story—discovers he has an important tale to tell us all. This tale, like most stories worth their breath, can be appreciated on various levels. At its most basic, "The Man Who Had No Story" is a wondrous tale, both mysterious and humorous. Children are delightfully frightened by the scenes at the wake and in the cemetery but tickled by the idea of being lifted by a gust of wind and flying through the air. At this level, the story is simply an engrossing adventure that has the power to entertain and hold the attention of an audience.

At another level, it is the tale of a man who has violated a taboo and must be punished for his transgression. The lesson here is "don't mess with the fairies." Within the folk culture of traditional societies, there is always a thin line between the natural and the supernatural. In the rustic regions of Ireland, fairies, leprechauns, banshees, elves and the like are not just superstitions but entities that many people have claimed to have seen.

But at another level, the story reminds us of the power and place of the arts in human society. Life is more than just working and making money. A "here again, gone again" routine may fill the pocketbook but it makes for a rather dull existence. It feeds the body but starves the soul. Life has its magic and the arts are an essential part of that magic. The bewildered Brian, cast into a series of situations, is forced to perform in creative ways that he never dreamed possible. No one is more amazed at his hidden talents than Brian himself. The arts make him whole and allow him to connect with his community. After all, what good is a man to himself or to others if he doesn't have a story, a song, or a few words of wit and wisdom to share with family, friends and strangers?

The arts should never be ignored or taken lightly. They are not throw away trinkets but valuable insights into the confusing environment that surrounds us and molds us. At a time when education is obsessed with online "literacy," the arts find themselves confined to the dusty corners of a curriculum that doesn't value their existence. This is disgraceful and not very wise. We fully suppose humans could live without singing, dancing, or painting, but what a sad and brutal existence that would be. Like Brian O'Brannigan, we may well be able to fashion a profitable living but not a very profitable life.

In the remainder of this chapter, we will attempt to tease out some of the important benefits that the arts have for the physical, social and intellectual development of children. We have sketched out ten reasons why the arts matter in the education and socialization of children but the imaginative reader will surely think of others.

Why the Arts Matter in the Education and Socialization of Children

(1) *The Arts Are Instruments of Motivation and Involvement.* There is an old adage that "you can lead a horse to water but you can't make him drink." Our classrooms (as well as our museums, theaters, and recital halls) are filled with "horses" who are uninterested or incapable of drinking deeply from the experiences to which they are being exposed. As any teacher knows, just because a child is sitting in a classroom, there is no reason to believe that she or he will be moved to imbibe the opportunities being offered. How often have we heard teachers complain that their students won't read, can't write, and don't take pride in the work that they submit? Physically the students may be present but, emotionally, socially and psychologically, they are someplace else, far far away.

The arts motivate interest and interest motivates participation. Human beings, and children in particular, are instinctively drawn by the powers of music, movement, dance, painting, stories and drama. A child's natural tendency to role play a story can become a portal to enter more deeply into the world of literature; a child's natural tendency to sing can become a motivator to participate in group activities; a child's natural tendency to dance can become an opportunity to build community in the classroom.

If one can harness this energy generated by participation in the arts and direct it towards educational goals, then a classroom becomes a vibrant counterenvironment that balances some of the influence of digital media in the lives of children. To sing, dance, draw and play make believe transports a child into experiences that are tactile, active, and intrinsically social. Unmediated by screens and lacking the electronic biases towards speed, individuality and immediate gratification, the arts cultivate a different way of being in the world. Besides the content, the arts change and refocus the pace, scale and quality of the learning experience.

Stories like the one that opened this chapter motivate children to listen, follow a narrative, ask questions, and share their thoughts. Was Brian merely dreaming all this or did it really happen? Were the fairies punishing Brian for entering their field or were they actually teaching him a lesson he needed to learn? Do you think Brian learned something from this experience? How was he changed? The story is filled with images that serve to motivate drawings and paintings. The story can be reenacted as an improvised drama with different children playing different parts. The teacher and the students can also role play characters in the story and respond to questions from the class.

A good story told well is an educational motivator. Like all the arts, it can be pedagogically crafted as a doorway to learning.

(2) *The Arts Tap into the Imagination.* Education doesn't begin in earnest until the student opens his or her heart and mind to the imagination. Without imagination, learning is uninspired and dead. "It is my conviction," Maxine Greene (1995/2000) writes, "that informed engagements with the several arts is the most likely mode of releasing our students' (or any person's) imaginative capacity and giving it play" (p. 125). Music, dance, drama and the like allow us to draw on aspects of our creativity that often lie ignored and unattended. When children become engaged in the arts, there is a change of heart and a shift in feeling that is tangible in the classroom and visible in their work. Like Brian in the story, we all have talents we don't even know we have.

Through the arts we experience a change of being and of perspective. But to cultivate that change, the creative teacher must introduce children to the symbolic forms that make it possible. Ordinary speech is not enough. Philosopher Susanne Langer described the artist as someone who puts "feeling into form" in a way that speech is unable to do. In her classic work, *Philosophy in a New Key*, Susanne Langer (1942) argues that music, myths, rituals and the arts are symbolic representations of emotional states that communicate through a different set of symbols than does speech and with a different intent and purpose:

> All language has a form which requires us to string out our ideas even though their objects rest one within the other; as pieces of clothing that are actually worn one over the other have to be strung out side by side on the clothesline. This property of verbal symbolization is known as *discursiveness;* by reason of it, only thoughts which can be arranged in this peculiar order can be spoken at all; any idea which does not lend itself to the 'projection' is ineffable, incommunicable by means of words. (pp. 81–82)

While the nature of language as a medium of communication requires us to-string-out-our-ideas-in-a-one-word-at-a-time-fashion, the arts work through different types of symbols that allow us to express the all-at-onceness of what we are experiencing. Logic, syntax, and the peculiar arrangement of verbal symbols demanded of language doesn't permit this. This is not to dismiss the importance of speech, only to reveal its limitations. Because of this intrinsic quality of speech, Langer (1942) argues that language "fails miserably in any attempt to convey the ever-moving patterns, the ambivalence and intricacies of inner experience, transient fantasy, or its more runic traces, all turned into nameless, emotional stuff ... Language is quite inadequate to articulate such a conception" (pp. 100–101).

The story of Brian O'Brannigan has the one-word-at-a-time quality of language, but its surreal images and magical twists transport the listener into a world that defies the relationships and occurrences expected by the rational mind. Like poetry, which also defies the discursiveness of speech, the story overwhelms our systems of logic and reason. We are enticed to leave behind the corridors of reason and enter into the more imaginative world of feeling.

Every teacher has had the unpleasant experience where students just sit there like lumps on a log. The arts, however, can tap into the imagination and transform the dormant energy into opportunities for learning. Introducing children to artistic experiences helps to expand their symbolic repertoire. Lacking the inhibitions and the narrow perceptions we develop as we mature, children are generally open and accepting of music, dance, drama and the arts. They are more prone to do these things spontaneously and freely. The imagination is alive and vibrating in the hearts of children and the arts actively engage, affirm and extend it.

(3) *The Arts Integrate the Brain Hemispheres.* Beginning with discoveries early in the nineteenth century, it has been gradually established that the human brain consists of two hemispheres, each with its own distinct and specialized capabilities. Of particular interest is the discovery of the critical role played by the right hemisphere (in left handed people, everything we say would be opposite) in mediating the cognitive abilities that relate to spatial relationships, visual processing and musical ability. Dismissed by scientists for many years as the "subordinate" or "minor" hemisphere, the right side of the brain has in recent decades been recognized to be of major importance when it comes to utilizing the imagination

and intuition. Releasing the imagination, therefore, inevitably means engaging the right hemisphere of the brain which psychologist Robert Ornstein (1997) describes as "the seat of creativity" (p. 2).

Because both sides of the brain are usually involved with most tasks, the distinctions in hemispheric specializations are easily over-simplified (Sylwester, 2008). Nonetheless, it has been repeatedly documented that different hemispheres play specialized roles in the processing of particular kinds of information. Although the left hemisphere has been shown to be dominant in the processing of speech (vocabulary, grammar, syntax and *literal* meaning), writing, and logical thought as well as the handling of analytical and sequential information, the right hemisphere is dominant in the processing of music, the tonality of speech, visuo-spatial information, metaphorical meaning and the ability of seeing the big picture.

It is for this reason that individuals who suffer brain damage on the left side of the brain often lose the ability to speak (*aphasia*) but retain the capacity to appreciate music. At the same time, damage on the right side of the brain may result in the loss of the ability to sing or do music (*amusia*) but leave the ability to speak totally unimpaired. Anthony Storr (1992) notes that damage to right hemisphere often leaves the capacity to speak intact but damages its musical or tonal quality. "Children with lesions in the right hemisphere may be competent at reading, but poor at communicating their feelings. Their speech is often monotonous and inexpressive, lacking those emotional/intonational aspects of speech recognized … as being important in communication between mothers and infants" (p. 37).

The right hemisphere also plays an important role in the processing of spatial information. Springer and Deutsch (1989) note that spatial recognition disturbances, known as "*agnosia*," sometimes result from damage to the right-hemisphere. "Such patients could be so disoriented in space that they were unable to find their way around in a house in which they have lived for many years … Some right-hemisphere patients have deficits in their ability to comprehend depth and distance relationships or to deal with mental images of maps and forms. One of the most interesting forms of agnosia is facial agnosia. A patient with this condition is unable to recognize familiar faces and sometimes cannot distinguish between people in general" (p. 16).

While, as we already noted, the significance of left/right hemispheric cognitive distinctions can be easily exaggerated, it would be foolish not to consider what we know thus far when attempting to engage the creativity and imagination of children and their teachers. The imagination lives in a part of the brain seldom touched by traditional pedagogical approaches which overemphasize left brain function. The right hemisphere—once diminished in science as the "minor" hemisphere—is not given its due. Art, music, poetry and dance make ample use of the right brain and, in so doing, children are given the opportunity to develop and connect both sides of the brain. As a result, they are more likely to become well-rounded with the enhanced capacity to look at issues and enjoy life from multiple perspectives.

(4) *The Arts Broaden Social Development.* The profoundly social nature of learning was uncovered by the philosopher and psychologist George Herbert Mead (1934) who maintained that the self is not a "given" at birth but has, in fact, a social basis that it is formed through its interactions with others. In other words, the self and the mind are essentially social creations, not biological givens that come to maturity in isolation. "The individual mind," Mead (1982) writes, "can exist only in relation to other minds with shared meanings" (p. 5). As we grow, we internalize in our minds the words and gestures of others who will, in turn, become a "generalized other" who influence our own patterns of thought and behavior throughout life. This generalized other gradually takes shape within us through three kinds of activities—language, play and games—which force us to understand and respond appropriately to those we encounter. "The internalization in our experience," Mead (1934) explains, "of the external conversation of gestures which we carry on with other individuals in the social process is the essence of thinking" (p. 47).

Keeping this in mind, it follows that children who are regularly brought into the company of storytellers, musicians, painters, dancers and so on, will have the opportunity to internalize these "others" as part of their own repertoire of possibilities. Duncan (1968) called this accumulation of others into our minds "the parliament of selves." His metaphor suggests that we do not blindly adhere to only one or two of the others we have internalized but that they constitute a varied presence who compete for prestige and influence within our personalities. By exposing children to artists and teachers not afraid to be creative in the classroom, children are much more likely to integrate creative ways of being into their own personalities. If we are socialized in situations with those who communicate through song, dance, humor, role play, poetic expression and so on, we are much more apt to absorb these experiences and make them part of our own minds.

Children learn best by example. When children encounter teachers who through their speech, demeanor, and everyday actions, exhibit creative behavior, they have the real possibility of internalizing inventive ways of being. If the teacher is creative in the classroom and is able to respond to students in creative ways, the children are much more likely to release their imaginations and become accustomed to putting "feeling into form." Through this routine exposure to artists working as teachers or teachers working as artists, the child begins to internalize "significant others" who can expand the psychic resources available to them.

(5) *The Arts Cultivate Multiple Forms of Intelligence.* The arts are a vital way of cultivating qualities of intelligence not normally recognized or sufficiently esteemed in a school environment. In his influential book, *Frames of Mind*, Howard Gardner (1983) argued that human intelligence is much more complex and varied than just linguistic and logical-mathematical intelligences. Beyond linguistic intelligence, that is, "sensitivity to spoken and written language, the ability to learn languages, and the capacity to use language to accomplish certain goals" (Gardner, 1999, p. 41) and logical-mathematical intelligence, that is, "the capacity to analyze problems logically, carry out mathematical operations, and investigate issues scientifically" (Gardner, 1999, p. 42), Gardner identified five other forms of intelligence. Musical intelligence is the capacity to appreciate, organize, identify, and create music. Bodily-kinesthetic intelligence is the capacity to control and creatively use bodily movement as demonstrated by dancers, actors and athletes. Spatial intelligence is the capacity to identify special patterns and to organize and navigate space. Interpersonal intelligence is the capacity to notice and respond to differences in others, "in particular, contrasts in their moods, temperaments, motivations, and intentions" (Gardner, 2006, p. 15). Intrapersonal intelligence is the ability to "access one's own feeling life, one's range of emotions, the capacity to make discriminations among these emotions and eventually to label them and to draw on them as a means of understanding and guiding one's own behavior" (Gardner, 2006, p. 17).

Gardner (1999) later expanded his original list of seven intelligences to include three more. Naturalistic intelligence refers to the capacity to identify and classify the various species found in our environment. Spiritual intelligence is the capacity to reflect on experiences "that are not readily apprehended in a material sense" (p. 54). Existential intelligence is "a concern with 'ultimate' issues" such as "the significance of life, the meaning of death, the ultimate fate of the physical and psychological worlds, and such profound experiences as love of another person or total immersion in a work of art" (p. 60).

In challenging the prevailing notion that intelligence can be narrowly confined in two qualities (linguistic and mathematical), Gardner was redefining intelligence much more broadly than is traditionally recognized by the educational establishment. With his theory of multiple intelligences, Gardner (2006) presents "an alternative vision—one based on a radically different view of the mind, and one that yields a very different view of school. It is a pluralistic view of mind, recognizing many different and discrete facets of cognition, acknowledging that people have different cognitive strengths and contrasting cognitive styles" (p. 5). The wide variety of the arts opens to these other intelligences by acknowledging their existence, nourishing their cultivation, and simply giving a time and a place for them to be.

It is also the case that many of the intelligences enumerated by Gardner are linked and can be developed more fully through the arts. Fletcher and Simmons (2016) point out, for example, that linguistic intelligence can be linked with musical intelligence through songwriting, "bodily/kinesthetic intelligence complements musical intelligence in choreography … [and existential intelligence] potentially connects to musical intelligence in the composition of sacred hymns, with bodily kinesthetic intelligence in dance performed for religious rituals, and with spatial and logical/mathematical intelligences in the design of holy places" and so on (pp. 34–35).

What the reader should take away from this section is that the arts are both forms of intelligence and a way to expand and enlarge it. They do not distract from linguistic, mathematical or other forms of learning. Rather, the arts in themselves are a form of learning that have the ability to connect, deepen and extend other ways of knowing.

(6) *The Arts Are Portals to Happiness and Well-Being.* The ability of the arts to foster health and happiness in everyday life is seldom taken very seriously. Art "therapy," music "therapy," or drama "therapy" is usually reserved for those with severe emotional problems but not sufficiently offered to the population at large. We tend to ignore the enormous benefits that come to us through participation in the arts. To sing, dance, paint or draw is to be more alive. We can actually feel the transformation in our beings and read it in our faces. The old maxim "laughter is the best medicine" strikes close to the truth as does Jimmy Durante's signature tune "You Gotta Start Off Each Day With a Song." It is quite obvious, both psychological and physically, that the arts are portals to happiness and well-being.

By supporting and expanding the arts, schools can put in motion a process that brings more cheerfulness and camaraderie to the classroom. It is not primarily about creating a future musician, dancer, actor or artist, but much more fundamentally about the creation of happy and healthy human beings. Music therapist Gary Ansdell (2014) notes that "The most valuable use of music is to maintain and enrich the quality of our personal, social and spiritual lives. This has been common knowledge and practice in many other times and places, but needs renewing in our culture today" (p. 304). Ansdell is referring, of course, to the benefits of actually *doing* music, not just listening to it. We do not reap the full benefits of music unless we are actively involved in its creation and its celebration. Participation in music brings a counterbalance to an environment that has cultivated us to be consumers of music but not generators of it.

As a result of not doing music on a consistent basis, we have never had the opportunity or the need to learn a repertoire of songs that can be readily shared with a group nor have we developed the custom of singing regularly with others. Strange to say, something so inherently human has become an alien experience.

There may well be music playing through our ear plugs or blasting in the places where we gather but the joyous act of collective singing is something of a rarity. The participatory musical experience advocated by Ansdell, therefore, is often marginalized by the more passive, electronic experience.

Participation in the creation of music, of course, is not the only means to "maintain and enrich the quality of our personal, social and spiritual lives." Art therapist Cathy Malchiodi (2003) emphasizes the importance of art in terms of "mind-body" medicine which tunes the physiological to the psychological. Lusebrink (1990) also stresses the benefits of art as "a bridge between body and mind, or between conscious levels of information processing and the physiological changes in the body" (p. 218). Similarly, drama therapists Landy and Montgomery (2012) see theater "as standing between body and spirit ... [in a way that] facilitates the dynamic flow of ideas, bodily sensations and images, and as such serves as a powerful exemplar of holistic education and wellness" (p. 168).

The arts introduced into the classroom as daily participatory activities has the potential to alter the scale and the patterns at which we normally experience music, dance, theater, and all the arts. The stage becomes smaller, the audience disappears, and our involvement is encouraged and affirmed. This new experience as participants in the arts rather than being just an audience forms a counterenvironment that is both social and psychological. We feel the difference; a part of us that has been dormant comes to life. As co-creators and live participants in an experience rather than as distant observers, we socially and psychologically inhabit a counterenvironment that contrasts with the digital experiences that circumscribe our daily lives. Abraham Maslow observes, "a musician must make music, an artist must paint, a poet must write, if he is to be ultimately at peace with himself." We would only extend Maslow's observation by adding that to be human we are all, in some very basic way, artists who need to create in order to be at peace with ourselves and each other. When Brian O'Brannigan plays the fiddle, improvises a homily and learns to tell a good story, he is not only a better person for doing it, he is a happier one.

In sum, creating a time and a space to sing, dance, and play have enormous health benefits for a child that are generally ignored within their schooling. The fact that children do not have the opportunity to be actively involved with the arts on a daily basis is a sad commentary upon our systems of education and socialization. Why aren't children, *every day*, singing songs and learning a repertoire? Why aren't children, *every day*, having the opportunity to dance and learn new steps? Why aren't children, *every day*, allowed to explore ideas and behaviors through role playing exercises? It is indeed an impoverished pedagogy that recognizes the value of technical proficiency and financial success but dismisses the beneficial qualities of doing the arts. Happiness and well-being have been left out of the equation.

(7) *The Arts Are Portals to Sociality.* On one level, "The Man Who Had No Story" can be understood as a folktale about someone who has not been responsible or attentive to the needs of his community. Brian O'Brannigan is an industrious man who has exhausted all the local resources he needed for his business and has had to resort to taking straw from the field of the fairies. He has busied himself serving his own needs but offered nothing to his community in return.

Although this is a traditional tale from the folklore of Ireland, it speaks compellingly to the modern situation. We each run in our own direction, exhausting our energies and the natural environment that surrounds us, but seldom do we take time to nourish our community with stories, songs and other forms of fellowship. The individual—his needs, his wants and his ways—reigns supreme. We each live isolated in our digital mentalities. The ubiquitous cellphone, ear plugs, and vacant stare are its constant testimony: "I am not with you. I am someplace else."

This loss of community life has serious ramifications. Without the need or the opportunity to learn the complexities of social interaction, it is now possible to say that not only do we have "no sense of place," as did Josh Meyrowitz (1985), but "no sense of other" as well. Restrictions on certain kinds of language and behavior that were once expected within "mixed company" wither away in public places and within the home. Even within houses of worship, people now feel free to use language, tone of voice, and behaviors that used to be unthinkable. Rules of decorum that were once absorbed as children are no longer expected or demanded. Even adults seem blissfully unaware of the differences between individual space and public space.

As life within the digital environment becomes more second-nature and commonplace, the arts have an important role to play. Whereas our growing dependency on cellphone communication tends to isolate and individualize daily life, the arts can be designed to nurture and re-establish our inherent sociality. Music, singing and dance are biased towards the social. They can be done individually and in isolation, of course, but they are characteristically interactive and, more importantly, function as socializing experiences. We meet the other through song; we touch the other through dance; we interact with the other through play.

Active involvement in the arts invites a child into an environment that educates and socializes quite differently than do digital technologies. Children will continue to be influenced and molded by digital media, but through *active* experiences in the arts, they will also have a greater opportunity to socialize and internalize real life others that have flesh, feelings, blood, and spirit. They are no longer in cyberspace but in social space.

(8) *The Arts Are Gateways to Ethical Behavior and Citizenship.* A primary obligation of public education is to cultivate and guide the ethical development of children and prepare them for the responsibilities of citizenship. As pedagogues,

we need to do more than just train children how to make money and efficiently use computers. To teach technological prowess but not social responsibility is a treacherous path. Howard Gardner (1999) is quite right when he notes that "we must figure out how intelligence and morality can work together to create a world in which a great variety of people will want to live. After all, a society led by 'smart' people might blow up itself or the rest of the world" (p. 11).

If democratic society is to survive the onslaught of the digital revolution, we must also develop a responsible and committed citizenry. In the digital age, when the stakes are so high and the technologies so powerful, Gardner's warning is particularly relevant. If there ever was a time we needed to act like citizens and be vigilant about the abuses of technology, it is now. The technologies that would make possible a totalitarian society are already in place and edging rapidly in that direction. Surveillance technologies have grown by leaps and bounds and we are now accustomed to having our lives monitored by invisible forces. This is a truly terrifying situation that seems to have come into place overnight. But what is most alarming is the lack of public discussion or interest in the possibility. As we pointed out in the previous chapter, artists have been trying to alert us to the threat of a careless faith in technology. Humans need to think, intervene, and make choices.

The arts can be especially helpful here. Without looking too far, we can see that moral and ethical dilemmas have always been amply represented in the arts. Shakespeare's *Richard III*, Goethe's *Faust* and Welles' *Citizen Kane* are warnings about blind ambition; Picasso's *Guernica*, Kubrick's *Dr. Strangelove*, and Serling's *Time Enough at Last* about the horrors of war; Nathaniel Hawthorne's *The Scarlet Letter*, Shekhar Kapur's *Bandit Queen*, and Ridley Scott's *Thelma and Louise* about the subjugation of women; Harper Lee's *To Kill a Mockingbird*, Ralph Ellison's *Invisible Man*, and Lewis Allan's "Strange Fruit" about racial oppression. The arts often point to ethical and moral challenges, make us see their existence, feel their textures and consider their consequences. It is not idle chatter that led George Orwell (1949/2001) to write that the most important purpose of the arts "is to make us more aware of ourselves and the world around us … I think it makes us more human, and I am quite certain it makes us more difficult to deceive, which is why, perhaps, all totalitarian theories of state … have deeply mistrusted the arts" (pp. 371–372).

In a nation that dares to call itself a democracy, the arts encourage us to act more like responsible citizens than like self-centered consumers. Through the arts, we meet those we might otherwise never encounter; we hear voices that we might never have heard in any other way. "One cognitive function the arts perform," writes Elliot Eisner (2002), "is to help us learn to notice the world … (T)hey enable us to step into the shoes of others and to experience vicariously what we have not experienced directly" (p. 10). By placing us in the shoes of others, literature, painting, photography, music and so on allow us to *feel* events. The arts bring us into other worlds.

(9) *The Arts Are Portals to Spirituality*. The intimate relationship between the arts, magic and spirituality is probably as old as art itself. The ancient art created by our ancestors is almost universally assumed to have been part of religious rituals. Richard Leakey (1994) writes that "It requires little imagination to think of Upper Paleolithic people chanting incantations in front of cave paintings. The unusual nature of the images, and the fact that are often deep in the most inaccessible parts of caves, begs the suggestion of ritual" (p. 111). Paleoanthropologist Steven Mithen (2005) adds "I am confident that the music played through the Geissenklösterle pipes [the oldest musical instruments yet discovered, dating to 36,000 years] and sung within ice-age painted caves had a religious function" (p. 271). In reacting to the oldest Paleolithic paintings thus far uncovered, several anthropologists in their exploration of Chauvet Cave in southern France remarked that they felt they had entered a spiritual space where rituals had been enacted some 32,000 years ago (Herzog, 2010).

The modern world, certainly with the spread of capitalism, has paid lip service to the spiritual dimension of existence but is far too connected to the material realm to take it very seriously. Art is only valued to the degree that it can support and extend wealth. Ernst Fischer (1963) reminds us that "the artist in the capitalist age found himself in a highly peculiar situation. King Midas had turned everything he touched into gold: capitalism turned everything into a commodity" (p. 19). The result is that artists are pressured to produce art for a particular market that sees art as symbols of status or objects of investment. "Art makes news today," Paglia (2012) quips, "only when a painting is stolen or auctioned at a record price" (p. vii).

Capitalism and technology are powerful companions that work together like two sides of the same coin. One of the tragic results of this coupling is that it despiritualizes the processes of art. Lewis Mumford (1952) writes that "the advancement of scientific and mechanical invention" celebrated by Francis Bacon, Isaac Newton, Faraday, Watts, Whitney and others of their ilk, "did not foresee that the humanization of the machine might have the paradoxical effect of mechanizing humanity; and that at this fatal moment the other arts, once so nourishing to man's humanity and spirituality, would become equally arid, and so incapable of acting as a *counterpoise* to this one-sided technical development" (pp. 4–5, italics added).

Mumford's choice of the term *counterpoise* is most interesting because it predates McLuhan's or Postman's use of the term "counterenvironment" but anticipates the same idea. The technologizing of humanity is in desperate need of balance.

Not Mumford, McLuhan nor Postman is saying that "technology is bad," they are only highlighting that it needs to be balanced. The arts, which traditionally has put feelings of spirituality into form, is now forced to suppress those feelings and conform to a materialist imperative promoted by the hybridization of technology and capitalism. Art is conceptualized as an economic good: if the art product cannot be bought, sold, accumulated and contained, it is not valued or supported.

In place of spirituality, this hybridization of capitalism and technology has promoted consumerism and entertainment. Electronic technology is increasingly brash and full of chatter. It doesn't allow us to experience the inner dimension. The ability to slow down, contemplate, and find moments of solitude, is being smothered in an environment dominated by nonstop amusements and hyperkinetic experiences. It is one thing to visit an amusement park; quite another to live in one. Paintner (2007) reflects on how the spiritual in the arts is being squeezed out in the contemporary environment:

> We live in a time when our capacity for imagining is being thwarted by television programs and video games that encourage us to tune out of life and become passive consumers rather than active imaginers. We have become paralyzed by our own busyness. Everything about our culture encourages us to keep busy. We do not slow down enough to really contemplate things and listen to the ways we are being drawn to live in response ... We are lulled into passivity, and our creative capacity is dulled through a constant barrage of media images and frenzied life pace. In a culture that demands we hurry up and do, produce, move faster and higher up the ladder, become breathless, worship speed and efficiency, it can be a real challenge to find space. And yet, for me, here is another important place where the spiritual life and the creative life converge—in the profound need and longing to make space and listen to the depths of experience that call me beyond myself in search of greater meaning in my life, into a relationship with mystery, and toward greater cultivation of spiritual practices. (p. 3)

The character of the technological environment in which we find ourselves calls out to be balanced by experiences that are not exclusively concerned with the practicalities of material gain. A pedagogy that doesn't esteem the arts as a central and necessary component in a child's education is tragically out of balance. The counterenvironments imagined by Marshall McLuhan and Neil Postman—using the arts and the schools as opportunities to question technology—can also function as a context where the spirituality, rather than the commerciality, of the arts can be cultivated and esteemed. The arts open up to a dimension that the technophile fails to appreciate or acknowledge. The arts help us to restore a balance.

(10) *The Arts Are Portals to Literacy*

The acquisition of literacy has never been easy. It is an arduous task that requires a very long and sustained commitment that takes years of study. First, we learn the names, sounds, and order of more than two dozen abstract marks called letters. We then learn how to skillfully hold a pen or pencil in our hands and how to write these letters on lined paper. It takes years to learn how to combine all these letters into words, how to string words into coherent sentences, how to mount the sentences into paragraphs and paragraphs into compositions.

Literacy demands as well that we learn to decipher these abstract symbols back into words and words into ideas and ideas into images in our minds. As we study more, the texts become longer and more involved. Often they are difficult to read. We build schools, train teachers, and organize school systems; it costs a lot of money to maintain and requires constant vigilance. The most challenging assignment for the student is often to read a book cover-to-cover or, even worse, to write a coherent research paper. And then, to move beyond the basics of reading, writing and coherent composition to a deeper level of command, eloquence and clarity, it will take decades of our lives.

No, the acquisition of literacy has never been easy.

Our intimacy with electronic media, and digital media in particular, has made the acquisition of literacy even a greater challenge. First, electronic media require little skill or dexterity to operate. Even toddlers soon figure out the basics of operating the radio, television and other digital devices. Push buttons and things happen. Second, as we adapt to technologies that don't require the laborious processes of learning to read and write, electronic media allow us to short circuit the use of literacy. Just as calculators allow us to short circuit the processes of basic arithmetic, the proliferation of digital media allow us to bypass the challenges involved in the learning of literacy. Third, the uses of electronic media cultivate an expectation for gratifications that are immediate, continuous, and always amusing. We are socialized to be distracted and entertained, not to focus, ponder and be patient. It's just so much easier to talk on a cellphone, play a video game or surf online.

This change in the communication environment creates an enormous dilemma for the classroom teacher. How do we teach literacy to students already acculturated to the speed and ease of electric mediation? Some would even argue that mass literacy is, in effect, dead. In an interview with Rachel Dretzin (2010), James Gee of Arizona State University accepts the decline of literacy as the inevitable cost of cultural progress. "There is always gains and losses ... Is it a loss? Sure. And to a certain extent getting people to be contemplative and a little bit slower, not to multitask all the time, paying avid attention over a long period of time, to a certain extent might be lost. But that's the price of gain."

This facile dismissal of literacy—by a university professor no less—is not something we should accept with such complacency. Many, ourselves included, are not so willing to abandon mass literacy nor do we think that such a loss is inevitable. Literacy changes how we think and how we speak. Literacy teaches us to organize our ideas in a logical and linear way. Literacy moves at a pace that allows us to examine more closely what we write and contemplate more carefully what we read. We can go back and reread passages, we can rewrite and correct that which we have already committed to paper. Literacy accustoms the mind to a way of thinking that is directly associated with philosophy, science, history, mathematics and, of course, literature. And so, before we turn our schools into "computer labs" and our libraries into "media centers," pedagogues need to rethink why literacy matters and how to teach it in an age that is biased against its very existence.

Conclusion

In this chapter, we have attempted to respond to the question "why the arts?" by outlining some of the multiple ways the arts contribute to a person's social, emotional and intellectual development. The story of Brian O'Brannigan—"here again, gone again"—isn't just a tale to entertain, it is a lesson to be learned. Brian is everyman; he is us.

Many of us are too absorbed in our day to day affairs to perceive the wider reality that surrounds us and suffocates our creative natures. How can a child nurture their creative nature if he or she seldom has the chance to actually participate in the arts? How can a child mature into a sense of community when they rarely have the opportunity to share songs, stories, and dances in social settings? It is not without reason that Elliot Eisner (2002) criticizes schools for putting "the arts at the rim, rather than at the core, of education" (p. xi). In the thirteen years since Eisner first published this lament, the emphasis on science, technology, engineering and mathematics—now enshrined in the acronym STEM—has calcified any attempt to give serious attention to the arts. We continue to think of the arts as "ice cream on Sunday" rather than the powerful food that nourishes the heart and fortifies the soul. We routinely attend to the "practical" but ignore the essential. "The arts," Eisner (2002) concludes, "are regarded as nice but not necessary" (p. xi). Like Brian, who could only see the fields of the fairies as an economic resource to be exploited, schools are losing sight of the transformative powers of the arts in narrowing their rightful and necessary place in the educational life of children.

Note

1. William Blake (1804–1820), *Jerusalem*, Plate 3, "To the Public."

References

Ansdell, G. (2014). *How music helps in music therapy and everyday life*. Burlington, VT: Ashgate.
Dretzin, R. (2010). *Digital nation: Life on the digital frontier*. A documentary film with Douglass Rushkoff.
Duncan, H. D. (1968). *Symbols in society*. New York: Oxford University Press.
Eisner, E. W. (2002). *The arts and the creation of mind*. New Haven, CT: Yale University Press.
Fischer, E. (1963). *The necessity of art*. New York: Penguin.
Fletcher, A., & Simmons, S. (2016). Creativity, collaboration, and integration: The ideas of Howard Gardner for education in the arts. In G. Humphries Mardirosian & Y. Pelletier Lewis (Eds.), *Arts integration in education* (pp. 31–54). Chicago, IL: University of Chicago Press.
Gardner, H. (1983). *Frames of mind: The theory of multiple intelligences*. New York: Basic Books.
Gardner, H. (1999). *Intelligence reframed: Multiple intelligences in the 21st century*. New York: Basic Books.
Gardner, H. (2006). *Multiple intelligences*. New York: Basic Books.
Greene, M. (1995/2000). *Releasing the imagination: Essays on education, the arts, and social change*. San Francisco, CA: Jossey-Bass.
Herzog, W. (2010). *Cave of forgotten dreams*. Documentary film.
Landy, R. J., & Montgomery, D. T. (2012). *Theater for change: Education, social action and therapy*. Portsmouth, NH: Heinemann.
Langer, S. K. (1942). *Philosophy in a new key: A study in the symbolism of reason, rite and art*. Cambridge, MA: Harvard University Press.
Leakey, R. (1994). *The origin of humankind*. New York: Perseus Books.
Lusebrink, L. (1990). *Imagery and visual expression in therapy*. New York: Plenum Press.
Malchiodi, C. A. (2003). *Handbook of art therapy*. New York: Guilford Press.
Mead, G. H. (1934). *Mind, self & society*. Ed. by C. W. Morris. Chicago, IL: University of Chicago Press.
Mead, G. H. (1982). *The individual and the social self: Unpublished essays by G. H. Mead*. Ed. by D. L. Miller. Chicago, IL: University of Chicago Press.
Meyrowitz, J. (1985). *No sense of place*. New York: Oxford University Press.
Mithen, S. (2005). *The singing Neanderthals: The origins of music, language, mind and body*. London: Weidenfeld & Nicholson.
Mumford, L. (1952). *Art and technics*. New York: Columbia University Press.
O'Cathain, S. (1980). *The bedside book of Irish folklore*. Cork: Mercier Press.
Ornstein, R. (1997). *The right mind: Making sense of the hemispheres*. New York: Harcourt Brace & Company.
Orwell, G. (1949/2001). Orwell notebook. In S. Orwell & I. Angus (Eds.), *The collected essays, journalism and letters of George Orwell*. Harmondsworth: Penguin.
Paglia, C. (2012). *Glittering images*. New York: Pantheon.

Paintner, C. V. (2007, January). The relationship between spirituality and artistic expression: Cultivating the capacity for imagining. *Spirituality in Higher Education Newsletter.*, *3*(2). Retrieved from https://www.spirituality.ucla.edu/docs/newsletters/3/Paintner_Jan07.pdf

Springer, S. P., & Deutsch, G. (1989). *Left brain, right brain.* New York: W.H. Freeman & Co.

Storr, A. (1992). *Music and the mind.* New York: Ballantine Books.

Sylwester, R. (2008). Alphabetical entries from how to explain a brain. In Jossey Bass Team (Ed.), *The Jossey-Bass reader on the brain and learning* (pp. 20–30). San Francisco, CA: John Wiley & Sons.

Yolen, J. (1986). *Favorite folktales from around the world.* New York: Pantheon.

PART TWO

Teaching as a Creative Activity

CHAPTER FIVE

The Oral Curriculum

A Prelude to Literacy and Learning

> When you plug something into a wall,
> someone is getting plugged into you.
> Neil Postman and Charles Weingartner[1]

Every Sunday afternoon for as long as I (Robert Albrecht) can remember, Aunt Flo and Uncle Mike would come to visit. They lived just down the block, but other than my mother's daily phone conversations with her sister, they lived in their world and we lived in ours. Sundays, however, were different. All the rhythms and routines of the week were interrupted by a new pattern. Usually my father would take my mother and Aunt Flo for a leisurely ride around town, while Uncle Mike stayed behind, read the Sunday paper, did the crossword puzzles, and puffed quietly on his cigar enjoying his day of rest.

The last stop on my father's tour was the bakery where he would pick up a loaf of rye bread for the evening's meal. Supper on Sunday was small—the big meal was taken earlier in the day—just some cold cuts, slices of cheese, pickles, bread and maybe a salad. The family who sat around me at the table exchanged gossip, commented on the news of the day, discussed celebrity scandals, chatted about upcoming weddings, joked about neighbors, reported sicknesses and lamented recent deaths.

Sooner or later, they always got around to telling stories about their childhood in Jersey City and New York. And this is what fascinated me most. With their words they drew pictures that fired my imagination and lured me into other worlds. There were tales of dark dingy tenements without windows or electric light, of immigrant parents and grandparents, of flu epidemics and hard times, of mischievous deeds and comic embarrassments.

And then, punctually at 8:45, my aunt would look down at her watch, stir in her seat and call out across the table "Mike, we better get going, it's almost 9 already." We all knew what that meant. Aunt Flo had to be home in time for *Bonanza* or else she would turn into a pumpkin. Dutifully, Uncle Mike would jingle the keys in his pocket, gather up his smoking materials and then they'd leave.

But then there were other Sundays. Sometimes they'd ask me to go get the guitar I was just learning to play, and between the stories, sandwiches, cold cuts, and beer, they would begin to sing. Mostly they harmonized to old Tin Pan Alley tunes and encouraged me to learn them so that I could accompany them: "Who's Sorry Now?," "Heart of My Heart," "My Gal Sal" and many other songs that I heard over and over again and can still recall to this day. Once in a while Aunt Mary and Uncle John would wander over from next door and the stories got better, the laughter grew louder, and the singing became even more spirited. The pressure was on me as I tried to finger chords that I had only recently learned. I struggled through the family's repertoire as best I could and gradually figured them out with the help of Aunt Flo. She was the most musical. My aunt had taught herself piano, ukulele and tenor guitar by ear and could sing and harmonize very well. She didn't even know the names of the chords I was supposed to be playing on the guitar, but she'd help me out by mimicking hand positions and guiding me with her eyes and words of encouragement.

As I got older, I was fortunate to hear many great musicians both live and on disc, but I will always remember those Sunday evenings singing along with my family as the greatest musical experiences I ever had.

***

The scene described above is no doubt tinged by nostalgia and idiosyncratic to the person who recounted it. Time distorts as well as illuminates. We didn't all come from families that sang together while sitting around a dinner table on Sunday evenings. Most of us do remember, however, a time in our childhood when we did sing songs, play games with friends, and exchange stories whether it was at home, on the corner, at school or in places of worship. Our lives were filled with a variety of interpersonal encounters that were a vital part of our early socialization. We needn't romanticize these interpersonal experiences but we shouldn't dismiss their importance either. They taught us how to interact with all kinds of people: new friends and old friends, the ice cream man, the neighbor who yelled at us, the bully down the block, the kids who wouldn't let us play with them, the teacher who disciplined us too severely, the friendly crossing guard, the ill-tempered bus driver, and on and on. More than just a series of pleasant or unpleasant memories, these interactions conducted face-to-face prepared us for a life lived in a community of others. In short, our passage through these labyrinths of social interaction was filled with experiences that marked and guided us for the rest of our lives. We got *here* only because we were *there* first.

In this chapter, we will argue that these multiple encounters experienced in face-to-face contexts form a necessary preparation for the transition from the informal learning of the home environment to the structured learning demanded of the school environment. Through these early interactive encounters, children learn their native language, the basic rules of conduct, and how to act appropriately within diverse contexts. They find their place in the world. In short, to try to school a child who has not been adequately exposed to the intricacies and breadth of oral communication makes the processes of education much more difficult.

We will begin by outlining what we mean by the "oral communication environment" and underscore the significant, but often ignored, role orality plays in preparing a child for the sociality of schooling and the rigors of academic learning. We will argue that orality—a mixture of speech, rituals, customs, artistic experiences and diverse interpersonal encounters—survived the rise of mass literacy but finds itself under siege and substantially weakened in the digital age.

Next, we will introduce a pedagogical concept we call the "oral curriculum." At a time when digital media and mobile technologies appear to be rapidly displacing the interpersonal experiences that were once common to childhood socialization, the oral curriculum acts as an effective counterbalance. Through the use of the arts, learning games and interpersonal activities, the oral curriculum helps to mold a set of attitudes and behaviors that are more amenable to the demands of education and a life to be lived in a social environment. In essence, the oral curriculum is the concept of the counterenvironment postulated by McLuhan and Postman applied to the primary school classroom.

Finally, we will outline some activities of the oral curriculum that can be implemented in the classroom and which function as powerful tools to help counterbalance the overwhelming influence exerted by digital media in the lives of children. They are by no means foolproof but they are designed to form an environment that extends and reinforces oral communication at a time when it is most needed. In sum, the oral curriculum helps prepare children for the transition from a context of individuality and accelerated pace fostered by repeated digital experiences to the slower and more social patterns required for literacy and academic learning.

The Oral Communication Environment

In his book *All I Really Need to Know I Learned in Kindergarten*, Robert Fulghum (1986/2003) recalls that in kindergarten he learned to play fair, share, put things back where you found them, clean up after yourself, wash your hands before you eat, take a nap, say you're sorry if you hurt somebody, and so on (p. 2). This all seems like pretty obvious stuff but apparently his simple comments struck a resonant chord with a great many people. His book went on to sell more than seven million copies in over one hundred countries and was translated into 37 languages. What's the deal? Why did so many people find this book worth the investment?

What Fulghum is actually describing is the oral communication environment. Orality is a form of socialization that was once common place but now appears to be on the wane. Oral communication is learned primarily, outside of school, through informal interpersonal interactions with others in acoustic settings like the one described in the story that opened this chapter. Orality teaches limits, responsibilities, and acceptable patterns of behavior and expression. It punishes transgressions and rewards compliance. Through orality, we learn to fit in and be part of something larger than ourselves: a network of family, friends, classmates and community acquaintances.

The dominant modality of oral communication is, as the term implies, speech. The ephemeral quality of the spoken word, however, requires a great deal of repetition as a means of maintaining cultural stability. In his important book *Orality and Literacy*, Walter Ong (1982) observes that "sound exists only when it is going out of existence" (1982, p. 32). Without literacy or electronic media to record and store speech in a fixed and retrievable form, vocalizations simply disappear as soon as they are uttered. It is for this reason that in oral cultures, that is, cultures without access or knowledge of literacy or electronic media, information deemed important and worth preserving must be constantly repeated or else it will be lost. Ong continues that within an oral environment "knowledge that is not repeated aloud soon vanishes" so that "oral societies must invest great energy in saying over and over again what has been learned arduously over the ages" (p. 41). A proverb is a proverb not only because it contains a bit of wisdom encapsulated in verbal form but because it is repeated through the ages. A saying, a song, a chant, a prayer, a poem, can only endure within an oral communication environment if it is repeated and passed on through face-to-face encounters. If not, it is gone forever. Barring this incessant repetition of what is known and what is important to remember, the continuity required of the oral communication environment is disrupted and lost.

But orality is much more complicated and varied than speech alone. Oral communication also includes music, dance, role play, make believe, synchronized movement, art, architecture, decorations, statuary, processions, parades, the preparation of food, rituals surrounding dining and drinking, and other sensory materials and experiences that intensify and underscore what is being communicated. These elements exist prominently side-by-side with speech and form an integral part of the oral environment. The sensory apparatus available to orality can also be enhanced through the use of candles, costumes, masks, incense, banners, drama, mime and customs that commemorate the passage of time, the cycle of the seasons, or whatever that culture chooses to celebrate. In oral communication, Strate (1986) reminds us, "Information is stored through all the senses, through the entire nervous system. Ritual, poetry, music, dance, pictures, smells, tastes, all combine to form one integrated system ..." (p. 243). When we speak of the oral tradition, therefore, we mean not only the spoken word in all its variant forms but also the whole array of symbolic and interpersonal experiences that constitute the social ecology of interpersonal communication conducted in face-to-face contexts. Like speech, all the direct sensory modalities mentioned above that are intimately involved in oral communication, are not one time occurrences: they are repeated constantly.

Within the context of orality, children learn and repeat the same nursery rhymes, sing the same songs, play the same games, chant the same words, and invoke the same rules as part of their routine interactions. A child doesn't play tag, stickball or hopscotch just once: these games and the rules of engagement that structure them are learned through routine repetition. This is the essence of orality and we have all experienced it in one form or another. A jump rope chant or the complicated hand play of patty cake is absorbed and is passed on through repeated face-to-face interactions and practice.

For most of our history as a species, human beings lived in what Walter Ong (1982) called a "pristine" or "primary" oral communication environment, that is, "a culture totally untouched by any knowledge of writing or print" or by electronic media (p. 11). Before the invention of writing, orality was the only show in town. Communication was necessarily direct and interpersonal. With the dramatic rise of literacy in the Middle East some five thousand years ago, and then its massive expansion via the printing press in the fifteenth century, orality was forced to share the stage with a medium that did not depend upon face-to-face interaction or human memory for its existence. Information could be recorded, stored, and shared outside the mind in a totally artificial way. The constant repetition of important information required by orality was no longer necessary for cultural preservation. Histories were etched in clay and stone, tales were written on papyrus and paper; knowledge no longer needed to be held in the mind and repeatedly shared in social contexts. The role of the bard waned and his feats of memory and composition could be put to rest. The book became the great mediator of civilization, not the spoken word, the improvised epic, or the ritualized interaction.

And yet orality endured. The culture of the common people—the folk—still relied heavily on the oral tradition as its primary form of communication. To be sure, the place of orality within the cultural hierarchy had been dealt a powerful blow but it was by no means fatal. Amongst the least literate—children, the poor and the unschooled—the routines and repertoire of orality continued to be practiced and passed on as they always had. Their songs and stories were still shared by word of mouth; their wisdom was still carried in proverbs, sayings and fables uttered orally; their beliefs and values still communicated through art, costumes, crafts and traditional rituals that they themselves organized and celebrated.

Beginning with the dramatic arrival of industrialization and electronic media in the nineteenth century, however, the enduring traditions of orality became more seriously challenged. Whereas literacy required a prolonged period of study to master its skills that discriminated against its adoption by the working and peasant classes, electronic media came ready made in a box that demanded no prerequisites. Anyone could watch a movie or learn to operate a radio, TV, phonograph or cassette recorder. Under such circumstances, it became increasingly difficult for the oral tradition to keep pace with the ease of interaction promoted by the electronic revolution. Many of the taken for granted folkways of orality disappeared or became spotty at best.

Despite the powerful surge of electronic media and its capture of culture, oral communication still played an important role in childhood and even retained a substantial presence within the interactions of adults. Children organized games and invented new ones, adults sang songs and shared stories, and orality did its best to retain its place in a rapidly changing communications environment. In the scene described at the opening of this chapter, the stories of an oral community competed with the weekly Cartwright saga broadcast on *Bonanza*, the humor rivaled that of the comedians on *The Ed Sullivan Show*, the Tin Pan Alley songs that had been heard on the radio were converted back into the oral experience, the events followed in the daily newspapers and on television became fodder for debate and discussion. Even the quirks and idiosyncrasies of characters viewed on TV and in the movies were translated back to fit the oral world around them. The neighbor who grew sideburns became "Elvis," the man who wore heavy soled boots to work was tagged "Frankenstein," the backyard sunbather in his leopard skin bikini was rechristened "Tarzan." These creative adaptations of electronic media by the ways of orality are tangible evidence of a vibrant system of oral communication that continued to exist within an environment increasingly dominated by electronic technologies.

What is most striking about the current moment is the speed at which orality is being challenged and displaced by digital media, especially in its evolution as mobile technologies. Electronic media have become a 24/7 experience that is increasingly present in every space we occupy whether it be at home, in the street, at leisure, in school or at work.

Children, who have not had sufficient time or the opportunity to absorb very much of the oral tradition, are especially effected by these changes. As they move back and forth between home and school, children necessarily bring with them the habits of mind and body cultivated by their socializing experiences with the digital. The ecological balance that once existed between the orality of home, family and neighborhood and the literacy of the school and the classroom is breaking down. Trying to keep pace, baffled school systems find themselves pressured to follow the technological imperative and adapt to the digital revolution, rather than search for ways to counterbalance it. More and more computers clutter the classroom while art, music, poetry, recess and other opportunities for social interaction are being reduced. In his only book to fully address the digital, Neil Postman (1992) comments:

> In introducing the personal computer to the classroom, we shall be breaking a four-hundred year old truce between the gregariousness and openness fostered by orality and the introspection and isolation fostered by the printed word. Orality stresses group learning, cooperation, and a sense of social responsibility ... Print stresses individualized learning, competition, and personal autonomy. Over four centuries, teachers, while emphasizing print, have allowed orality its place in the classroom, and have therefore achieved a kind of pedagogical peace between these two forms of learning, so that what is valuable in each can be maximized. Now comes the computer, carrying anew the banner of private learning and individual problem-solving. Will the widespread use of computers in the classroom defeat once and for all the claims of communal speech? Will the computer raise egocentrism to the status of a virtue? (p. 17)

Postman's questions were essentially rhetorical ones. He already knew quite well that this emergent state of affairs would have serious consequences upon the education and socialization of children and that schools needed to be more mindful of this.

From the point of view we are developing in this chapter, a child's transition from a home environment saturated with digital technology to a school environment focused on literacy and academic learning is greatly impeded if a child has not been fully exposed to the interpersonal socialization of orality. The kindergarten experience memorialized by Fulghum was only a small part of the process. If children do not have prolonged and repeated opportunities to absorb oral forms of expression during their formative years, it becomes more difficult for them to develop the patterns of patience, decorum and tolerance that are essential to the learning of literacy and being in school. Rather than accentuate the use of computers across the curriculum, therefore, we would urge that schools become counterenvironments and employ methods that cultivate orality in the classroom. As we shall see, there are good reasons for this.

The Oral Curriculum

Some years ago on *Oprah*, an audience consisting entirely of school teachers from Chicago was discussing the challenges of contemporary education. One teacher stood up and remarked, "give me a class with one or two discipline problems and I can work with them. But if half the students are discipline problems, it becomes impossible to teach." The teacher's words drew an enthusiastic response from her peers. She was spot on. How could she teach literacy or anything else if students have yet to learn discipline, decorum and the basics of social behavior? How could she proceed with the rigorous processes of learning when her class was largely distracted, unruly and disrespectful?

There are, of course, multiple factors we could point to that help explain this change in the attitudes and behavior of children. Poverty, the breakdown of the family, exposure to violence, drug abuse, and multiple other problems certainly figure prominently in a child's behavior and readiness for school. But it would be very foolish indeed to overlook the fundamental and far-reaching shift in our communication environment that we are currently experiencing. What happens if a child arrives at school never having been exposed in a substantive and prolonged way to the oral tradition? What if their childhood has been spent in front of a TV or sitting before a computer screen or playing on a mobile phone? This is important. Television doesn't teach discipline, laptops don't require cooperation, and what's so social about social media?

"We need to know in what ways," Neil Postman (1992) writes, "[the computer] is altering our conception of learning, and how, in conjunction with television, it undermines the old idea of school" (p. 18). Electronic technologies not only undermine "the old idea of school" but, just as importantly, they also undermine the old idea of orality upon which schooling was built and was able to thrive. Children need to bring something to the class that allows the teacher to do her job of educating young minds. There needs to be a deeply ingrained sense of decorum, self-restraint and mutual respect. These values are not, and cannot be, taught through videogames and cellphones. Quite the opposite.

We need to consider another approach. It seems reasonable to suggest that something should be offered to counterbalance this grand shift in our communication environment. Digital media are indeed powerful tools for learning but for someone who has not mastered the arts of orality and literacy, they can be quite dysfunctional. How will a child learn to behave in the company of others when they have grown up with mobile devices constantly in reach? Why would a child make the prolonged and tedious effort to become fully literate when they are accustomed to the speed and ease of the internet?

In the aftermath of the inspirational work of McLuhan and Postman, we are left with a baffling set of questions that remain unanswered. The loquacious McLuhan, who seemed to have an opinion on everything, was uncharacteristically mute on the subject of pedagogy while Postman outlined the problem quite thoroughly but never adequately responded to the question of "how." Although he took several stabs at suggesting pedagogical solutions to the questions that he himself raised, even Postman seemed overwhelmed by the enormity of the problem. In *Teaching as a Subversive Activity*, Postman and Weingartner (1969) passed the ball and concluded that it was a task for schoolteachers to solve, not academics. It's not "reasonable to expect the 'intellectuals' to do it, for they do not have access to the majority of youth. But schoolteachers do, and so the primary responsibility rests with them" (p. 13). In his introduction to *The Disappearance of Childhood*, Postman (1982) once again punted the ball downfield. "There is one question of great importance that this book will not address—namely, What can we do about the disappearance of childhood? The reason is that I do not know the answer ... Professional educators are, I believe, supposed to do that sort of thing" (p. xiii). In sum, Postman understood that this "how" had to take place in schools but the connecting of the ideas he suggested to actual classroom practice was a task he left for others.

If one accepts the premise of McLuhan and Postman that our culture would greatly benefit from the existence of vibrant counterenvironments from which to identify, discuss and question the nature of rapid technological change, we in education are left with the enormous problem of translating their ideas from the printed page into classroom praxis. To begin with an emphasis on academic learning and the rigors of testing, or the vain hope that more technology will cure the ills of more technology, is pure folly. We already know that digital technologies can be addictive, are filled with distractions, and can impact negatively on the acquisition and the sustenance of literacy. Why would we at this juncture insist that computers be integrated even more thoroughly across the curriculum?

In our own work with children, therefore, we have found it useful to start with the cultivation of orality as a prelude to literacy. Before a child can learn how to read, write, and perform academically, they need to learn decorum, patience and what it means to be in a social environment and not in front of a screen. To jump ahead to a full-fledged literate curriculum makes the adaptation to school almost impossible for many children and challenges the patience and skills of the classroom teacher. It is planning for failure.

Applying the Oral Curriculum in the School Environment

To Sir with Love (1967) is not generally considered to be a classic movie—probably not on anyone's list of the one hundred greatest movies of all time—but it is nonetheless a very important one. Especially for teachers. Confronted by a class of unruly high school students in a tough London neighborhood, a well-intentioned but inexperienced teacher (Mr. Thackeray played by Sidney Poitier) is rapidly burning out. He could have become mean and angry (he was heading there), he could have quit (he was thinking about it), or he could have become resigned to failure (as were many of his colleagues). Instead, he was inspired to come up with a creative response. Convention and custom were not working. After the proverbial "last straw," the fuming Mr. Thackeray blurts out "Kids!" This is his moment of insight, his epiphany, his creative breakthrough. He suddenly realizes that in order to be a successful teacher, he must cease his failed attempts to teach according to the dictates of the assigned curriculum and respond creatively to the actual students he is facing in the classroom. Rather than blame his students, Mr. Thackeray seeks ways to engage them in the joys of learning.

In the digital age, we must do the same. The inability of our students to read well and write coherently may not be so much a personal failure but the result of a dramatic change in our media environment. They are not the "dumbest generation" as Mark Bauerlein (2009) so provocatively labeled them but a generation of young people who have been socialized and educated in an environment that has worked against literacy and the orality on which it depends. The oral curriculum we outline below is an attempt to add balance to the curriculum. It builds upon oral practices that were once common to childhood but which have since eroded and in many cases disappeared. These activities are not intended as a "cure-all" but they are a step in the right direction in transforming the kinds of classrooms inhabited by teachers in Chicago and elsewhere throughout the world.

Play

One of the most alarming casualties of the digital revolution is the decline of the spontaneous and unsupervised outdoor play of children. We shouldn't breeze by this too quickly for it has enormous ramifications. Writing for *The Economist*, Barbara Beck (2019) notes that contemporary "children will spend most of their time indoors, often with adults rather than with siblings or friends, be supervised more closely, be driven everywhere rather than walk or cycle, take part in many more organized activities and, probably for several hours every day, engage with a screen of some kind." Most adults of a certain age would probably agree with Beck's observation. The playful interactions a child encounters when online are of a qualitatively different nature than those mediated face-to-face. The physical and intimately social nature of play has been superseded by a vicarious and distanced one.

The assault on traditional forms of childhood play comes at three distinct but interrelated factors. On one level, many parents are reluctant to allow their children to play freely outdoors because of fears regarding automobile traffic, dangerous characters on the streets, pedophiles, bullies and so on. There may well be some cause for concern but parents may also be reacting to what George Gerbner (1998) called "the mean world syndrome." Gerbner argued that the violence sensationalized and over represented on television cultivates an exaggerated fear in the audience about the dangers lurking outside their doors. As a result, many responsible parents feel obliged to keep their children inside where it is safe. The alternative is to taxi and chaperone their children to and from a whole host of adult supervised activities ranging from ballet class to soccer practice. It has also become common for parents to schedule "play dates" for children who no longer meet spontaneously outdoors in public areas but at times and places set, chaperoned and controlled, and once again, taxied to, by adults.

On a second level, schools, which are increasingly under the gun to raise scores on standardized tests, have responded by restricting the time allotted to play during recess and at lunch while increasing the time focused on academics and in preparation for endless tests and evaluations. The scores on these tests are crucial for all concerned from administrators down to the children in kindergarten. Teachers are oft times pressured into conformity while the principal of a "failing" school can easily be demoted, fired, or simply exiled to an even more challenging school.

But it is on a third level that traditional forms of play confront their biggest threat. Increasingly, children have abandoned bats, balls, miniature tea sets and other forms of interaction and replaced them with an array of entertaining digital gadgets. At the very least, this is a very radical departure from what play has always meant to the countless generations that have engaged in it. Play is embedded in our collective heritage as human beings. Unlike speech, writing or the internet, there was never a time in human history when children didn't interact through play. Johan Huizinga (1938/1955) in his influential meditation on play went as far as to suggest that we rename our species *homo ludens*—"man the player"—to emphasize the centrality of play in the evolution of humanity. For Huizinga, play was not just a frivolous pastime or a marginal activity but a deeply precious and complicated one. According to the Dutch scholar, it is through play that we gave birth to language and poetry, music and dance, ritual, drama and art, our games and our sense of fair play, our laws and our civilization:

> Ritual grew up in sacred play; poetry was born in play and nourished on play; music and dancing were pure play. The rules of warfare, the conventions of noble living were built up on play-patterns. We have to conclude, therefore, that civilization is, in its earliest phases, played. It does not come *from* play like a babe detaching itself from the womb: it arises *in* and *as* play, and never leaves it. (p. 173)

Early psychologists as well emphasized the importance of play in a child's development and well-being. For Carl Jung, play released the imagination and was a necessary activity that should be cultivated and enjoyed not only in childhood but throughout our entire lives. Jungian historians Segaller and Berger (1989) write that "childhood and playing were of lifelong importance to him" (p. 80). Jean Piaget (1928, 1955, 1962), writing in the early and middle years of the twentieth century, noted at the very initiation of his career that young children learned not through logic or rational thought but through hands on experiences made possible by the trial and error of play. Lev Vygotsky (1931/1978) also emphasized the importance of play as a tool for children to develop intellectually by drawing them into creative and imaginative experiences. Bruno Bettelheim (1975) maintained that childhood play was of great psychological importance for it provided young children a vehicle to explore in symbolic form unsolved problems "which are too complex, unacceptable, and contradictory" to deal with directly (p. 55). Robert Sternberg (1998) adds that play is significant because the "relationships with peers during childhood are important not only for the child's well-being but, eventually, for the well-being of the adult that the child will become" (p. 440).

Research has systematically demonstrated the importance of play in a child's physical, social/emotional and cognitive development. Multiple studies, for example, have shown that outdoor play helps to promote a child's physical well-being (Isenberg & Quisenberry, 2002; National Association for the Education of Young Children & the National Association of Early Childhood Specialists in State Departments of Education, 2002) and that active experiences in play are associated with the socio-emotional development of children (Nielsen, 2012;

Saracho & Spodek, 1998; Smilansky and Shefatya, 1990; Steen & Owens, 2001; Sutherland and Friedman, 2013). Others have published research demonstrating that play allows children to practice various cognitive capacities, including self-control (Blair & Diamond, 2008; Savina, 2014; Vygotsky, 1967), narrative abilities (Pellegrini, 1985), theory of mind abilities (Harris, 2000), and creative abilities (Carruthers, 2002; J.L. Singer, 1995). Some have argued that pretending allows children to learn about how things in the world could be different than they actually are (Gopnik, 2009; Lillard, 2001). Research also supports the notion that play teaches turn-taking, collaboration, following rules, and empathy (Bodrova & Leong, 2007; Krafft & Berk, 1998).

At the same time that play is essential to a child's physical, socio-emotional and cognitive development, several authors maintain that play has an important effect on the development of basic language, literacy and advanced academic skills (Dansky, 1980; Dansky & Silverman, 1973; Fromberg & Bergen, 1998; Frost, Wortham, & Reifel, 2001; Pepler & Ross, 1981; D.G. Singer, 1973; Sutton-Smith, 1986). Several studies conclude that play and creative thought are related behaviors because both rely on children's ability to use symbols (Johnson, Christie, & Yawkey, 1999; Saracho & Spodek, 1998; Singer & Singer, 1998).

For all these reasons and many more, play is a significant form of socialization and learning. Children learn by doing and by doing play children absorb the attitudes, assumptions, and habits of mind, body and spirit that will guide them as adults. A group of children making a sand castle at the beach are not wasting their time. They are channeling their energies in an imaginative way. They are in perpetual but coordinated motion, working together, making new friends, negotiating procedures and designs, identifying problems and inventing solutions. Their play is a spontaneous "happening," an opportunity to meet, greet, and celebrate life.

Any pedagogical approach that ignores the active involvement of children in play is necessarily a very fragile one. Despite a huge literature testifying to its importance to childhood development, schools in the United States have routinely dismissed the pedagogical importance of play. Play is not a piece of junk jewelry that merely adorns the neck of childhood. It is, as Huizinga maintained, the very basis of civilization. For all these reasons, play is allotted a prominent position in the oral curriculum. All the other modalities of the oral curriculum—storytelling, games, art, drama, music, movement and dance and so on—are but different ways of playing. When they become too serious, they lose their character as play. The activities that follow are conceptualized as play. While they teach important skills and cultivate behaviors amenable to academic learning, they are meant to be enjoyed, shared and repeated as forms of play.

Storytelling

"Once upon a time" is an irresistible invitation to enter a world where the normal rules of the universe do not apply and the imagination reigns supreme. Animals talk, horses fly, cows climb on roofs, beanstalks grow up into the clouds, villains shift form, warriors fight dragons, and invisible forces guide the hero from the depths of failure to the lofty heights of triumph. Since time immemorial, fairy-tales, folktales, fables and myths have been told and retold to children who have delighted in stories that warned of the perils of jealously, envy, sloth, malicious trickery, empty pride and uncontrolled desire, as well as those celebrating the deeds of great heroes to be emulated and honored. The story of "David and Goliath" is forever the tale of the small overcoming the powerful; "King Midas," the folly of greed; "Pinocchio," the pitfalls of dishonesty; and "Little Red Riding Hood," a warning to be wary of strangers. Each tale is an opportunity to teach, each story is a reflection of our psychic and social reality, each narration a bit of wisdom and poetry to which generations return again and again over the course of their lives.

A well told story is also about the community formed between the storyteller and the storylistener. The words from the mouth of one vibrate in the ears of the other. The images the storyteller forms with words creates pictures in the minds of the listeners. There is eye contact, the exchange of facial expressions and body gesture, the sharing of laughter and awe. The storyteller molds the tale to her audience, hearing them just as much as they hear her. A collective vibration can be tangibly felt. In its essence, a social bond is being created.

We still have stories in the digital age, of course, but these stories are generally being told by images on a screen. The bond of storyteller and listener has been broken. Rather than having to absorb all the complicated social routines, rites and responses that are necessary for life within an oral community, digital media have made it more convenient and comfortable to go online. When in cyberspace, one doesn't have to deal with an actual person or, if they do, can do so in ways that would be inappropriate, disrespectful and even impossible in an oral setting. The mobile device held prominently in the hand distracts the child and prevents the oral bond from fully forming.

Stories, even those told in childhood, often have a great psychic depth. Both Freud and Jung seized upon the idea that stories were not just childish tales easily dismissed as fantasy but significant illuminations of our unconscious minds. Thus Freud could draw on Greek mythology and talk about Oedipal complexes and narcissism while Jung explored a vast array of ancient and medieval stories as key elements in the formation of his psychoanalytical theories. In outlining what he called "the journey of the hero," Joseph Campbell (1949) understood these tales as archetypal adventures symbolizing our own journeys through life as we struggle to mature from childhood into a full and vibrant adulthood. Bruno Bettleheim (1975) offered penetrating analyses of classic children's fairytales such as "Jack and the Beanstalk," "Hansel and Gretel," and "Snow White" that illuminate the inner workings of the young psyches of children. In fact, the very word we use for the study of the human mind is borrowed from the ancient Greek myth of Psyche. "The curiosity of Psyche," writes Robert Sternberg (1998), "and her search—for both knowledge ... and for love—are symbolic of our spirit of inquiry as we go in search of the human mind. The story of Psyche exemplifies many of the phenomenon that psychologists seek to study: curiosity, envy, love, compassion, altruism, and perseverance" (p. ii).

It is as if some of the most creative minds of the twentieth century were pointing us toward the importance of story and yet, paradoxically, the educational establishment has walked away from it. Whether this is for indifference or for ignorance, no theory of pedagogy should discount the power of classic stories in the formation of a child's character. Children need stories that affirm their higher selves and illuminate the difficult pathways of life with an array of examples of great heroes who have stood firm for the good and the true. "Our genius," Postman (1995) observes, "lies in our capacity to make meaning through the creation of narratives that give point to our labors, exalt our history, elucidate the present, and gave direction to our future ... The purpose of a narrative is to give meaning to the world, not to describe it scientifically" (p. 7).

Like childhood play, the art of storytelling is a part of our ancient heritage that has suffered with the transition to the electronic media environment. Stories of the commercial variety that children routinely consume via electronic media are generally there to flatter, thrill and sell a product, not to instruct them on how to become a better person. Whereas stories told on television, in the movies or online are there to attract and hold an audience, stories of the oral curriculum are there to teach values that the culture believes a child should learn. In constructing the oral curriculum, therefore, repeated exposure to stories, told orally or read aloud from books, is essential. "Not any kind of story," Neil Postman (1995) adds, "but one that tells of origins and envisions a future, a story that constructs ideals, [and] prescribes rules of conduct ..." (pp. 5–6). Stories of the oral curriculum are chosen to stir the imagination, inspire curiosity, and help give children a reason to learn.

At the same time, by hearing stories told repeatedly, children learn to transform words from abstract sounds into images and follow an oral narrative—a skill necessary for the successful transition to literacy. Stories also extend vocabulary by putting words into a context and showing how they are properly pronounced. A well told story can increase attention span and lead to questions that are the keys to learning and basic to intellectual development. Without curiosity, education is dead in the water and schools become tedious dungeons not houses of learning.

In their book *Asking Better Questions*, Morgan and Saxton (1991) outline different levels of questions, from the most concrete to the most abstract, that a teacher can ask her class in response to the shared experience of a story. These questions can range from those which merely ask students to recall what they heard to those which demonstrate the degree to which the story impacted their levels of understanding, reasoning and judgement. Questioning sharpens the mind and creates a more exciting learning experience not only for the students but for the teacher as well. "All our knowledge," Postman (1979) observes, "results from questions, which is another way of saying that question-asking is our most important intellectual task" (p. 140).

We are fortunate enough to live at a time when our "global village" has provided us with ample versions of tales gathered from every historical period and corner of the planet. There are tales for every occasion, season and situation. Within the oral curriculum, teachers learn to become storytellers who can reach down and pull out appropriate stories to share with children on a daily basis. Their listening improves, their focus is sharpened, their imagination is stimulated. They learn narrative structure and are moved to ask questions. Stories can be, and should be, repeated: the children will demand it. Well-chosen stories open the doors of perception and invite children to enter worlds populated with characters, moral dilemmas, challenges and triumphs that nourish young minds in a very beneficial way. Stories are metaphors to live by.

Art

It is one of the great curiosities of history that many of the most important discoveries of Paleolithic art were made by children engaged in the act of play. "Boys are officially credited with the discovery of about a dozen art caves," writes John Pfeiffer (1969), "but the unofficial count would be considerably higher, since archeologists often receive sole credit for caves they originally learned about from boys in the neighborhood" (p. 251).

The very first discovery of Paleolithic art, however, was not made by a boy but by a nine-year-old girl name Maria Sautuola. In the summer of 1879, Maria set out with her father Marcelino to explore the caves of Altamira in northern Spain. While her father was scouring the floor of the caves in search of ancient artefacts, Maria was playing with the flickering light from her candle. As she cast shadow puppets on the walls that surrounded her, Maria suddenly squealed in surprise at seeing the painting of a bull on the ceiling above her. As she whirled about and studied the walls around her, the little girl saw paintings of several other animals. And thus it was that the first modern discovery of Paleolithic art was made by a nine year girl playing with a candle.

Just 16 years later in the spring of 1895, the second major discovery of Paleolithic art was made a group of boys exploring inside a cave near La Mouthe in France. "One by one they crawled into a hole just big enough to worm through," Pfeiffer (1982) notes, "kept crawling for more than 100 yards, and came out with news of an engraved figure seen by candlelight ... a bison with great curving horns" (p. 26). As it turned out, the second great discovery of Paleolithic art with more than 200 engravings and paintings was also made by children who were playing.

But the greatest discovery of them all would have to wait until 1940. Four boys out for a walk followed their dog who had crawled into a hole covered over with thick vegetation. The dog led the boys down a tunnel and into a cave where they found over 600 of the most spectacular paintings ever discovered. For the quantity and sheer beauty of these depictions, Joseph Campbell (1959) and many others have referred to this particular cave as "the Sistine Chapel of the Paleolithic" (p. 300). And so it was, this magnificent trove of Stone Age art at Lascaux was also uncovered by children.

At present, hundreds of these caves have been found, some of which contain art that dates back as far as 32,000 years ago. We may never know exactly why our ancient ancestors crawled through holes and down narrow tunnels, risking life and limb, to paint on the walls of caves. It does demonstrate rather convincingly, however, that the impulse to create art resides deep with our very nature. We do art because we must.

There is also a direct historical connection of the innate drive to create art and the development of writing. It is not too much to suggest that the manual dexterity required in making art contributed to the manual dexterity required to write. Nor is it too far-fetched to propose that the coordination of eye and hand necessary for the creation of art was also applied to the earliest forms of writing. We should not ignore as well that the first technologies employed to write—chisels, brushes, paints and so on—had all been developed as tools in service to art. While the origins of writing can be traced back to the accounting needs of ancient Mesopotamians over 5000 years ago, the earliest forms of art are at least fifteen times as old. Necklaces crafted from shells, flutes fashioned from bone, horses sculpted in ivory, and literally hundreds of "Venus" figurines carved from stone pre-exist by several millennia the first efforts at writing.

We should also note that the earliest forms of writing—in Sumer, Egypt, China and Central America—were all image based. In ancient Sumerian cuneiform, the written word for "fish" was a drawing of a fish; in ancient Egyptian hieroglyphs, the written word for "foot" was a drawing of a foot; in Chinese writing the written word for "center" is a drawing of a box with a line drawn through its middle. Only very gradually did images become stylized abstractions and the nonfigurative squiggles we call letters. Originally, the letter A had been the drawing for ox, B a drawing of a house, H a drawing of a fence, M a river, S a snake, and so on down the line. Since the word for ox was "aleph" and for house was "bet," we call this system the "alphabet" based upon the first two letters much as we sometimes say the "ABCs."

As with the case of play and storytelling, it strikes us strange that a modality with such a powerful appeal to children and with a historical correlation to writing is not taken more seriously in schools. Writing is just one step away and already exists in embryonic form as art. From a very early age, children love to play with chalk, pens, pencils, paint and crayons. They draw on walls, sidewalks, and in the margins of their notebooks. These kinds of simple activities improve cognitive development, refine motor skills and aid visual learning. Finger painting, sculpting clay and playing with sand are tactile experiences that develop hand-to-eye coordination and support mental growth. Along with scribbling, such activities must be appreciated as important precursors to writing and early literacy. Holding and grasping pencils, crayons and paintbrushes, as well as organizing blocks and boxes, help children develop the important motor skills needed for writing as well as accomplishing future everyday tasks like setting the table, cooking, and constructing and repairing useful objects.

As the art skills of a child develops, their ability to plan, understand cause-and-effect and complete projects becomes integrated into their future academic and cultural endeavors. Mathematical concepts like size, shape, proportion, counting and spatial awareness also have their roots in making art. Art is also a gateway to language and social abilities. Encouraging children to describe their work and their process can become an early way to develop metacognition, verbalization and the ability to interact socially.

In one activity we developed specifically for the oral curriculum, "Everyone Has Stories," each child is assigned a partner and asked to respond to a series of prompts offered by the teacher: tell your partner about your favorite relative (or a time you got into trouble, or about a special place you went, or about a time when you had to go to the hospital, etc.). After conversing for a few minutes with their partner, the child is asked to draw a picture of the experience they had been conversing about with their partner. Once they have completed their art piece, children may then be given a chance to explain the drawing to the class. This public speaking extension would be on a volunteer only basis because some children may be reluctant or intimidated by having to talk in front of the entire class. But for those who do want to take the plunge, the exercise can lead to confidence in speaking in front of a group.

An alternative approach also connects art to storytelling. After telling a story to the class, children are given a chance to draw a scene from the story. When children illustrate a scene from a story they've heard in class, they reach into their imaginations and are able to connect more deeply to the tale. Applying art to story opens a dialogue about what has taken place, leads to questions about what will happen next, and fosters the ability to look more carefully into the story's meaning, its complexity and its use of symbols. This way of working can reveal to the teacher each student's level of understanding and the different kinds of meaning a child brings to a tale. The classroom can also be transformed into an art gallery where children pretend to be museum goers or art critics discussing the merits or meaning of the work they are encountering. This encourages children to develop a wider vocabulary and, once again, creates opportunities to speak in public before a group in a non-threatening way.

Art in the life of a child begins as play. A child scribbles on the wall, makes airplanes from clothespins on the kitchen floor, builds castles of sand at the beach. When children pick up a stick, a stone or a piece of chalk and spontaneously draw shapes on any surface they can find, they are connecting to this same drive that inspired our Paleolithic ancestors. Children simply love to do art. The oral curriculum encourages this love of art not because we expect to turnout future Picasso's or as a reward for "being good," but because we want to develop the child's full potential as a human being and prepare them for the gradual transition to academic subjects, literacy and critical thinking.

Games

Games are a form of play that comes with a set of rules and procedures that participants agree to respect. If these rules are violated by one or more of the participants, say by a cheater or someone who doesn't pay attention, then the informal contract is broken and the game is abandoned. Although some games, such as solitaire, are played alone, these are the exceptions. Nearly all games—board games, card games, street games, field games, court games and so on—are meant for two or more players and, therefore, are social by nature.

It is not often that we think of the classroom as a place to play games but, in the digital environment in which we now find ourselves, it may well be the only place where children have the opportunity to do so on a regular basis. By games in the oral curriculum, we are specifically referring to games that are conducted face-to-face, without some form of electronic interruption or mediation, and which teach important skills and attitudes required for successful learning. In such a way, games can become powerful tools for absorbing the basics of interpersonal behavior and preparing children for the sociality and discipline that schooling requires. All games have rules, procedures, and restraints that demand self-control. Games also require the negotiation of conflicts in order to proceed, the ability to wait one's turn, and an overall respect for group process. These are not natural inborn behaviors; they need to be learned, passed on, and reinforced through constant repetition.

In our use of games in the classroom as part of the oral curriculum, we often begin our workshops by simply having the class rearrange their desks into a circle. The circle eliminates the corners where timid children hide and forces those who would withdraw from a social experience into a position where it is more difficult to do so. Once in a circle, we go around and allow each child to say their name—thus asserting their membership in the group—which is usually accompanied by a simple rhythm that is slapped on the knee. One by one, each child announces his or her name, the group repeats it three times, and thereby making the process a sort of musical affirmation game. As simple as this sounds, it serves to break the ice, brings smiles, and lays the foundations for a successful workshop.

Another game we use is called "Seat on my Right." This game helps split up the cliques that form in all groups and often impede group participation. A seat is left vacant to the right of the teacher who then invites a child by name to come over and sit next to him. The teacher may also ask the child to tell him one thing about herself: her birthday or a favorite color, hobby, subject, TV show, food, singer, etc. The seat left vacant by the child who has changed position allows another student to repeat what the teacher has just modeled. One by one every child in the circle is involved, affirmed, and switches seats. The cliques have been broken and the class is ready to proceed more openly with the next activity.

Besides creating a greater sociality in the classroom, games of the oral curriculum can also be used to enhance the ability to listen, observe, follow and give directions. "Change 3" is an observation game we adapted from a book by Viola Spolin (1963) which places children in pairs and requires them to briefly observe the attire of their partner. The partners then turn away from each other and quickly change three things (changing a bracelet from one wrist to the other, removing a belt, an earring, or a shoe, rolling up a sleeve of a shirt, etc.). Partners then turn back again to face each other and must describe what has been changed in their partner's appearance. A new set of partners is then formed, the number of things to be changed is increased and the game quickly becomes very interactive and quite silly. Within the fun, however, children are learning to work with others, be observant, and change their appearance in creative ways.

"Tiger and Ox" is a game that teaches listening skills. Two children are blindfolded, placed within the circle, and each given a rattle. One child is assigned the role of a tiger who must capture the ox while the other child becomes the ox and must try to escape. The tiger shakes the rattle and the ox responds but then quickly changes location. If after three attempts, the tiger cannot capture the ox, the ox escapes and is victorious. Each child, of course, gets his or her turn to play while the group has the important task of remaining silent so that the tiger can listen to the movements of the ox. The group also forms the circle that contains the tiger and ox and must gently guide any child who begins to wander outside back into the center. As such, the game contributes to the building of trust and support within the classroom while teaching children to listen carefully and restrain their impulses to shout.

In another listening game, "Airport," the teacher blindfolds a child while his or her partner guides them with a series of verbal commands through an obstacle course of books, pencils and random objects strewn about on the floor. If a child steps on an object, the airplane crashes and the partners switch roles. Children need to speak loud and clear enough for their partner to hear. The directions that guide the blindfolded partner encourage an accuracy in verbal command.

In "Who Started the Motion," a volunteer is asked to leave the circle while the teacher secretly designates a child to be the leader. The leader will start to make a motion that the rest of the circle mirrors. The leader is instructed to seamlessly change the motion from time to time while the other children, for their part, are instructed not to look directly at the leader. When the volunteer returns to the circle and sees everyone doing the same motion, she is given three guesses to determine who the person is who has started the motion. At that point, a new leader is chosen and the process is repeated.

There are multiple other learning games of the oral curriculum that teach children social skills, listening and observation skills, decorum, patience, kinesthetic expression, verbal skills, self-confidence and so on (see Fluegelman, 1976; LeFevre, 2002; Luvmour & Luvmour, 2019). In the digital age, the acquisition of these skills should not be taken for granted. Children who spend a good portion of their day interacting with some sort of screen or with a mobile device fixed in their hand may not have had much experience in face-to-face communication conducted in a truly social context. Such games are easily learned, require no money, and can be played outside on the playground or at home without the intervention of an adult.

Music, Movement and Dance

Within this very real conflict between oral and digital communication environments, music, movement and dance have an important role to play. As part of the oral curriculum, the irresistible appeal of music encourages children to focus their collective energy in a single, sustained and shared activity. At a time when digital media and mobile phones are splintering groups into collections of disconnected individuals, music transforms a room of individuals into a gathering of community. Singing, movement and dancing encourage us to raise our voices and move our bodies in a joyful way that challenges isolation. Music, movement and dance forge a group that is able to sustain an activity to its completion and then follow it with others that build on the one that preceded it. There is a continuity of effort. In short, music, movement and dance make the many one.

Music, movement and dance are seamlessly joined together in a follow the leader game from Ghana in West Africa called "Che Che Kole." In this activity, the teacher sings a short string of nonsense syllables which the children repeat. The teacher then adds a motion to accompany the words and the children imitate the movement. Classroom volunteers can then take turns at being the leader of the group. Children will often use this platform as a stage to show off their dance moves and agilities.

"Bumper Cars" is a simple music, movement and dance game that works well with younger children. The teacher asks the children to imagine that they are bumper cars in an amusement park that can only move when she hits the small drum she is holding in her hand. If she taps slowly, they can move slowly; if she taps the drum quickly, they can move quickly. When the teacher stops tapping, the children have to freeze in place no matter what position they are in. If a car continues to move once the drum has stopped, then the bumper car has to be sent to the "repair shop" and the child misses a turn. When the children are moving to the beat of the drum, the teacher can ask them to imagine they are "rabbits" (or clouds, or fish, birds, lions, zombies, etc.) or to move like "butterflies" (or horses, bees, robots, etc.). This simple activity teaches restraint at the same time it allows children to move in creative ways.

The learning of songs is also a central part of the oral curriculum. It promotes focused attention, group process, social interaction, and enhances the development of memory. Foreign languages can also be introduced through singing—learning not only vocabulary but the correct pronunciation and the rhythm of phrases. Singing on a regular basis allows children to develop a repertoire of singable tunes that can be shared with others and steadily expanded. If the singing is accompanied by a musical instrument, the experience is sure to fill some children with the desire to learn to play an instrument. In our 40 years of work, we have *never* been in a class when at least one child did not ask to hold or touch the guitar.

Learning songs from other times and places connect children with people and events of different cultures and different historical periods. "Cielito Lindo," a well-known Mexican song from 1882, has a chorus that children can learn quite easily. "I'm Henery the Eighth, I Am" is a 1910 British music hall song sang with a Cockney accent. "Does Your Chewing Gum Lose Its Flavor?" is a comic reworking of a song from American vaudeville in the 1920s. "I've Been Working on the Railroad" is a song from 1894 that can be used as a platform to discuss the building of the transcontinental rail system. Woody Guthrie's "This Land Is Your Land" can be used to teach history, citizenship, American geography, and the hardships of the Great Depression. "Sixteen Tons" invites a dialogue about the way of life of those who labor in coal mines; "Jambalaya" offers an opportunity to discuss the cuisine and customs of a different region of the United States; "Clementine" opens a conversation about the Gold Rush of 1849. Depending upon the resourcefulness, interests and abilities of the teacher and her class, this repertoire can be steadily expanded upon.

Group singing also connects quite naturally with literacy and higher forms of learning. Memorization is one of the most tedious requirements of learning but the act of singing jubilantly improves a child's ability to recall a series of words and access them on a later occasion. Children who are singing in a group and following a written text learn to read as part of a group in which the abilities of the slow reader are enhanced rather than be made the source of public embarrassment. Written songs show children how words are spelt and allows them to hear how they are properly pronounced. Songs can also be copied by hand, gathered together, and placed in notebooks that are creatively decorated. This not only teaches writing and reading, but the basics of organization upon which higher learning depends.

In sum, group singing, movement and dance enhance memory, the ability to keep rhythm, inspire interest in learning to play an instrument, release joy, and contribute to the formation of a functioning group within the classroom. At just the point in their lives when they are most physically active, children are eager to channel their energies into music. Children are normally much less inhibited about the use of movement, dance and song than are older children and adults. Such activities enhance sociality in the classroom and provide a bridge for children to connect to other children, generations and cultures.

School systems that attempt to leapfrog over music, movement and dance in order to get to the "more important" STEM (science, technology, engineering and mathematics) subjects may find that they have lost half of their students in the process. Active involvement in music (as opposed to passive listening or watching) is by no means a "magic bullet" solution to the problems posed by the massive influence of digital media, but it does help to create an environment that is much more social, collectively focused and ultimately more conducive to learning. Like Aunt Flo of yesteryear who would forego the pleasures of *Bonanza* if she were engaged in the act of music making, contemporary children can be weaned off of their electronic devices and related behaviors if given more opportunities to sing, move and dance to music.

Drama

Playing pretend, re-enacting stories, and imagining ourselves in different roles and situations is a natural part of childhood. Digital media places the pretend world on a screen; the oral curriculum brings it to life in the classroom and converts it into a vehicle for learning. In Chapter Six, we will discuss at length the pedagogical role that drama can play in the cultivation and deepening of literacy but, for now, we will confine our remarks to using drama as part of the oral curriculum. This natural childhood impulse to play pretend can be transformed into fertile ground for learning a wide variety of skills necessary for the adaptation to schooling and as a helpful prelude to literacy.

Our use of drama in the classroom consists of a mixture of theater games, mime, improvisation, and role play. "I'm Thinking of a Word," for example, is a simple drama activity, based on mime, that teaches children to rhyme, to be creative with their bodies, to raise their hands and be patient as they wait their turn. Sitting in a circle, the teacher states that she is thinking of a word that rhymes with (for example) "sat." "I will only call on those children with their hands up." The children make suggestions—cat, flat, hat, mat, rat—until one child guesses what the teacher is thinking. In the second round, the game becomes more fun. Rather than *say* the word, the children have to *act it out*. Children who may not be adept with what Gardner (1983) calls linguistic or mathematical intelligences may find that they excel in this type of activity and are thus given a chance to shine in front of their teacher and classmates.

"Story drama" allows children the opportunity to act out a story that has been told to the class. Children can be assigned different parts in the tale with the teacher acting as narrator. Better yet, the class can be broken into smaller groups, thus creating more opportunities for the children to participate both as characters in the story and as the narrator. The classroom itself can be rearranged so that desks and chairs become walls, mountains, stores, or whatever. In re-enacting the first discovery of Paleolithic art in Altamira, we created a workshop in which the lights in the room were dimmed, children formed tunnels by moving furniture, and blindfolds were used to simulate darkness.

The fullest expression of the oral curriculum can be found in the creation of grade-wide or school-wide pageants that integrate stories, games, art, songs, dance, mask making, costume making and theatre in a collective celebration. This is a total artistic emersion that requires a great deal of cooperation at various levels, but the rewards are truly impressive. Such pageants are an opportunity to collectively commemorate a holiday, a great hero, a season of the year, or other significant events.

One such project that we developed was called "Children of the World." In 1981, we were invited by the Jersey City Public Schools to develop an arts in education program that would address on-going ethnic conflicts in schools throughout the city. The result was a seven-week series of workshops that concluded with a grand pageant that brought children from different fifth grade classes together in a shared multi-sensory experience. In preparing the program, we researched the art, music, stories, crafts, and costumes of various cultures and eventually came up with a wide range of activities that would channel the creative energy of children and provide a powerful intercultural narrative celebrating ethnic diversity.

The "Children of the World" series began with an adaptation of the Tower of Babel story which we presented as a theatrical piece to an assembly of all the classes. An idyllic community becomes confrontational and non-cooperative and suddenly finds that it is unable to communicate amongst its members. The monoculture of Babel was then cast to the four corners of the earth and the beginnings of our multicultural world are set into motion. The children—who had been an audience up until now—were then divided into one of four groups representing the great cultural regions of the world: Africa, Asia, the Americas and Europe. Each of the four classes selected for the program was then assigned a region to study. The children began the seven-week workshop series focusing on the arts, dances, music, games and stories of the particular culture to which their class had been assigned.

At the conclusion of the seven-week series, the four groups were reunited for the first time since the Tower of Babel dramatization that had initiated the program. None of the groups knew exactly what the other groups had been working on and there was usually a burst of delighted surprise as each witnessed the other file into the space set aside for the pageant. The children entered in full regalia, carrying banners and wearing costumes and masks, parts of which they had made themselves. Art work created during the series was incorporated into the scenery for each story and each group sang a song to welcome the others to the circle. After the initial greetings, each class performed a dramatization of a story from the cultural group to which they had been assigned.

The "Children of the World" pageant went on to tour several different schools, neighborhoods, churches, and day camps in Jersey City. The program proved enormously popular with children, teachers, and parents and, to a large extent, it succeeded in its goal of introducing children to the varied traditions of the world's different cultures and symbolically healing the rifts of ethnic misunderstanding.

Perhaps most importantly, however, "Children of the World" incorporated all the arts in a stunning illustration of the power and appeal of the oral curriculum. Sociality was enhanced, focus and attention were sharpened, and school became an exciting place.

Conclusion

Orality is often taken for granted as if it were inborn and natural. It isn't. It is learned through countless face-to-face experiences with others around us. We learn it, and can only learn it, by doing it. It was once an intrinsic part of childhood but, with the advance of digital media into our communication environment, children have less exposure to interpersonal experiences that earlier generations lived on a daily basis. Orality teaches children how to live in community and helps them develop certain habits of mind and body that allow them to move on to the rigors and routines of literacy and schooling.

The family anecdote that introduced this chapter illustrates the vital role that families have traditionally played in the preservation and passing on of orality. Through repeated family encounters, we learn to speak, sing and share stories. Values and beliefs are passed on and a repertoire of interpersonal modalities, experienced face-to-face in a shared context, are internalized, honored and become a part of who we are and what we will become. Like the kindergarten environment praised by Fulghum, the family has traditionally been an important agent of socialization in the ethos of orality. When electronic media come to replace these interpersonal experiences as the prime source of socialization, there are undoubtedly consequences for a child's development. To ignore these consequences, to refuse to even discuss them or experiment with other approaches, is to abandon our role and our responsibilities as pedagogues at a crucial point in the history of our species.

Digital media tend to individualize the user. Along with their speed, convenience and easy access to information, a large part of their appeal is the accentuation on individuality. It is very easy to become self-involved on a cellphone or a laptop. Even people dining together will often be more engaged with their phone than with the person sitting directly across from them. We are clearly arriving a time when every environment imaginable, from the local fast food joint to the city park to all forms of transportation, has Wi-Fi access. In fact, we already expect it. The discourse that ensues in such an environment is oblivious to what goes on around it. At the same time, it becomes more and more difficult to participate in conversation that is not broken up by digital disruptions. We are becoming a new species of being that is no longer *here* where we sit but *there* in cyberspace.

The culture of the classroom necessarily leans in the opposite way. Schooling is not about there, but about here. It is an environment that demands continuity and sustained attention as the price of learning. Rather than individualize, interrupt and scatter attention, schooling exists to train students to collectively focus on a serious purpose called "education." Although there will be opportunities to have fun and socialize with classmates, school is not about being entertained or talking to my friends. It is about learning. The teachers from Chicago we met earlier think they have hit a brick wall. But they haven't. They have actually hit an electronic one. Like teachers everywhere, they are caught in a battle of media environments that needs to be more carefully acknowledged and discussed. Their vocation requires they guide their students to adapt to the rigors of schooling. The students they teach, however, have been socialized in an electronic media environment that promotes constant amusement, banter with friends and incessant channel changing. They are in the same room but in different worlds. Neil Postman's (1992) remarks about television's impact on schooling can easily be extended to the transformative role currently being played by digital media:

> Children come to school having been deeply conditioned by the biases of television. There, they encounter the world of the printed word. A sort of psychic battle takes place, and there are many casualties—children who can't learn to read or won't, children who cannot organize their thought into logical structure even in a simple paragraph, children who cannot attend to lectures or oral explanations for more than a few minutes at a time. They are failures, but not because they are stupid. They are failures because there is a media war going on, and they are on the wrong side … (pp. 16–17)

The question becomes, then, what do we do about it?

In this chapter, we have explored the concept of an oral curriculum centered on cooperative games, interpersonal experiences and, most especially, the arts. Taken together, these activities form the core of a curriculum that acts as a counterenvironment to the overwhelming dominance of digital technology. Orality—the ability to interact within a group, communicate verbally, and develop a repertoire of socially based competencies—is the foundation upon which schooling and the acquisition of literacy depends. Why not begin and end the school day with a group song that assembles the students and makes them feel like an integral part of the class? Why not cultivate a child's natural impulse to play in a way that has educational benefits?

McLuhan knew the arts were the key to a vibrant counterenvironment and Postman never wavered from the belief that a viable counterenvironment had to evolve amongst young people in schools. As academics, however, they were remote from the everyday challenges of the primary school classroom. We need to move from theory to experimentation, from "probe" to practice.

The oral curriculum we outlined in this chapter is an effective step in constructing such a countervailing force. More technology is not the solution to a problem caused by more technology.

Note

1. Neil Postman and Charles Weingartner (1969), *Teaching as a Subversive Activity*, p. 7. New York: Delta.

References

Bauerlein, M. (2009). *The dumbest generation: How the digital age stupefies young Americans and jeopardizes our future*. New York: Penguin.
Beck, B. (2019). Why children's lives have changed radically in just a few decades. *The Economist*. Retrieved from https://www.economist.com/special-report/2019/01/03/why-childrens-lives-have-changed-radically-in-just-a-few-decades
Bettleheim, B. (1975). *The uses of enchantment: The meaning and the importance of fairy tales*. New York: Knopf.
Blair, C., & Diamond, A. (2008). Biological processes in prevention and intervention: Promotion of self-regulation and the prevention of early school failure. *Development and Psychopathology*, *20*, 899–911.
Bodrova, E., & Leong, D. (2007). *Tools of the mind: The Vygotskyian approach to early childhood education*. Upper Saddle River, NJ: Pearson Education.
Campbell, J. (1949). *The hero with a thousand faces*. New York: Pantheon.
Campbell, J. (1959). *Primitive mythology: The masks of the god*. New York: Viking Penguin.
Carruthers, P. (2002). Human creativity: Its evolution, its cognitive basis, and its connections with childhood pretence. *British Journal for the Philosophy of Science*, *53*, 225–249.
Dansky, J. (1980). Make-believe: A mediator of the relationship between play and associative fluency. *Child Development*, *51*, 576–579.
Dansky, J., & Silverman, I. (1973). Effects of play on associative fluency in pre-school-age children. *Developmental Psychology*, *9*(1), 28–43. Retrieved from http://dx.doi.org/10.1037/h0035076
Fluegelman, A. (1976). *The new games book*. Garden City, NY: Dolphin Books.
Fromberg, D. P., & Bergen, D. (1998). *Play from birth to twelve and beyond: Contexts, perspectives and meanings*. New York, NY: Garland Publishing Inc.
Frost, J., Wortham, S., & Reifel, S. (2001). *Play and child development*. Upper Saddle River, NJ: Merrill/Prentice-Hall.
Fulghum, R. (1986/2003). *All I really need to know I learned in kindergarten*. New York: Ballentine.
Gardner, H. (1983). *Frames of mind: The theory of multiple intelligences*. New York: Basic Books.

Gerbner, G. (1998). Cultivation analysis: An overview. *Mass Communication & Society, 1*, 175–194.
Gopnik, A. (2009). *The philosophical baby: What children's minds tell us about truth, love, and the meaning of life.* New York, NY: Picador.
Harris, P. L. (2000). *The work of the imagination.* Oxford, England: Blackwell.
Huizinga, J. (1938/1955). *Homo ludens.* Boston, MA: Beacon Press.
Isenberg, J., & Quisenberry, N. (2002). Play: Essential for all children. A position paper of the *Association for Childhood Education International.* Retrieved from www.acei.org/playpaper.htm
Johnson, J. E., Christie, J. F., & Yawkey, T. D. (1999). *Play and early childhood development* (2nd ed.). New York: Longman.
Krafft, K. C., & Berk, L. E. (1998). Private speech in two preschools: Significance of open-ended activities and make-believe play for verbal self-regulation. *Early Childhood Research Quarterly, 13*(4), 637–658.
LeFevre, D. (2002). *Best new games.* Champaign, IL: Human Kinetics.
Lillard, A. S. (2001). Pretend play as twin earth: A social–cognitive analysis. *Developmental Review, 21*, 495–531.
Luvmour, J., & Luvmour, B. (2019). *Everyone wins!: Cooperative games and activities.* Toronto: University of Toronto Press.
Morgan, N., & Saxton, J. (1991). *Asking better questions: Models, techniques and classroom activities for engaging students in learning.* Markham, ON: Pembroke Publishers.
National Association for the Education of Young Children & the National Association of Early Childhood Specialists in State Departments of Education. (2002). *Early learning standards: Creating the conditions for success.* Washington, DC: United States Department of Education.
Nielsen, M. (2012). Imitation, pretend play, and childhood: Essential elements in the evolution of human culture? *Journal of Comparative Psychology 126*(2), 170–181.
Ong, W. (1982). *Orality and literacy.* New York: Routledge.
Pellegrini, A. D. (1985). Relations between preschool children's symbolic play and literate behavior. In L. Galda & A. Pellegrini (Eds.), *Play, language, and stories* (pp. 107–121). Norwood, NJ: Ablex.
Pepler, D. J., & Ross, H. S. (1981). The effects of play on convergent and divergent problem solving. *Child Development, 52*, 1202–1210. doi: 10.2307/1129507
Pfeiffer, J. E. (1969). *The emergence of man.* New York: Harper & Row.
Pfeiffer, J. E. (1982). *The creative explosion.* Ithaca, NY: Cornell University Press.
Piaget, J. (1928). *Judgment and reasoning in the child* (3/2002). (M. Warden, Trans.). New York: Harcourt, Brace.
Piaget, J. (1955). *The language and thought of the child.* New York: World Publishing.
Piaget, J. (1962). *Play, dreams and imitation in childhood.* New York: Norton.
Postman, N. (1979). *Teaching as a conserving activity.* New York: Delacorte.
Postman, N. (1982). *The disappearance of childhood.* New York: Delacorte.

Postman, N. (1992). *Technopoly: The surrender of culture to technology.* New York: Alfred A. Knopf.
Postman, N. (1995). *The end of education: Redefining the value of school.* New York: Vintage.
Postman, N., & Weingartner, C. (1969). *Teaching as a subversive activity.* New York: Delta.
Saracho, O. N., & Spodek, B. (1998). Preschool children's cognitive play: A factor analysis. *International Journal of Early Childhood Education, 3,* 67–76.
Savina, E. (2014). Does play promote self-regulation in children? *Early Child Development & Care, 184*(11), 1692–1705.
Segaller, S., & Bergen, M. (1989). *The wisdom of the dream.* Boston, MA: Shambhala Publications.
Singer, D. G. (1973). *The child's world of make believe: Experimental studies of imaginative play.* New York: Academia Press.
Singer, J. L. (1995). Imaginative play in childhood: Precursor of subjective thought, daydreaming, and adult pretending games. In A. D. Pellegrini (Ed.), *The future of play theory: A multidisciplinary inquiry into the contributions of Brian Sutton-Smith* (pp. 187–219). Albany: State University of New York Press.
Singer, D. G., & Singer, J. L. (1998). Developing critical viewing skills and media literacy in children. *Annals of the American Academy of Political and Social Science, 557,* 164–179.
Smilansky, S., & Shefatya, L. (1990). *Facilitating play: A medium for promoting cognitive, socioemotional and academic development in young children.* Gaithersburg, MD: Psychological and Educational Publications.
Spolin, V. (1963). *Improvisation for the theater.* Evanston, IL: Northwestern University Press.
Steen, F. F., & Owens, S. A. (2001). Evolution's pedagogy: An adaptationist model of pretense and entertainment. *Journal of Cognition and Culture, 1,* 289–321.
Sternberg, R. J. (1998). *In search of the human mind.* New York: Harcourt Brace.
Strate, L. (1986). Time-binding in oral cultures. ETC: A Review of General Semantics, *43*(3), 234–246.
Sutherland, S. L., & Friedman, O. (2013). Just pretending can be really learning: Children use pretend play as a source for acquiring generic knowledge. *Developmental Psychology, 49*(9), 1660–1668.
Sutton-Smith, B. (1986). *Toys as culture.* New York: Gardner Press.
Vygotsky, L. S. (1931/1978). *Mind in society: The development of higher mental processes* (M. Cole, V. John-Steiner, S. Scribner, & E. Souberman, Eds.). Cambridge, MA; Harvard University Press.
Vygotsky, L. S. (1967). Play and its role in the mental development of the child. *Soviet Psychology, 7,* 6–18.

CHAPTER SIX

Building a Bridge to Literacy

Drama in Education as a Pedagogical Method

Once you learn to read, you will be forever free.

Frederick Douglass

Learning to read is probably the most difficult and revolutionary thing
that happens to the human brain.

John Steinbeck[1]

If Neil Postman's work could be summarized in just a few words, they might very well be "language, literacy, and the consequences of technological change." There's not a book, essay, lecture or interview in which these elements do not play prominently in his questioning of media environments. Postman's worst nightmare was that speech was devolving into meaningless babble while schooling had lost its way in the wake of the electronic revolution. He tried to warn us in as many ways as he knew how that we were on a collision course with disaster. Yet, most of us remain indifferent to the possibility that technology isn't always a friend. "In America, especially in American education …we love our technology …." Postman (1992) stated in his keynote address before the New York State Speech Communication Association, "And as you know, when people are in love, they see no faults in their beloved, are willing to sacrifice everything for the sake of their beloved, and, as a result, know nothing whatever about their beloved" (p. 17).

But it wasn't just technological change that worried Postman, it was the speed at which it was being hurled at us. "We've reached the stage," Postman wrote early on with his collaborator Charles Weingartner (1969), "where change occurs so rapidly that each of us in the course of our lives has continuously to work out a set of values, beliefs, and patterns of behavior that are viable" (p. 11). As a consequence, our social ecology has become seriously unstable. "The primary value of any ecological system is balance," writes Lance Strate (2014), "and Postman identified late 20th century American culture as dangerously out of balance" (p. 4). We were, in the titles of some of his books, entrapped in a "technopoly" where we were "amusing ourselves to death" and witnessing "the disappearance of childhood" as we rapidly approached "the end of education." Postman always urged that we should be expressing some "conscientious objections" about this technological onslaught and be willing to take measures to protect ourselves by "building a bridge to the 18th century" in order to restore some measure of sanity and reason to our lives. With great eloquence and clarity (and not infrequently a sense of humor), Postman labored to reveal the significance of our diminishing ability to ask meaningful questions, make intelligent statements and develop compelling reasons to learn. Not to resist the obvious would be moral and intellectual cowardice; to meekly acquiesce would be cultural suicide.

The thorny question for Postman, however, was always the "how." How do you teach students to ask good questions and write coherent sentences? How do you excite students to read books and become engaged with all the transformative processes involved in becoming truly literate? Throughout his career, Postman made some general suggestions but, by the time of his last full book on the subject of education, *The End of Education* (1995), it appears that he had just about given up on the "how" question by dismissing it as something of an engineering problem:

> In considering how to conduct the schooling of our young, adults have two problems to solve. One is an engineering problem; the other a metaphysical one. The engineering problem ... is essentially technical. It is the means by which the young will become learned ... But it is important to keep in mind that the engineering of learning is very often puffed up, assigned an importance it does not deserve. (p. 3)

There is a bit of an irony in this statement for the "how" question is characteristically of primary importance to media ecologists. In all fairness to Postman, however, he was principally referring to the myriad of methods proposed and debated that aim at improving the quality of education without ever wrestling with the more fundamental question: what is the purpose of education. "What this means," Postman (1995) explains, "is that at its best, schooling can be about how to make a life, which is quite different from how to make a living" (p. x). While Postman was focused on the deeper purposes of education, it is necessary to uncover methods that translates these purposes into actual classroom praxis.

In this chapter, we will offer our own response to the "how" question by outlining how the arts, and especially drama, can be used as a bridge to literacy. By using drama as a means of teaching children how to ask questions, absorb new vocabulary, expand attention spans, work in groups, increase their knowledge of narrative, feel confident to exert their voice in public, develop a love of the printed word and write with a point of view, we are in effect preparing children to become fully literate, questioning and critical thinkers. In short, drama in education can act as a transition from habits unconsciously shaped by electronic technologies to a deeper learning that develops a questioning mind and inspires a critical spirit.

We will begin by reviewing the rationale that underscores this approach known as "drama in education" and then proceed to illustrate, through description and analysis, a small selection of workshops with which we have experimented in the primary school classrooms of Jersey City. We do not wish to suggest that this is the only approach that can be employed to counterbalance a child's increasing exposure and dependence on the digital, but we do believe that it is a most effective alternative. In effect, drama in education constitutes a counterenvironment that works against some of the habits and biases that are unconsciously absorbed by our socialization in the electronic environment that surrounds us.

Approaching Literacy through Educational Drama

John Dewey famously emphasized that we "learn by doing" as the essential element of a fully progressive education. "Give the pupils something to do, not something to learn," Dewey (1916/1922) wrote over one hundred years ago, "and the doing is of such a nature as to demand thinking … learning naturally results" (p. 181). Neil Postman, especially in his early work with Charlie Weingartner (1969, 1971), also stressed a pedagogical approach that reached far beyond trying to stuff students with facts and figures. Their approach sought to engage students as active participants in the process of meaning making, not just repeaters of it.

But how do we get there from here?

Over the years in our work with children, we have increasingly gravitated towards using drama in the classroom, not as a means of putting on a play for an audience, but as a method of teaching. While all the arts are important in the cultivation of the oral curriculum we discussed in the previous chapter, drama is especially potent in teaching the full range of skills and attitudes demanded by literacy. Drama in education builds naturally upon a child's natural propensity to play make believe. By placing children in role as characters in an unfolding and flexible story, drama in education allows the creative instructor to introduce challenges and complexity as a means of teaching academic subjects, skills, attitudes and literate habits of mind. In short, in the words of O'Neill and Lambert (1982), drama in education is "a mode of learning. Through the pupils' active identification with imagined roles and situations in drama, they can learn to explore issues, events and relationships" (p. 11).

Educational drama, therefore, is definitely *not* about acting in a play, following a script or putting on a theatrical production for an appreciative audience. Much more importantly, educational drama is using "make-believe" as a means of probing the meaning and depth of a story. In role as characters in a story (and thereby achieving some distance from who they are in real life), children converse, respond, argue, write and discuss as would the characters they are playing and bringing to life in the classroom environment. The ability to ask questions and linguistically frame different points of view is thus put into a dramatic context which allows students to play roles, commit to a situation, and explore different points of view. Drama in education, then, accentuates the central role of language in a student's development and allows the teacher—also in role—to expand and contextualize the vocabulary available to children while engaging and molding their processes of critical thought. O'Neill and Lambert (1982) continue:

> One of the most positive contributions which drama makes to the curriculum is that it provides a facilitating atmosphere for many kinds of language use. Language is the cornerstone of the drama process and the means through which the drama is realized. Whenever any kind of active role-play takes place, language is directly and necessarily involved. Drama can provide a powerful motivation to speech, and this speech does not occur in isolation but is embedded in context and situation where it has a crucial organizing function. (pp. 17–18)

Educational drama as a means of teaching academic subjects is not a new pedagogical method but has its roots in the early part of the twentieth century when Winifred Ward (1930, 1957) developed an approach she called "creative drama." Creative drama was introduced as a way of improving a student's self-expression, their appreciation of literature, and proficiency in spoken English. Ward's work was furthered by Nellie McCaslin (1968) in her widely read *Creative Dramatics* which included lessons using improvisation, movement, and mime activities that often culminated in a story dramatization centered on a poem, fairytale or folktale. While the dramatizations sometimes became scripted and shared with a small group of children or family members and friends, most often, the group creating the drama shared their story with each other and not an audience.

Perhaps the most influential practitioner of educational drama, however, was Dorothy Heathcote. Although she published rather sparingly during her lifetime, her innovative work with children in Great Britain redefined and expanded the field beginning in 1950 when she was just 24 years of age. Heathcote pioneered a technique she called "mantle of the expert" which, in an article she co-authored with Herbert (1985/2009), she defines as a "system of teaching [that] involves a reversal of the conventional teacher-student role relationship in which students draw on the knowledge and expertise of the teacher. When the mantle of the expert is used in drama, the teacher assumes a fictional role which places the student in the position of being 'the one who knows' or the expert in a particular branch of knowledge" (p. 173). In other words, as Morgan and Saxton (1987) explain, "the students are working as themselves, but 'as if' they were experts. The role is a general one (we are all engineers, advisors, the tribe, anthropologists …), which implies special skills, particular information and/or expertise which can be brought to bear upon the task" (p. 31).

Heathcote's innovative methods have influenced scores of teachers who followed and expanded on her example in England (Bolton, 1984; Neelands, 1984; O'Neill, 1995; O'Neill and Lambert, 1982), in Canada (McCaslin, 1968; Miller & Saxton, 2004; Morgan & Saxton, 1987; Tarlington & Verriour, 1991), and in the United States (Polsky, Shindel, & Tabone, 2006; Tabone & Albrecht, 2000, 2002; Wilhelm & Edmiston, 1998). When Newcastle University invested her as an honorary Doctor of Letters, John Burn (2005) stated that Heathcote was "famous for almost single handedly introducing drama into UK secondary education: She dared to challenge the orthodoxy that children were blank slates on which their teachers could write. She argued that to truly communicate, teachers must begin with that person's existing knowledge, learning together" (p. 1).

The field of educational drama allows us to take on imaginary roles and invites us to explore multiple perspectives within the safe space of "make believe." Children are naturally drawn to this form of play; educational drama merely transforms it into an opportunity for learning literacy and the art of asking questions. It builds on what children already know and then expands outward and inward. Students are not conceptualized as empty vessels that need to be stuffed with knowledge but as human beings who have already learned a great deal that needs to be processed, organized, articulated and brought to light. "Children are not seen as passive recipients," writes educational dramatist Jonathan Neelands (1984), "but as active meaning-makers who have already made considerable learning progress in their immediate environment before they ever come into classrooms" (p. 2).

By fashioning learning experiences that enhance social interaction, verbal articulation, and active problem solving, drama in education molds a powerful interpersonal and uniquely literary counterenvironment in the classroom. In short, drama in education is a viable and practical response to the "how question" left unanswered by both McLuhan and Postman.

A Selection of Drama Workshops

In reviewing the following workshops, the reader will get a clearer idea of how educational drama can be used in the classroom. It is important to keep in mind that this approach requires flexibility. A creative teacher will necessarily make adjustments and additions that reflect the needs of her class, the demands of the curriculum, and most importantly, the teaching moments that occur. An educational drama workshop, like a jazz performance, functions best when there is a strong sense that each workshop is a unique process. The following outlines give direction, but the teacher should always bear in mind that spontaneity, imagination, and improvisation are key. For those who may wish more extensive and detailed descriptions of various educational drama workshops, we would suggest Bowell and Heap (2013), Burke (2013), Dawson and Lee (2018), Miller and Saxton (2004), Neelands (1984), O'Neill (1995), Tandy and Howell (2009), and Toye and Prendiville (2000) as well as any of our own series of handbooks for teachers (Educational Arts Team, 2008, 2010, 2013).

Lesson 1: Orson Welles and the War of the Worlds

The drama activities we used in this workshop were selected to motivate participation, engage the imagination, and stimulate probing questions. The workshop also sought to create a non-threatening space where children would be able to speak with relative comfort before a group and be inspired to write enthusiastically. The choice of Orson Welles' historic radio dramatization of H.G. Wells' novel, *War of the Worlds*, was made for three reasons: (1) the story was included in the classroom literature book and therefore enabled us to build upon content already in the curriculum (Cooper & Pikulski, 1996); (2) the story of the broadcast could be easily adapted to a format that included reading, writing, questioning, and public speaking; and (3) the historical occurrence provided material for a number of simple drama activities that could be learned by the classroom teacher and hopefully applied to other stories in the future. Below we have broken down the workshop into a series of steps that can be adapted and modified as needed by the classroom teacher.

Step One: Motivating the class's interest and involvement. The success of role-play in the classroom depends entirely upon the students' commitment to the drama. If the students do not enter the imaginary world of the story, the workshop will lack energy and be unproductive. In order to stimulate curiosity and involvement, we begin by employing a word puzzle. The teacher draws a simple rebus on the blackboard constructed of broken lines that represent letters and ideograms. It is a format with which children are familiar from watching television and through such guessing games as "hangman."

The teacher allows the students to ponder the cryptograph for a moment and then explains that she has written a message on the board that the class will work on together to solve. Children are invited to raise their hands and suggest a single letter. If the letter is included in the cryptogram, she fills in the appropriate space and reveals the letter(s); if not, the letter is written down next to the cryptograph so that the letter will not be suggested again. Eventually, a child will decipher the intended message: "Are there really such things as UFOs?"

The collective solving of the puzzle immediately opens a discussion of a subject usually of great interest to children. Indeed, are there really such things as UFOs? Children freely share stories they have seen on TV, in the movies or heard from friends and relatives. Now, they are engaged and ready to participate in that which follows.

Step Two: Introducing War of the Worlds. After discussing the question of the existence of UFOs and life on other planets, the teacher introduces the topic of Orson Welles' radio drama of 1938. The teacher may wish to begin with a simple statement, such as, "During the 1930s before there was television, people used to listen to programs on the radio. It was the night before Halloween and Orson Welles, an actor and future movie director, decided this would be a good time to play a scary trick on the people who were listening to his show. He began the show

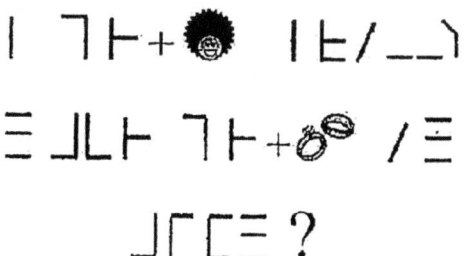

Figure 6.1. War of the Worlds Puzzle by Albrecht, R. and Tabone, C., 2002, retrieved from Martians invade the classroom: a workshop in language learning. The Journal of the Imagination in Language Learning. V11, 4–8.

as if it were just a regular music program. But then he played his prank. He broke into the music program with a news bulletin that strange explosions were being observed by scientists on the surface of the planet Mars. He then brought onto the show what people thought was a real astronomer, named Professor Pierson, and asked him some questions. If I brought Professor Pierson to this classroom, what would be some of the questions you would ask him?"

After the students have shared several questions, the teacher may wish to stop and ask them to write down three or four on a sheet of paper. This is a good opportunity to teach children about the "5 W's and 1 H" (what, where, when, why, who and how) used by news people all around the world in formulating questions.

Step Three: Moving into role as reporters. The teacher then asks the children, do they know what a reporter is and what a reporter does? What kinds of things are reporters good at? Do you feel that you know enough about reporters to be in role as a reporter in a drama? Most likely, some students will be ready and feel comfortable to join in the drama. The teacher explains that those who aren't, can join in as they become ready.

Step Four: Setting the space and the context for a press conference. The teacher can then ask if the students know what a press conference is. What happens at a press conference? The teacher then asks the children what modifications can be made to the classroom so the space can look like a place where a press conference could be held. During this step, the students may suggest they move desks and chairs or employ classroom fixtures such as plants, globes and the like to dress the dramatic playing space.

Step Five: Distinguishing in-role and out-of-role. After rearranging the space for the news conference, the teacher explains to the class that they will be moving in and out of an imaginary situation. When she steps to the front of the room, she will be in-role as a character in the story; when she steps to the side—out of the "spotlight" so to speak—she will be out-of-role. While in role, the teacher may wish to make some minor changes in her appearance (put on a sports coat or a laboratory frock) but remember, this is an informal drama, not a theater piece. Keep it simple.

In sum, the teacher is moving to create a "dramatic playing space" in front of the class that enables her to establish when she is in role as a character in the story and when she is not. When in role, she steps inside this space; when out of role, she steps outside this space and can reflect with the class on the action that just took place in the drama.

Step Six: The news conference. Having rearranged the playing space for the news conference and having explained the difference between in and out of role, the drama can begin to unfold. Professor Pierson (the teacher in role at the front of the room) begins with a short statement explaining that she is an astronomer and has personally witnessed a series of explosions on the planet Mars that were reported earlier this evening through a telescope at the Princeton Observatory in New Jersey. The professor downplays the questions of the children by assuring them that the explosions are purely natural in origin and certainly do not suggest the existence of extraterrestrial life. The teacher's tone could evoke very subtly that she is hiding what is truly going on while steadfastly denying that there is any cause for alarm. The idea here is that the teacher in role as an astronomer is challenging the students to ask questions and probe more deeply into the facts.

After a few rounds of questions, Professor Pierson steps to the side of the room and out of the spotlight so as to address the class out of role. The teacher then discusses what has just happened by asking a number of questions such as, "What are some of the things that Professor Pierson had to say? What did you think about what she was saying? Do you trust her?" The teacher then asks the students to write down some of the things that they learned from Professor Pierson about the strange explosions as if they were reporters covering the story.

Step Seven: "Science Beat." The teacher explains that there is going to be a science show on TV about the strange explosions of incandescent gas that were reported on the planet Mars. She asks the students what types of people should be included as guests on the show. Next the teacher and students again make some minor changes to the classroom that would suggest a set for a TV program: perhaps a desk with a globe or a plant on it flanked by a chair on either-side. The teacher in front of the room (in-role as the TV host) announces:

> Ladies and gentlemen, welcome to another edition of 'Science Beat' the show that investigates curious phenomenon in the world of science. Last week we discussed Global Climate Change and asked the probing question, 'Is the climate of the earth really changing?' On tonight's show, we will be discussing one of the most unusual stories to take place in recent years in the world of science. I am referring, of course, to the strange explosions on the planet Mars that were witnessed earlier this week by astronomers from around the world. In order to help us to get to the bottom of the matter, we are privileged to have with us tonight, a number of world-famous scientists and other guests.

The host may wish to introduce her guests (children who have volunteered to play these roles) as experts in the field. She may ask them a few background questions about their careers in order to relax the children and to help establish their characters. The moderator then begins to ask their opinions of what has occurred on Mars earlier that week. The class, as the studio audience, can then ask their questions.

Step Eight: The news bulletin. At some point during the discussion on "Science Beat," the host receives a piece of paper from an assistant. The host stops the action and, in a very grave voice, announces: "Ladies and Gentlemen, I have just been handed a news bulletin and I will read it to you: 'The Governor of New Jersey has confirmed that aircraft, apparently of extraterrestrial origin, have landed on a farm owned by a Mr. Joseph Wilmuth near the state capital in Trenton.' We will now interrupt our regularly scheduled program and go directly to our action reporters who are on the scene at Grover's Mill where State Police have blocked off the site to keep people from panicking."

Step Nine: On the scene at Grover's Mill. The teacher (out-of-role) asks the students who might a reporter interview at the scene in Grover's Mill. She can write their responses on the board and thereby affirm and encourage more suggestions. She then divides the students into pairs and explains that one of them is a reporter and the other, an eyewitness. The reporters should take notes on what they observe as well as on the information she or he receives from the eyewitness. After a few minutes, the teacher can ask the reporters what they have learned from the eyewitnesses they interviewed.

The teacher then asks the class who are some of the other people at the site that a reporter would want to interview. Together they can add the possibilities on the board and once again using the 5 W's and the 1 H, the students can draw up a list of questions they might want to ask of those on the scene. The teacher can then divide the class into a new set of pairs and allow them to continue the work of interviewing eyewitnesses who are present at the scene.

Step Ten: Preparing the evening news. The teacher announces that the students have very little time before the evening news starts and that the reporters must prepare their stories immediately. In classes where there are children of different cultural backgrounds, the teacher may wish to leave open the possibility of a child writing the report in a different language. The students write up their reports and prepare to present them at an improvised news desk that has been set up in the front of the room. The teacher is in role as anchor so as to clearly establish a news format and to keep the action moving. "Good evening. This is Jill Jenkins with the Six O'clock News. The Knicks win, the Mets lose, more rain is on the way, and right now I have Carl (or Carla) Phillips with me who has breaking news about an extraterrestrial landing in Grover's Mill, New Jersey. Carl(a), take it away." This brief introduction by the teacher clearly invokes a familiar television format and allows the child to speak comfortably and believably in role to the rest of the class.

After a few of the students have finished reading their reports, the teacher could suggest to the class that they look at the coverage on another channel. The news could also contain actual footage of the interviews whereby students can reenact scenes of their meetings with eyewitnesses including police officers, scientists, and neighbors. In classrooms where children have written their reports in a different language, this is a good time to allow them to read their reports. Since the children are already familiar with the story, they will have a good idea of what is being said even if they don't speak the language. This confirms the validity of languages other than English and permits the English-only children the opportunity of hearing a foreign language report.

Step Eleven: Closing the action. Stepping out of role, the teacher returns to the story of Orson Welles and the infamous *War of the Worlds* broadcast of 1938. On Halloween Eve, Mr. Welles fooled more than one million people who were listening to his radio program into believing that Martians had actually landed in New Jersey and were making their way toward New York City. People were so scared that they were running through the streets with wet towels wrapped around their heads to protect themselves from the poisonous gases that Orson Welles said the Martians were supposedly using to kill people.

The teacher then asks the students to open their readers to Howard Koch's script used by Orson Welles in his presentation of the *War of the Worlds*. The teacher can then assign parts to different students, including the making of sound effects, and then direct a dramatic reading of the script (a fragment of the script was included in the class's reader by Cooper and Pikulski, 1996; the entire script is included in Cantril, 1982).

Step Twelve: Extending the story. To extend the interest generated by this drama workshop, the teacher could have the students create a newspaper that chronicles the story of the Martian invasion complete with headlines, feature stories, comic strips, interviews, advice columns and drawings of the events. The workshop also leads naturally into a whole host of art activities including picture books, portraits of Martians, sculptures of creatures from other planets and so on. Teachers wishing to continue with the theme of extraterrestrial life can explore the outer space drama workshops developed by Neelands (1984), O'Neill and Lambert (1982) and Wilhelm and Edmiston (1998).

The workshop also lends itself to several areas of social studies. The students may be assigned to do some archival research at their local libraries and asked to do a report on how newspapers covered the event on the day following the historic broadcast. The teacher may wish to use this workshop to communicate some of the fears that people had during the era immediately preceding World War II. The ability of this historic newscast to terrify the audience has often been linked to the rise of Adolf Hitler in Germany.

Most obviously, the workshop can be a jumping off point for a discussion on the role of media in contemporary society. Students may wish to debate whether limits should be placed on the kinds of things that the media are allowed to broadcast. The teacher may also wish to play the actual recording of the broadcast (readily available online or CD) to the class and ask them to analyze what it is that made the broadcast so believable.

Lesson 2: The Pied Piper of Hamelin

When mediated by educational drama, a folktale like "The Pied Piper of Hamelin" becomes an opportunity to read, write, question, debate, and speak in public before a group. At the time we developed this workshop, a version of the story was published in the readers used in fourth grade classrooms in Jersey City. There are multiple ways of approaching the story as educational drama, so the reader should be aware that what follows is just one possibility. As always, the workshop we outline here can be modified as needed with particular steps added, deleted or extended.

Step One: Engaging the class's interest. The teacher asks the class if anyone has ever seen a rat. After a brief discussion, children are divided into pairs and asked to talk about what rats look like and anything else that they know about rats. This question allows city children to describe an experience that many may have heard about or have even seen with their own eyes. This exercise starts the process of building belief in a context about a town overrun by rats.

Step Two: Entering the story. The teacher tells the class that today we will be doing a drama about a small town that was suddenly invaded by rats. "Once upon a time," the teacher narrates, "there was a beautiful little village where people lived together in peace, prosperity and harmony." This short statement opens the doors to the imagination and becomes the portal into a dramatic space. The teacher can involve the students by asking such questions as "What do you think the village might have looked like?" "What kinds of buildings and places might we find there?" The children offer ideas and these suggestions become possible settings for the drama. The teacher can write the suggestions on the board which affirms their participation and provides examples of places that may come into play in the drama.

Next, the teacher asks the children what kinds of people might be living in this village. For example, there may be shopkeepers, bakers, school children, teachers, policemen, and so on. Once again, the teacher can write their suggestions on the board.

Step Three: The townspeople see the rats. The teacher narrates that many of the villagers have reported seeing large rats at various locations in the town. Divide the children into pairs and ask them to become villagers at the moment that they first saw a rat. Children need to discuss where they were at that moment, indoors or outdoors, and what they felt. The teacher then gives a signal and everyone at the same time is asked to become a statue that reflects that moment.

Step Four: The meeting with the mayor. The teacher explains that the mayor has been asked to meet with the villagers concerning the rat infestation problem. The teacher asks the students where this meeting would take place. Children may suggest the town hall, the mayor's office, a local school, or some other place. Once the location has been agreed upon, the teacher asks the children how we could rearrange the classroom to look more like that space. The teacher may also wish to ask the students how the mayor would enter the space. Is she frightened, confident, arrogant, humble, etc.? As the villagers wait for the mayor, what is their attitude? Are they friendly or hostile, sullen or frightened?

Once again as in the previous workshop outline, the teacher is creating a "dramatic playing space" that enables her to establish when she is in and out of role. When playing a character in the story, she steps inside this space; when she steps outside this space, she can reflect with the class on the action that just took place in the drama.

The teacher in role as the mayor thanks the villagers for coming out to meet with her. After some good-natured banter, the mayor asks the villagers to express their concerns and then assures them the problem is a minor one and that they should not worry. The mayor responds to the citizens, repeats and restates their questions, elevates the level of the dialogue, introduces new vocabulary, and guides the discourse. The mayor attempts to persuade the citizens that everything is under control and verbally spars with the citizens who want immediate action.

At some point, the mayor excuses herself saying she has other pressing matters to attend to and exits.

Step Five: Reflection out of role. Out of role, the teacher asks the students how they would describe the mayor. How would they describe the villagers? Do you feel that any progress had been made addressing the rat problem?

Step Six: The problem gets worse. The teacher divides the class into pairs and asks them to become a two-person sculpture or tableaux showing that the rat problem, despite the mayor's assurances, has gone from bad to worse. Upon the teacher's signal, everyone at the same time becomes that tableaux. Volunteers are given the opportunity to share and explain their tableaux to the class.

Step Seven: The letter. The teacher explains that the mayor has been avoiding meeting with the villagers. As a consequence, the villagers decide that each one should write a letter to the mayor explaining their concerns and demand that she hold a meeting. The students are then given time to compose a letter. The teacher may wish to use this opportunity to show students the proper way of addressing, writing and closing a formal letter. After the letters have been completed, the villagers walk silently through the town on their way to post their complaints on the doors of the town hall.

Step Eight: A town hall meeting. The teacher narrates that despite what the mayor has said about solving the rat infestation problem, numerous people have reported seeing the rats throughout the town and in their own homes. The teacher reads some of the comments that the villagers wrote in the letters that they had posted on the door of the town hall. Due to this outcry from the citizens of the town, the mayor has reluctantly agreed to meet with the townspeople once more. At the meeting, the children in role as citizens stand and address the teacher in role as mayor. At some point during the town hall meeting, the mayor reveals that she has received a letter from a mysterious person who claims to have ability to rescue the town from the rats. She reads the letter aloud:

> *Dear Mayor and Townspeople of Hamelin,*
>
> *I have heard about the tragic rat infestation that has beset your unfortunate village. I wish to inform you that I can rid your village of the rats, but I will require a fee of thirty gold guilders for my services. My work is fully guaranteed or else I will not accept payment.*
>
> *In closing, I look forward to meeting with you.*
>
> *Sincerely,*
>
> *The Pied Piper*

After reading the letter, the mayor tells the students that the Pied Piper is just outside the room and wants to meet with the townspeople. "Should we invite him in to speak with us?" "What kinds of questions should we ask him?" After getting their assent, the students write down their questions and the mayor exits the room to invite the Pied Piper to enter.

Step Nine: Meeting with the Pied Piper. When the teacher in role as the Piper enters, he introduces himself, explains his abilities, and asks for their questions. The Piper insists he will not take the town's money if he is unsuccessful, that his work is fully guaranteed. After gaining the agreement of the townspeople, the Piper exits the room.

Step Ten: Paying the Piper. The teacher (out-of-role) discusses with the children (also out-of-role) what the Piper said. She then explains she will now go back into her role as mayor. The mayor and the villagers discuss what just transpired with the Piper. The mayor announces that she has just received a message from the Chief of Police stating that when the Piper began to play his flute the rats followed him down to the river. And, as the Piper continued to play his flute, the rats jumped one by one into the water and drowned. The rat infestation is over! The message also states that the Piper is on his way to pick up a fee of thirty gold guilders.

The teacher in role as mayor begins to renege on the agreement that was made and reels of a litany of excuses not to pay: "Who agreed to pay the Piper thirty gold guilders? I don't remember making any such promises. Besides, there's no written contract so our agreement isn't legal. We were just discussing it, we didn't actually agree to it. Think of all the other things we could do with that money! Besides, if we don't pay him, what can he do? The rats are already dead and gone. What can he possibly do?"

By discussing and debating with the children in role as citizens, the teacher in role as mayor is leading a discussion in ethics. By giving the children all the excuses for not doing the right thing, the children must respond to the mayor's craftiness with their own reasons and arguments.

Step Eleven: Closure and extensions. At this point, the teacher can either continue with the story or start to bring it to closure. If she wishes to continue, the students can create a newspaper with up-to-date reports, human interest stories, and illustrations that summarize all that has happened thus far. If she wishes to move towards closure, the students can be asked what kinds of things might the Piper do if he isn't paid the amount that was agreed. In either case, the children will be excited to read the story to find out exactly what happens.

The enthusiasm generated by this educational drama lesson can easily be a springboard to explore questions of ethics, public sanitation, and ecology. This workshop is also a lesson in civics. What kind of qualities should an effective political leader possess? Did the mayor live up to these expectations? Why not? What does it mean to make a promise and give your word?

The workshop can also be directed towards concerns of public sanitation. What do you think attracted the rats to Hamelin and what could have been done to prevent the invasion? What is our responsibility as citizens to keep our city clean? What should we do with our garbage? How can we reduce our trash? What is recycling? What is composting? Can measures be applied to our classroom? Our schools? Our homes? Our towns? Who should we speak to? How should we address them? Should we write them a letter outlining our complaints? Can we invite them here for an interview to speak with us? What questions would we ask?

Lesson 3: Pop-up Puppet Theater

Shadow puppets, hand puppets, rod puppets, marionettes, and so on, have delighted audiences throughout the ages and have functioned as carriers of folk stories, legends, myths and various forms of educational content. Children love puppetry, which is why this approach is such an effective form of educational drama. "Puppetry," writes Robert Landy (1982), "is a total dramatic art experience, since it involves design and construction, movement and speech, playwriting and improvisation, performance and viewing" (p. 225).

Pop-up Puppet Theater (PPT) originated in observing the enthusiasm with which children sketch and play at their classroom desk with paper drawings to create fantasy dramas. Building on those playful impulses, we developed a project that could help students improve their oral presentation skills, count. Bruner (1986) studied the relationship between play and the acquisition of symbol systems. He believed that it is not so much *formal instruction* in either language or thinking that develops these skills, but the opportunities to *play* with language and thinking. He held that the symbolic playing and transforming of objects into persons, situations, and events accompanied by verbal practice could provide an important source for literacy development. In this workshop, children transform storytelling into verbal communication, art, puppets, scenery and handwritten scripts which are then presented to children in younger classes as mini-theater productions.

Step One: Telling two simple stories. The teacher begins by telling the children two short and simple stories, usually two Aesop's fables, containing not more than two characters. Here are two that we used:

(1) "Hercules and the Wagon Driver." One day, a wagon driver was on his way to town transporting a heavy load along a very muddy road. For whatever reason, he wasn't paying attention to where he was going, and the wheels of his wagon got stuck in a hole full of mud. The more the driver urged his horses to pull the wagon free, the deeper the wheels sank into the mud. Exasperated, the wagon driver threw down his whip, dropped to his knees, and prayed to Hercules the god of strength. "O Hercules," he cried, "Have pity and help me get my wagon out of this mud." With those words, the clouds parted, and Hercules appeared to him and said: "You lazy wagon driver! Why are you begging me for help? Get up and put your shoulder to the wheel!"

The moral to this story is: "The gods help those who help themselves."

(2) "The Boy Who Went Swimming." On a very warm day in spring, a young boy was on his way to school. As he passed a lake, he thought to himself that he'd much rather go swimming than go to school. And so, he jumped into the water, but since it was early spring, the water was still very cold. Soon he was swallowing a great deal of water and gasping for air. Just then a man was passing by. When the boy saw him, he cried out: "Help me! Help me! I'm drowning!" The man looked sternly at the boy and said, "Aren't you supposed to be in school young man?" The boy, frantic that he might die, yelled, "But please mister, help me I'm drowning." To

which the man shouted at the boy "I'm going to tell your mother that you didn't go to school today!" With that the boy pleaded: "Please save the lectures for later. Right now, help me get out!"

And the moral of this story is: "There's a time and place for everything."

Step Two: Class reviews the two stories. After the teacher tells both stories, the group reviews the sequence of each story. "What was the first thing that happened in the story? What happened next?" Look for very short responses so that many children have a chance to tell a line or two. In classes in which the children are not confident or seem confused by the question, they may need more prompting before responding. The teacher may need to start by saying "one day a wagon driver was off to market and what happened next?" Each time the class becomes stuck, the teacher may need to provide the next line and then ask for one of the students to tell what happens next.

Step Three: Students retell one of the stories to a partner. The children are then divided into pairs and asked to decide who is A and who is B. The teacher explains that A will go first and tell "Hercules and the Wagon Driver," adding that B must be a good audience and listen carefully. The teacher asks "What does it take to be a good audience?" (Look at the storyteller, use your eyes to watch, listen carefully with your ears, and please don't talk, so your mouth needs to stay closed). When the A group has finished telling the Hercules story to their partners, the B group tells the second story, "The Boy Who Went Swimming," to their partner. Once again, they are reminded what it takes to be a good audience: look, listen and be silent.

Step Four: Creating the puppets. Each child then does a simple drawing of the two characters in their story. Taking a piece of 8 ½ by 11 white paper, the children fold it in half and then fold it again, so they have four rectangles. They cut on the creases so they have four rectangles of equal size. Each student gets two of the rectangles. If A told "Hercules and the Wagon Driver," they will be making a pencil drawing of Hercules on one of those pieces and of the wagon driver on the other. In "The Boy Who Went Swimming" story, one of the drawings will be of the boy and the other of the man. Explain to the students they should not be doing any scenery on the paper just the character; one on each sheet.

When the students have finished doing the drawings, give each student two strips of white paper, approximately a half inch in width and about four inches long. Give out glue sticks to the students so they can attach each paper puppet to one of the four-inch-long strips of paper. The strip is attached to the head of the puppet so that when you hold the strip the puppet dangles below. In effect, the strips are the strings to the marionette. At this point students can begin to use crayons or markers to make the puppets more visually interesting.

Finally, using scissors, students can trim around the outside of their drawings to give some shape to the paper puppet.

Step Five: Students retell the story using their puppets. The teacher asks the students who are in the A group to stand and face their partners in the B group who remain sitting. On the signal, "one day," the A group will tell their story to their partner using their two puppets. The teacher reminds the students in the B group to be good audience members. When the A group has finished, the B group stands and, on the signal, "one day," they tell the story of the boy who went swimming to the A group.

Learning to speak comfortably in front of a group is a difficult process that usually requires time, repeated experiences and some nurturance. Children need to acquire the confidence to do this and the first step is to present their story to an audience of one and then, only gradually, increasing the size of the audience. In this step, the child can practice being in the role of presenter to an audience by telling their story to a single person, their partner, using the paper puppets that they themselves have constructed. Since it's an audience of just one child directly across from them, it makes the task very easy.

Step Six: Making the scenery. Having told the story with the puppets they created, students are now ready to create the scenery for their mini-theater productions. Review the stories with the class and ask them to discuss possible settings for their puppet production. You can list the possibilities they suggest on the board, such as, mountains in the distance, a muddy road, a lake, clouds in the sky, trees, etc. Explain to the students that the scenery they make is their choice and there are no right or wrong ways of doing this. On a piece of 8.5 × 11 paper (preferably a heavy weight paper stock) turned horizontally, students draw and color their scenery. When the students are finished, they can fold in each side of the paper approximately an inch and a half so that the scenery can stand horizontally and become the stage for their presentation.

Step Seven: The play production. Now that students have their puppets, scenery and the ability to tell their story, they are able to put on a show. First the A group goes so that each individual student can present to his or her partner. Once that is completed, the B group goes.

Step Eight: Writing the script. The teacher explains to the class that they will be writing a script based on the stories that they've been working on. She asks them if they know what a script is, and then outlines the very beginnings of a format that can serve as a model in converting the stories from oral presentation into a written form. This simplified format would include just the dialogue for narrator and the two characters so that the students, already familiar with their story, are able to confidently complete a script.

Step Nine: Reading the script. The teacher places the students with new partners. One child reads his or her script and then their partner does the same. By reading aloud to a new partner, the student-writer will hear mistakes and omissions that they will be able to correct before finalizing their script.

Step Ten: Taking your show on the road. Adventurous teachers can take their students with their puppets and puppet stages to a class of younger children to present their play productions. In this case you can divide the class you are visiting into small groups of two or three children. Each student in group A presents their story to an audience of two or three younger children. When they're finished, group B gets their turn. In all these cases make sure that everyone is completely attentive and ready before your students begin telling their stories. The teacher can act as master of ceremonies and help her students by announcing to the younger audience something like, "Ladies and Gentlemen! We now present to you the story of 'Hercules and the Wagon Driver!' or 'The Boy Who Went Swimming'."

Step Eleven: Extensions. Having learned the basics of telling a story that includes memory, a simple narrative and oral expression followed by the making of puppets, constructing scenery, writing a script and putting on a play before a small audience, this workshop can be repeated with any number of stories. Each repetition will increase the student's confidence in oral and written communication as well as their ability to perform before a group. It is a total learning environment that develops verbal and written skills as well as manual dexterity and the confidence to interact with others. Depending upon the needs of the class, this process can take stories from history, literature, science and so on, and put them up on the puppet stage.

Conclusion

Since its inception as a field of study, media ecology has remained largely confined within the walls of academia. Its ideas and debates have been elaborated almost exclusively within academic journals, at academic conferences, and in books with an academic readership. The great challenge that McLuhan and Postman have left to us is how to transform their profound insights into pedagogical experiences. Not everyone can fathom the meaning of McLuhan; not every student is motivated or prepared to respond to the generative questions asked by Postman. Do we continue to talk over their heads or is there a way to bring them into the discussion? In short, the counterenvironments and thermodynamic experiences they envisioned must somehow be operationalized and translated from words on a page into ideas that come to life in classrooms.

In this chapter, we have outlined one such approach based upon the educational use of drama. The introduction of drama into the classroom curriculum—*not as subject matter per se but as a pedagogical method*—is a viable way of teaching the kinds of things that McLuhan and Postman found so important. By extending a child's natural tendency to play make believe, the educational use of drama places children in roles and situations that open exciting possibilities to explore other worlds and to think in other ways. Based upon the characters and contexts in which the students find themselves, students learn to speak in role, incorporate perspectives of historical and literary characters, and make critical decisions that guide the drama. They are able to respond to the dramatic moments and conflicts in which they are engaged through writing, conversation, public speaking, reflective reading and various forms of artistic representation. The key to remember is that the driving purpose of educational drama is not to put on a show followed by applause and curtain calls but to learn how to ask questions, become more confident in oral and literate expression, and develop a deep appreciation and love of literacy.

Note

1. John Steinbeck (2003), *America and Americans and Selected Nonfiction*, p. 123. New York: Penguin.

References

Bolton, G. (1984). *Drama as education*. Essex, England: Longman.
Bowell, P., & Heap, B. S. (2013). *Planning process drama: Enriching teaching and learning*. New York: Routledge.
Bruner, J. S. (1986). *Actual minds, possible worlds*. Cambridge: Harvard University Press.
Burke, M. (2013). *Gavin Bolton's contextual drama: The road less traveled*. Bristol, England: Intellect.
Burn, J. (2005). Dorothy Heathcote, DITT. Retrieved from http://www.ncl.ac.uk/congregations/assets/documents/DorothyHeathcote.pdf
Cantril, H. (1982). *The invasion from Mars: A study in the psychology of panic*. Princeton, NJ: Princeton Legacy Press.
Cooper, J. D., & Pikulski, J. J. (Eds.). (1996). *Explore*. Boston, MA: Houghton Mifflin.
Dawson, K., & Lee, B. K. (2018). *Drama-based pedagogy: Activating learning across the curriculum*. Bristol, England: Intellect.
Dewey, J. (1916/1922). *Democracy and education: An introduction to the philosophy of education*. New York: MacMillan.
Educational Arts Team. (2008). *The magic circle of drama: A handbook of 40 lesson plans*. Jersey City, NJ: Educational Arts Team.

Educational Arts Team. (2010). *Bringing literature to life: Theater strategies and sample lesson plans for middle school literacy.* Jersey City, NJ: Educational Arts Team.

Educational Arts Team. (2013). *The artful learner: A theater arts and literacy handbook for 2nd and 3rd grade teachers.* Jersey City, NJ: Educational Arts Team.

Heathcote, D., & Herbert, P. (1985/2009). A drama of learning: Mantle of the expert. *Theory Into Practice, 24*(3), 73–180. Retrieved from https://www.tandfonline.com/doi/abs/10.1080/00405848509543169

Landy, R. J. (1982). *Handbook of educational drama and theatre.* Westport, CT: Greenwood Press.

McCaslin, N. (1968). *Creative dramatics.* New York: David McKay.

Miller, C., & Saxton, J. (2004). *Into the story: Language in action through drama.* Portsmouth, NH: Heinemann.

Morgan, N., & Saxton, J. (1987). *Teaching drama.* Cheltenham, England: Stanley Thornes.

Neelands, J. (1984). *Making sense of drama: A guide to classroom practice.* Portsmouth, NH: Heinemann.

O'Neill, C. (1995). *Drama worlds.* Portsmouth, NH: Heinemann.

O'Neill, C., & Lambert, A. (1982). *Drama structures: A practical handbook for teachers.* Portsmouth, NH: Heinemann.

Polsky, M., Shindel, D., & Tabone, C. (2006). *Drama activities for K-6 students: Creating classroom spirit.* Lanhan, MD: Rowman & Littlefield.

Postman, N. (1992). Seven ideas about media and culture. *The Speech Communication Annual, 6*, 7–18.

Postman, N. (1995). *The end of education: Redefining the value of school.* New York: Vintage.

Postman, N., & Weingartner, C. (1969). *Teaching as a subversive activity.* New York: Delta.

Postman, N., & Weingartner, C. (1971). *The soft revolution.* New York: Delta.

Strate, L. (2014). *Amazing ourselves to death: Neil Postman's brave new world revisited.* New York: Peter Lang.

Tabone, C., & Albrecht, R. (2000). Harriet Tubman and the underground railroad: A drama workshop for junior high and high school students. *Stage of the Art, 2*(3), 12–16.

Tabone, C., & Albrecht, R. (2002). Martians invade the classroom: A workshop in language learning. *The Journal of the Imagination in Language Learning and Teaching, VII,* 4–8.

Tandy, M., & Howell, J. (2009). Creating drama with 7–11 year olds: lesson ideas to integrate drama into the primary curriculum. London: Rutledge.

Tarlington, C., & Verriour, P. (1991). *Role drama.* Portsmouth, NH: Heinemann.

Toye, N., & Prendiville, F. (2000). *Drama and traditional story for the early years.* Oxon, Great Britain: RutledgeFalmer.

Ward, W. (1930). *Creative dramatics.* Boston: D. Appleton.

Ward, W. (1957). *Playmaking with children from kindergarten through junior high school.* Boston: Appleton-Century-Crofts.

Wilhelm, J., & Edmiston, B. (1998). *Imagining to learn: Inquiry, ethics and integration through drama.* Portsmouth, NH: Heinemann.

CHAPTER SEVEN

The Seesaw Principle

Summer Camp as Counterenvironment

A little girl sat silently on a swing. It was mid-July, the sun was shining, and all around her children were jumping, singing and chanting to the syncopated rhythms of a morning in summer. A counselor at the day camp passed by. The little girl suddenly sprang to life, looked back and gleefully cried out, "Give me a push!" The counselor stopped short in his tracks, turned to the little girl and gave her a push. And the little girl laughed. He pushed her again and the little girl laughed even more.

"What's so funny Zoraida?" the counselor asked. "Let me in on the joke."

When the little girl finally caught her breath, she explained that she had never had the opportunity to play outdoors for such a long period of time. Up until this point, she had been spending her entire summer locked in an apartment with her little brother while her mother was at work. She watched TV, played video games, and took care of her little brother. Now she was outdoors all day long at a summer day camp. She could play in an environment under the sky and surrounded by other children.

Zoraida was like a little bird who had been let out of her cage.

For city kids like Zoraida, summer camp has always served as a kind of counterenvironment to the harsh urban milieu in which they live. In the age of digital media, however, summer camp takes on an added function. The experience of being outdoors and actively engaged in play can also be conceptualized as a counterenvironment that balances the influence of electronic media in the lives of children who may be confined indoors for twelve long weeks. Little children like Zoraida cry out for alternative kinds of experiences.

In this chapter, we will argue that summer camp—either a "sleep away camp" or a "day camp"—can act as an important counterenvironment to the dominance of digital technologies in the lives of children. We will introduce our concept of the "seesaw principle" which understands summer camp as a counterweight to the heavy presence of electronic forms in the play routines of childhood. Too much of anything—academics, athletics, television, computers or whatever—disrupts the equilibrium necessary for a child's development. Rather than think of digital media in strictly damaging terms, therefore, the seesaw principle allows us to conceptualize them as entities that require a compelling counterweight in order to balance them in a sane and healthy way.

Next, we will explore the world of childhood play from a media ecological perspective that considers not only what new technologies do to play, but also what they undo. What new ideas do digital technologies bring to play and how do they compete with the ideas and worldview embodied in more traditional, pre-electronic forms of play. These questions are questions raised by Neil Postman, but never before have they been applied in a systematic way to childhood play. Indeed, how does digital technology change the nature and character of play?

Finally, we will outline our own attempt to design a summer day that would act as a counterbalance to the influence of electronic media in the lives of children. What kind of activities should it include? How should it be organized? What restraints need to be put into place and what patterns of interaction should be cultivated and reinforced? It is our contention that only by offering children a wide array of orally and interpersonally mediated experiences that are enjoyable can the tremendous weight of digital media be brought into balance.

The Seesaw Principle

A seesaw functions, and can only function, if there is a counterbalance of similar weight sitting at the other end of the plank. When contemporary pedagogues speak of "integrating digital technology across the curriculum" and then advocate extending its influence to include the summer months, the seesaw principle is violated. What we are doing in such a case is creating a situation that places an enormously heavy body at one end of the seesaw while leaving the other side vacant. The child is left dangling in the air.

A child's school year, in class and out, is already saturated with electronic experiences. The summer months, as well, are becoming progressively more influenced by things digital. Besides informal contexts at home and at play, children are being assigned to more formal learning contexts designed to extend a child's mastery of computers. Although the number of "computer" camps and academically oriented summer camps are on the rise, many would argue that children need a chance to escape those kinds of environments. Writing for the *New York Times*, Kristen Race (2016) notes that "summer is an opportunity to undo some of the damaging effects that school year screen time has on the developing brain … Unstructured outside play is one of the best ways for children's brains to recover from school pressures and excessive screen media. Inventing games, building forts or just playing a pick-up game of soccer are all ways to not only increase their imagination, creativity and social skills, but also their critical thinking skills."

A second point the seesaw principle forces us to consider is that in constructing a workable counterenvironment, the counterweight employed must have sufficient appeal to balance the power and prestige of the digital environment. In other words, it is not enough for the weight just to be counter, it also needs to be an alternative that generates enthusiasm and engagement. It is quite clear that digital media have an enormous place in the lives of children and so the question necessarily becomes what has sufficient appeal to counterbalance that influence. The full array of the arts and recreation working together in harmony with the warmth of the summer and the outdoors can surely produce enough appeal to create an equilibrium. Certainly this combination forms a potent mixture.

This brings us to a third point. In creating a counterbalance during the summer months, camp can be creatively designed to function as way of introducing and reinforcing the oral curriculum discussed in Chapter Five. Through their daily participation in a wide range of arts and recreation, children are learning behaviors and attitudes that will help to broaden and socialize them. While building upon a child's natural desire to play, to touch the earth and do the arts, an outdoor summer camp can act as a force that contributes to a child's emotional, social and intellectual development.

The Media Ecology of Play

While media ecologists have written extensively about how various techniques and technologies have restructured our social environment, few have treated at length the question of play. Indeed, how do changes in technologies effect the who, how, when, what and where of a child's play? What can we say of the current technological environment and its influence on play?

Changes in technology have always changed childhood play. Surely there were major differences in play as it moved from pre-linguistic interactions (tag, races, peek-a-boo, wrestling, tree climbing, and other nonverbal forms) to ones that necessitated the adroit use of verbal communication (the evolution of riddles, rhymes, poetry, songs, guessing games, and so on). The introduction of literacy also changed the ways in which childhood play was mediated. Fairytales which had been passed down via the oral tradition in a multiplicity of versions moved from word of mouth to standardized versions codified on the printed page decorated with illustrations. In such a way, one version of the story—the printed version— would become the "correct" version, while the visualizations that were once created in the child's mind, would now be influenced by an artist's conceptualizations. Poetry as well came to be written down and experienced visually rather than being shared and celebrated orally and through song. Children's literature was born and became a significant influence in the imagination of young readers. New forms of play became codified and experienced through literacy. Playing cards came with printed symbols that had to be deciphered by the players, board games required the reading of directions, and sporting contests were guided by instructions recorded in the "rulebook."

In the electronic age of communication, childhood play was transformed once again. Indeed, what happens to childhood play in the electronic age when it becomes more than an occasional TV show or a brief encounter with an online computer game but something that is habitual and practiced for several hours on a daily basis? No experience of this proportion can enter a culture and not have far-reaching consequences on the socialization and learning associated with play. Moreover, whereas earlier pre-electronic changes happened quite gradually over a period of centuries, even millennia, and had time to integrate with earlier forms of play, electronic media have emerged so suddenly and forcefully that they threaten to devour and displace other forms of childhood play.

But how do we assess these changes and their impact on the socialization molded by play? This question, of course, is only partially about the act of playing itself. More fundamentally, it is really about the nature of the environment that surrounds it. Over the course of his career, Neil Postman often returned to this point and made several suggestions as to how to proceed with an approach that gave precedence to the central role that media play in the construction of that environment. Sometimes phrased as a series of interlocking ideas (Postman, 1992, pp. 7–17), or basic principles (Postman 1995, pp. 192–193), or generative questions (Postman, 1999, pp. 42–43), Postman's suggestions provide a useful schema in which to map an analysis of some of the major differences between traditional forms of children's play and those which are mediated through electronic technology. For the purposes of brevity, we will limit ourselves here to the application of just three taken from his table of principles.

The first principle that Postman (1995) offers is the one we employed in the discussion that opened this book. "*All technological change,*" Postman writes, "*is a Faustian bargain. For every advantage a new technology offers, there is always a corresponding disadvantage*" (p. 192). There are no doubt multiple benefits to the electronic technologies that we place in the hands of children but there is another side of the story that shouldn't be overlooked. If children are heavily engaged with television and other forms of electronic media, they are not fully entering the world of play and all the learning that is associated with it. Singer and Singer (1990) maintain that educational television stifles a child's natural curiosity and that time dedicated to TV watching would be put to better use in creative activities that require actual participation. Vandewater, Bickham, and Lee (2006) quote research demonstrating that "television viewing is … negatively related to creative play, especially among very young children (younger than 5 years)" (p. 1). Elkind (2007) adds that "children's play—their inborn disposition for curiosity, imagination, and fantasy—is being silenced in the high-tech, commercialized world we have created …" (p. ix). In other words, even educational television has the power to undo some of the basic activities that we have always associated with childhood play and learning. Along these same lines, Urie Bronfenbrenner reasons:

> Like the sorcerer of old, the television set casts its magic spell, freezing speech and action, turning the living into silent statues for as long as the enchantment lasts. The primary danger of the television screen lies … in the behavior it prevents: the talks, the games, the family festivities, and the arguments through which much of the child's learning takes place and through which his character is formed. Turning on the television set can turn off the process that transforms children into people. (In Winn, 2002a, p. 8)

As powerful as television has been and continues to be, digital media in recent years have emerged on the scene and have added immensely to the presence of electronic media in a child's life. In Chapter Two, we noted the association between electronic media and the atrophy of physical activity. Digital play is "active" in that children may become intensely involved with play they experience on screen but, characteristically, it is not physically engaging. In fact, it is the opposite. The vicarious sense of movement experienced online is not the same as actual movement. At the same time, children rarely have regular opportunities to be physically active outdoors and in the elements, and in spontaneous and sustained interactions with friends.

Digital technology also exerts an important role in the undoing of the intense social rituals that were once part and parcel of traditional forms of play. Much of the playing associated with digital technology is either done alone or in isolation from others who may not even share the same space. A digital game, even when played with others, can be a very individualistic experience. It is not at all uncommon for each set of eyes to have its own individual screen, each set of ears its own phone, ear plugs, and music. Thus children who are the best of friends may actually spend more time playing apart from one another than in a cohabited space.

The multitasking discussed in Chapter Two may also play a role in determining the quality of the ensuing interpersonal interaction. Conversation, when it manages to take place, is subject to constant interruption and fragmentation. The very transportability of mobile devices allows children to carry them in their pockets or backpacks so that even during play with others, they are continually distracted and distanced from their immediate environment. Even when in a face-to-face context, playmates expect that their interaction can be, at any moment, pushed aside with a text message, phone call, or some other digital interruption. The term "social media," then, is misleading because how social is communication amongst people who may never have had met face-to-face, can be permanently "unfriended" from one's life with the push of a button, and can be routinely ignored or dropped from conversation in mid-sentence?

Traditional children's games, in contrast, are deeply social events that necessarily teach the basics of group dynamics. In a pick-up game of stickball, for example, children must agree on the selection of captains, the just division of players into teams, a fair procedure for deciding who gets first pick, the assignment of appropriate field positions and the designation of a batting order which must be monitored and maintained throughout the game. Children will also have to collectively arbitrate whether a ball is fair or foul, a pitch is a ball or a strike, a runner is safe or out, and other potentially conflictive situations that inevitably arise during the course of the game. The players will have to agree as well on the number of innings to be played, when a game is to be called off because of rain, darkness, dinner or some other intervening factor. Are "new players" allowed to join the game once in progress and on whose side? Who will pay for the ball ("chips" or "no chips") should it get lost or roll down into a sewer? Failure to agree on anything noted above or the inability to settle a dispute will mean that the game cannot continue. The negotiations may be resolved peacefully or may result in heated arguments which may even incur fist fights, hurt feelings and bloody noses. There are no buttons to push that allow for immediate disengagement from an uncomfortable situation. There are no adults to appeal to, no video cameras for the purposes of review, no umpires other than the children themselves. Cheaters and bullies will have to be dealt with collectively by the group or by an individual who assumes a position of leadership. The process of working in groups and of resolving conflicts is not always easy or automatic but it's a necessary part of social development in traditional forms of play.

At the same time, many children have become so intensely involved in the digital play world that they have difficulty turning it off and returning back to the real world. Online gaming has become recognized as a serious malady and is now being treated in many quarters as a form of addiction (Graham, 2014; Hussain & Griffiths, 2009; Sanders & Williams, 2016; Weinstein & Lejoyeux, 2015). This addiction will no doubt be exasperated exponentially with the development of virtual reality which, in effect, represents the undoing of reality altogether. It would seem almost certain that "personal" relationships in the virtual world will, in many instances, become more valued than family, friends and interpersonal ones in the real world.

A second principle that Postman (1995) suggests we consider in understanding the intricacies of the media environment relates to the disguised ideological content of technology. For Postman, technologies are not neutral entities but human creations put to purposes laden with meanings. "*Embedded in every technology,*" he states, "*there is a powerful idea, sometimes two or three powerful ideas*" (p. 192). In his lecture "Seven Ideas About Media and Culture," Postman (1992) noted

> (E)very technology has a prejudice. Like language itself, it predisposes us to favor and value certain perspectives and accomplishments. In a culture without writing, human memory is of greatest importance, as are the proverbs, sayings and songs which contain the accumulated oral wisdom of centuries … But in a culture *with* writing, such feats of memory are considered a waste of time … The writing person favors logical organization and systematic analysis, not proverbs … The television person values immediacy, not history. And computer people … value calculation, not judgment. (p. 12)

Indeed, upon closer examination, there does appear to be numerous ideas embedded in the electronic technologies used by children as media of play. For now, we will mention just two. First of all, consider the idea of *commercialization*. From the very beginning, there has always been an admission price to the electronic arcade and that price has steadily increased with each new invention, innovation and generation. Telegraphy charged customers per word; telephony charged for time, distance, and the rental of the technology; phonographs and motion pictures started out as coin operated machines that rapidly evolved into multi-million dollar industries promoting fortune, fame and glamour; the radio industry sold its device to consumers and charged advertisers for time and the privilege to enter audiences' homes in order to make a sales pitch. Television repeated and expanded on radio's business plan and eventually charged not only advertisers but customers who now pay large amounts for the privilege of watching the commercial propaganda that was once beamed in for free.

With each turn of the screw, the commercialized form of interaction digs deeper into the culture of childhood. "Children," writes Sterin (2012), "particularly those younger than 12 years of age, are a very special and lucrative media audience, especially for television and now the Internet" (p. 290). Whereas in the past, advertisers had to go through the parents to get to the kids, electronic media allows advertisers direct access to young minds still in the process of being formed. "With children either spending or influencing 500 billion worth of purchases," Sterin continues, "marketing techniques have been turned upside down" (p. 290). The growing presence and sophistication of digital technology allows corporations to surveil, study, and market to children with little or no interference from their parents. Indeed, it has become virtually impossible for a child, no matter how small, sheltered or smart, to stand totally outside the advertiser's pitch.

Realizing that children, with all the insecurities and enthusiasm of youth yet lacking in mature defenses against the sophisticated rhetoric of pervasive advertising, are an easy mark, corporations have seized the opportunity with a gusto that boggles the mind. In 2003, Rideout, Vandewater, and Wartella noted that "recent years have seen an explosion in electronic media marketed directly at the very youngest children in our society: A booming market of videotapes and DVDs aimed at infants one to 18 months, the launching of the first TV show specifically targeting children as young as 12 months, and a multi-million-dollar industry selling computer games and even special keyboard toppers for children as young as nine months old" (p. 2). A more recent assessment by Hanson (2014) adds, "Marketing to children in the twenty-first century goes far beyond the traditional print and thirty-second television ads. Companies are instead pouring money into product placement, in-school programs, mobile phone ads, and video games" (p. 280). Hanson (2014) notes that "in 1983 companies were spending $100 million a year to reach children. But by 2008 spending on advertising directed at children had grown to $17 billion a year. That means that marketers are spending 170 times more today to reach children than they were a generation ago" (p. 279). In sum, via promotional toys, magazines, radio music programs, TV cartoons, finely honed commercials, product placements, and so on, children are being expertly groomed to think and act like consumers.

Digital gaming is enormously popular with children and profitable for those who design and sell them. Describing the lucrative potential of digital games, *Statista* (2018) estimates that "the entire worldwide market is projected to grow from an estimated 1.72 trillion U.S. dollars in 2015 to 2.2 trillion U.S. dollars by 2021." Digital games, regardless of their content, are designed as commercial products that routinely entice the user to buy constant upgrades. Just as salt and sugar are added to foods to entice its consumption regardless of its detriment to health, digital games are designed to be sold in massive quantities to children regardless of their impact on physical or psychological health.

We could outline ad infinitum the tremendous costs incurred with the purchase of various digital technologies as well as the cost to repair, upgrade and replace them, but the main point is that we have grown to accept the idea that play in the electronic media environment is a commercialized form of transaction. The simplicity of traditional forms of play that relied on a discarded broom stick and a 15-cent rubber ball, have been replaced with the idea that if you want to play, you got to pay. Play is big business.

Stemming directly from the idea of commercialization, there is another idea embedded in the electronic mediation of children's play: *immediate gratification*. From the outset, electronic mediated have promoted the idea that the first rule of engagement was to gratify audiences as fast and as often as possible. Vaudeville, with its variety of rapidly changing short acts, was a primitive introit into this unfolding drama. The phonograph allowed us to have music anytime, anywhere without being involved with its production. Early motion pictures with their pie in the face humor gave the audience quick and easy laughs. And television, of course, is constantly attempting to gratify us instantaneously less we zap the show or, God forbid, turn it off.

The case of the pinball machine is an interesting one to ponder. In that pinball machines are coin operated, they vividly represent a form of childhood play that has been commercialized; in that they are a game with an alluring array of bells, buzzes and whistles in exchange for a child's coins, they also underscore the idea of immediate gratification. The cacophony of sound, the mesmerizing flashing of lights, the frenetic din of the arcade housing the machine, the fantastic images lying on top of the table and the ever accumulating score on the back panel bringing the player closer and closer to the promised land of "free replay," immediately and continually gratify the player in a virtual orgy of stimulation.

Contemporary computer games have tossed this primitive electronic device into the dustbin of nostalgia and have made online gaming a portable and nearly constant feature in the lives of many young people. One no longer needs to go to an arcade to be gratified, only to reach into their back pocket. With virtual reality just around the corner, the idea of gratification will surely become more intense and more alluring. And remember, we are only at the dawn of the digital age. These games will only become more seductive and what we hold today as the "best new thing" will very soon find its place in a collector's basement next to the juke boxes, old radios, windup phonographs, cassette players and pinball machines.

Digital games, which are now on every cell phone and held in every hand, have gone a long way in diminishing collective and quiet pursuits. Whereas electronic mediation continually aims at immediate gratification, the idea of delayed gratification is typically embedded in both oral and literate forms of communication. Baseball proceeds slowly, jumping rope requires each child to wait their turn, chess cultivates patient pondering, etc. The hare-like pace of digital media contrasts sharply to the tortoise-like pace required by literacy and deep reading. It is no accident that the careful deciphering of black marks on a white page is rapidly being replaced by scanning and by the immediate gratification of icons, imagery and talking screens.

A third principle that Postman proposes concerns the dramatic tension that exists between old and new forms of technology. "*A new technology,*" Postman (1995) writes, "*usually makes war against an old technology. It competes with it for time, attention, money, prestige, and a 'worldview'*" (p. 192). Just as vaudeville died in the wake of the talkies and the influence of radio waned with the arrival of TV, traditional forms of children's play have rapidly been sidelined or made obsolete with the dawn of the digital. We have already noted the extent to which children spend huge amounts of time engaged with television, computers, cell phones, video games and other electronic devices. But as these new technologies enter the lives of children, what forms of communication are pushed out in order to make room? In an article entitled "What Television Chases Out of Life," Marie Winn (2002b), notes that

> Without conjuring up fantasies of bygone years with family games and long, leisurely meals ... the ordinary daily life is diminished: those hours of sitting around at the dinner table, the little games invented by children on the spur of the moment, the scribbling, the chatting, and even the quarreling—all the things that form the fabric of a family that define a childhood. (p. 42)

Family and community sing alongs, which are almost non-existent today, were once an activity where a child learned a varied repertoire of songs that fostered social bonding and active participation within a cross-generational context. Today, it is difficult to find a group of people who are not totally embarrassed to sing or who are willing to sing a song to its completion. And, if a group is disposed to sing, it is increasingly difficult to identify songs to which all would know the lyrics. Songs, which once bound generations together, are discarded almost as soon as they are created and consumed. Rather than bind us, music marks a line that divides us. How can we sing each other's songs if we don't know them or, even worse, if we continually ridicule them as yesterday's leftovers?

At the same time, singing is now commonly conceptualized as the exclusive province of the professional who must be paid huge amounts not only to sing but to perform. This transferal of singing from a communal activity to a spectacle has been expanding in presence and in prestige throughout the rise of electronic media. At midpoint in the twentieth century, Lewis Mumford (1952) made an important observation relevant to our discussion:

> The very growth of mechanical facilities has given people a false idea of technical perfectionism so that unless they can compete with the products of the machine or with those whose professional training qualifies them for such a public appearance, they are all too ready to take a back seat. (pp. 6–7)

The very popular TV show *American Idol*, which has inspired imitations throughout the world, is a good example of the way electronic media has put the professional in the driver's seat and left the rest of us in the back seat gazing out the window at a landscape we once inhabited but are now leaving. The whole premise of the show is to catapult amateur "nobodies" into the elevated realm of professional "somebodies." The appeal of the program is intense and the illusion of active participation is enhanced all across the media spectrum. Jack Lule (2014) writes that

> *American Idol* hit the airways in 2002 and became the only television program ever to earn the top spot in the Nielsen ratings for six seasons in a row, often averaging more than 30 million nightly viewers … Newspapers put developments on the show on their front pages. New cell phone technologies allowed viewers to have a direct role in the program's star-making enterprise through casting votes. Fans also could sign up for text alerts or play trivia games on their phones. In 2009, AT&T estimated that *Idol*-related text traffic amounted to 178 million messages. (p. 28)

Time and attention spent on media phenomenon like *American Idol* or other such shows represents time and attention not focused elsewhere. Although the synergistic web surrounding the show encourages enthusiastic audience participation, it is not at all the same quality of participation that traditional children's songs and activities insure. Moreover, what does this teach a child about singing and its place in society and human psychology? Is singing nothing more than a ladder to fame and fortune? Is the sharing of songs among families and friends just an embarrassingly poor substitute for professional performance? It would appear, almost undeniably so, that the place and the prestige of one form of communication, such as communal singing by amateurs, is marginalized and made to look ridiculous or, at best, oddly quaint by the growth and expansion of electronic media.

This same loss of prestige suffered by communal singing is paralleled throughout the oral world of children. Hop-scotch, board games, patty-cake and other childhood activities are one by one discarded and replaced with electronic ones. This is not just a change of fashion or style but constitutes a change in worldview. The worldview fostered by this shift, as Mumford (1952) correctly points out, is the enshrinement of celebrity and the diminishment of an actual community. The common use of words such as "idol," "star" or "icon" underscores this change in worldview as we learn to worship an ever-changing array of anointed individuals who have attained a quasi-religious status. Like the stars in the heavens that we once gazed upon, we now avidly gaze at the razzle dazzle of performers who shoot across our screens like comets, only to disappear as suddenly as they have appeared. Moreover, since these idols or stars are commercially created and sustained entities, children are being acculturated not only to a professionalized form of interaction that excludes them but to a profit oriented one as well.

The evolution of American pop culture from Elvis Presley and Annette Funicello to Justin Bieber and Miley Cyrus and from *Father Knows Best* and *Leave It to Beaver* to *Keeping Up with the Kardashians* and *South Park* also reflects a profound shift in world view and our conceptualization of youth. Whether children watch these shows or not, they are being socialized into a society that does. And, as Postman emphasizes in his book *The Disappearance of Childhood* (1982), television has eroded the information walls between childhood and adulthood. These sorts of contemporary idols and programs—jaded, materialistic and featuring characters totally lacking in self-regulation—did not create the shift in worldview: they are symbolic representations of it.

Summer Camp as Counterenvironment

When Marshall McLuhan and Neil Postman spoke of artists and educators as creators of "counterenvironments" that balance the disequilibrium born of technological change, it is doubtful that they were thinking of play or the joys of a children's summer camp. Frankly, we can think of no better example. With a little imagination and the willingness to experiment, a summer camp can be designed as an "environmental installation," a pageant, an outdoor "happening," and an opportunity to explore various ways of communicating not mediated by digital technologies. In the section that follows, we will be repeatedly referencing Johan Huizinga (1938/1955) whose generative and influential work on play emphasized its centrality in the socialization of children and even its essential role in the creation and sustenance of civilization.

Summer camp, whether a sleep away or day camp, takes a child out of their ordinary world and places them within an alternative universe. Camps are designed to overturn the grind of the normal routine and replace it with novel experiences. For Zoraida, camp was enough to provoke waves of laughter. It gave her the one thing that the dominant environment had denied her: a time and place to play outdoors with other children.

For over forty years, we have been developing a day camp to give city children an opportunity to make new friends, discover their creative talents and play in an outdoor environment. The program we founded has evolved from a very simple summer program originally located on an abandoned city lot into a very sophisticated blend of art, music, dance, theater, gardening, board games, field games, drama and puppets. We conceptualize every activity as a learning experience, every day as a work of art in motion. The children are outdoors for the entire day in an environment not mediated by digital technology and a panoply of screens. Youngsters are instructed to leave their cellphones and electronic devices at home and for six hours a day, five days a week, the children inhabit a non-cybernetic environment free from the distractions and allure of the digital.

The camp is dedicated to the cultivation of play in its various forms and circumstances. "Summing up the formal characteristics of play," Huizinga (1938/1955) observes, "we might call it a free activity standing quite consciously outside 'ordinary' life as being 'not serious,' but at the same time absorbing the player intensely and utterly ... It proceeds within its own proper bounds of time and space according to fixed rules and in an orderly manner" (p. 13). At camp, several varieties of play are available and it's not difficult for a child to find an activity that draws their enthusiastic attention, intense involvement, and commitment so that it may proceed "according to fixed rules and in an orderly manner."

The morning at Camp Liberty begins at 8:00 a.m. when some children are dropped off by parents on their way to work. Children climb monkey bars, play tag, converse, organize games. If they have cellphones in their hands, they are asked to put them away. Around 9:30 a.m., the majority of the children arrive on buses provided by the camp.

Shortly after 10 a.m., a hand rung bell calls all the children and the staff to stop what they're doing and gather for a short assembly program in a large outdoor pavilion. Regular assemblies throughout the day remind both children and staff that they are part of a community, not a conglomeration of individuals or small isolated groups. The use of an acoustic bell to call assembly is intentional. Similarly, we never utilize microphones or public address systems to communicate with the children but only use the acoustically mediated voice. Historically, a sonorous object has frequently been employed to gather the community. Lewis Mumford (1961) reminds us that "Mesopotamian cities had an assembly drum, just as medieval cities used a bell in a church tower to call their citizens together ... Plato limited the size of his ideal city to the number of citizens who might be addressed by a single voice" (p. 63). The ringing of the bell at the camp, then, is a simple practice that reinforces the idea that the children and the staff are in fact a community, not simply a mass of individuals pursuing personal interests.

The pavilion, where the camp assembles at various points during the day, is totally open on three sides to allow for the illumination of natural sunlight and the circulation of air. The children (approximately 200) range in age from 6 to 12 and are divided into four groups based on their age. The staff (approximately 30) consists of high school and college students, teachers, and artists who range in age from 17 to 75. This age differential in the staff forces a great deal of intergenerational communication and sharing, something not normally experienced in a digital environment. Following the assembly bell, the day beings with a couple of songs ("Jambalaya," "The Cat Came Back," "This Land Is Your Land," etc.) and a few necessary announcements. The benefits of starting the day with a song are enormous. Singing makes the many one, it integrates isolated individuals into a group and transforms the group into a community. Singing effects our mood (Magill, 1980; Pignatiello, Camp, & Rasar, 1986), heart rate (Landreth & Landreth, 1974), the secretion of hormones (Spintge, 1988) and various other aspects of our physiological and psychological beings. At the same time, by singing collectively on a daily basis, we develop a repertoire of songs that will serve us long after we leave that space. Parents often tell us that the children sing the songs they learned at camp in the car and around the house. The intergenerational repertoire (folk songs, songs by the Beatles, old pop and rock 'n' roll songs, contemporary hits) connects the children with their parents and grandparents. Singing is sharing: children teach the songs to their friends and to their siblings. Finally, and perhaps most importantly, by doing this every day, the act of singing becomes a natural part of who we are. We learn by doing. By regularly raising our voices in song, we are not as intimidated by the act of singing as are people who rarely have the opportunity to sing with others. Collective singing becomes a natural part of who we are and what we regularly do.

The day is divided into four periods, about one hour each, two in the morning and two more after lunch. From the stage, counselors announce a wide range of age specific activities from which the children can select which one they will join. Activities include drawing, painting, crafts, singing, dancing, drumming, drama, vaudeville, puppetry, gardening, playground, soccer, volleyball, board games, swimming, softball, handball and so on. Not all activities, of course, are offered each and every period but are dispersed throughout the course of a day. The emphasis in all the activities, whether arts or recreation oriented, is on participation, enjoyment and mutual respect. We are not interested in cultivating professional artists or star athletes but in creating an environment where recreation and the arts can be experienced on an everyday basis by all. "Play," Huizinga (1938/1955) argues, "lies outside the reasonableness of practical life; has nothing to do with necessity or utility, duty or truth …" (p. 158). At the camp, children are able to explore what it is that they like and to do so in a playful way with no other end than pure enjoyment.

Singing at the camp retains its character as play rather than as aesthetic perfection: the emphasis is on involvement not performance. The same can be said of music's most faithful companion, dance. Children are given ample opportunity to participate in dance: in plays and in rehearsals where they are exposed to dances from different cultures and different historical periods, in unsupervised moments where they can improvise and share dance moves with each other, and in periods during the day where they can dance freely with friends as a way of playing. Dancing is presented primarily as a form of play, of enjoyment, not as a performance to be evaluated. Huizinga (1938/1955) emphasizes the playful character of dance:

> If in everything that pertains to music we find ourselves in the play-sphere, the same is true in even higher degree of music's twin sister, the dance. Whether we think of the sacred or magical dances of savages, or of the Greek ritual dances, or of the dancing of King David before the Ark of the Covenant, or the dance simply as part of a festival, it is always at all periods and with all peoples pure play, the purest and most perfect form of play that exists. (p. 164)

At the same time that there is ample opportunity to experience music and dance, recreation is on-going in multiple forms throughout all four periods. Recreation is a chance for children to run, jump, skip, and shout in a way not usually possible on a city street or when locked indoors, sitting in front of a computer screen or a texting on a mobile device. Athletics—soccer, softball, basketball, handball—teach commitment to an activity and its rules, the cultivation of endurance, strength and speed, a graciousness in victory and the acceptance of defeat. All children, regardless of their ability, are encouraged to play. Competition is inevitable in the sports activities but we attempt to keep it to a minimum. We do not form leagues, award trophies or medals, and never allow competition to take the fun out of games. Teams dissolve at the end of the game and are re-formed differently in the next game. Huizinga (1938/1955) emphasizes the on-going dangers of play being corrupted by competition when he notes that "ever since the last quarter of the nineteenth century games, in the guise of sport, have been taken more and more seriously ... with the increasing systematization and regimentation of sport, something of the pure play-quality is inevitably lost ... The spirit of the professional is no longer the true play-spirit; it is lacking in spontaneity and carelessness" (pp. 196–197).

How much more compelling is Huizinga's warning in the present day! It is clear that this professional ideal of winning at all cost has filtered down to the children at the camp. In games of soccer, for example, some of those who play in leagues outside of the camp have learned to "flop"—intentionally throwing themselves down in order to draw a penalty—much as their heroes do in professional matches broadcast on TV or how their coaches have taught them. "In the case of sport," Huizinga (1938/1955) concludes, "we have an activity nominally as play but raised to such a pitch of technical organization and scientific thoroughness that the real play-spirit is threatened with extinction" (p. 199). If children do not have a time, a place and a chance to experience the "real play-spirit" that Huizinga advocates, they are much more likely to be influenced by the win at any cost role models they see in the media in professional games.

Another activity, gardening, is offered once or twice a day and, like all the activities at the camp, children have the choice of joining the activity or choosing another. There are several gardens at the camp, some with flowers, some with fruits, some with vegetables. Gardening, however, is not just about planting, weeding, and watering, but the feel of the earth on the hands, the discovery of different kinds of bugs, the coolness of water on the skin, the sense of stewardship and nurturance of life, the conversation and negotiation with companions as they work together cooperatively, the learning to use a variety of tools—shovels, hoes, pitchforks, watering cans, wheel barrows—and improvising new ones with sticks and stones found on the ground. When the cultivated food is ripe, the children are allowed to pick it and eat it fresh off the vine. Many of these children, born and raised in an urban environment, are amazed that edible fruits and vegetables actually come from the ground and can be eaten.

There are also wild berry bushes and trees from which the children are allowed to gather the fruit once it is ripe. Gathering wild fruit includes developing a sharp eye to discover it hiding in a bush or on the branch of a tree. It is also about having the forbearance to wait until the berries are ripe and about remembering where the best bushes and berry trees are located.

Board and table games are offered every period and include chess, checkers, dominoes, Monopoly, Chutes and Ladders, Scrabble, card games and so on. Each one of these games is interactive and each one teaches a host of skills: reading and following the directions, waiting one's turn, how to negotiate disagreements about rules and procedures, commitment to the game until completion, how to lose without having a meltdown. Board games also teach children to clean up and be responsible for the condition in which they leave the game and its pieces.

At the same time that athletics, gardening and board games are going on, children also have the opportunity to choose between several art, drama and music workshops. The art workshops are conducted by artists and art teachers who instruct children in the basics of 2D and 3D design. Some music workshops teach singing while others focus on the basics of drumming. The drama workshops conducted by actors employ theater games, puppets and improvised role play. Once a day, there is "vaudeville practice" where children prepare to participate in a camp talent show where they can perform songs, jokes, skits, magic tricks and so on, before an audience that will include parents as well as other children. Taken together as a group, art, music, drama and vaudeville workshops are open invitations to children to explore their creativity with artists. Once again, it is intended as a socializing experience that encourages face-to-face conversation, opportunities to meet and make new friends, the assignment and sharing of responsibilities, and the negotiation of conflicts.

At the end of each one-hour period, the hand rung bell rings, the camp reassembles, new activities are announced, and once again the children are free to select which one they wish to join. When we first started Camp Liberty, children were required to join certain activities during particular periods—"art period," "softball period," etc. Noticing the resistance of children and staff, we reorganized our schedules to allow children to choose their preferred activities. Huizinga (1938/1955) maintained that "first and foremost … all play is a voluntary activity … (T)he first characteristic of play: that it is free, is in fact freedom" (pp. 7, 8). By having the freedom to choose from a wide variety of options, children learn how to make decisions, explore different activities, negotiate with friends which activity they will join, and have the opportunity to make new friends. Moreover, within Camp Liberty, not only do the children have the freedom to choose their activities but even the staff has a great deal of leeway in choosing which activities they will coordinate and their level of involvement.

At lunchtime, the bell is rung once more, the "play world" in which the children have immersed themselves all morning is interrupted, and they are called to re-enter the "real world." Huizinga (1938/1955) writes that "play is distinct from 'ordinary' life both as to locality and duration … It is 'played out' within certain limits of time and place … The umpire's whistle breaks the spell and sets 'real' life going again" (pp. 9, 10).

Once outside the play world, children assemble in the pavilion for lunch. From the stage, there is a mini performance by two counselors who do a short routine, sing a couple of songs and tell corny jokes, some of which the children themselves have contributed. The songs serve to reassemble and calm the children who have spent the morning in diverse activities while the jokes appeal to and help develop a child's sense of humor in a positive way. Humor, of course, lifts the spirit, nurtures the body and sharpens the nimbleness of the mind.

After the comedy act, the children take their seats at the picnic tables located at the rear of the pavilion. In recent years, many of the children have also spread out towels in the field adjacent to the pavilion and have organized their own picnic lunches with friends. Eating is a ritual guided by rules of decorum that are not normally taught or respected in the frenetic and individualistic atmosphere of the digital environment. No one begins to eat until everyone has been seated and all have been served. A counselor leads the camp in a breathing and relaxation exercise that calms the children before eating. The staff sits and eats with the children. This gives adults a chance to chat informally with the children, exchange jokes and riddles, learn something about them, share food and make sure they eat orderly and clean up after themselves. Here too, we are engaged in a muted but very important form of play. Huizinga (1938/1955) notes the importance of verbal word play:

> Culturally speaking, advice, riddle, myth, legend, proverb, etc., are closely connected … The riddle, we may conclude, was originally a sacred game, and as such it cut clean across any possible distinction between play and seriousness. It was both at once; a ritual element of the highest importance and yet essentially a game. As civilization develops, the riddle branches out in two directions: mystic philosophy on the one hand and recreation on the other. (pp. 110–111)

Once again, this form of social interaction, practiced on a routine basis, is not something that digital technology readily cultivates. The art of conversation, questioning and negotiating outcomes is learned through initiation, imitation and habit. It is learned by doing. Much as Neil Postman repeatedly emphasized the importance of learning to use language intelligently, simple and focused conversation with a child not distracted by a cellphone can become a learning experience.

After lunch, a group of children who have volunteered collect left-over scraps of half-eaten pieces of fruit and vegetables and takes them to the garden area where they will be turned into compost. The other children put their things away, return to their benches and a counselor will tell a story from the stage. These stories give the children and staff a few moments to rest and digest their food before entering the afternoon's activities. The stories include a selection of age appropriate folktales, fairytales, myths and fables from the four corners of the world. These stories allow us to explore various points of view that contrast rather dramatically with the stories children normally see on television or in the movies. While the stories are meant to be entertaining, there is always a worthy lesson embedded within each tale. Mythology, as Freud and Jung grasped early on, uncovers a great deal about the human psyche and plants in us terms and motifs with which to discuss and understand the human condition. Fables and folktales reveal human folly and foibles and help to cultivate in children a sense of ethics and moral behavior. Fairytales take the imagination of children into magical kingdoms and assure young hearts that righteousness will be restored, that virtue will triumph over evil, and that goodness will live "happily ever after."

As a medium of communication, storytelling is an ancient practice that enhances a child's capacity to listen and to follow an extended narrative that has no images other than the ones created in the child's mind. Storytelling can be said to support the acquisition of literacy which also requires an individual to focus on a narrative and turn words into mental pictures. Electronic media, in contrast, shortcuts the process. By providing the viewer with pictures, electronic media makes the learning of literacy more of a challenge to children who are accustomed to having the images provided for them. Moreover, the bias of electronic media, as we have said, is to entertain and amuse not educate. The media are preoccupied with commercial goals, not educational ones. With oral storytelling, the community re-appropriates its responsibility to be the one who passes on important knowledge and values to children. Rather than abandon this power to anonymous entities more concerned with financial gain than social development, the face-to-face community reasserts and reclaims that role.

Once the story is completed, the staff reassembles on stage, the next period's activities are announced, and the afternoon proceeds in mirror image of the morning. At the end of the day, around 3:00 PM, the bell is rung for the final time. A few announcements are made, lost articles of clothing are distributed from the stage, and a couple of songs are sung before dismissal. One of these songs is usually a quiet tune ("Down in the Valley," "Stand by Me," "Redemption Song") which functions as kind of a lullaby for children (and staff) tired after a long day of physical activity. The second song, in contrast, is a lively one that functions as the camp's "theme song" and sends the children happily on their way.

The culminating event that caps each one of the summer's four sessions is the presentation of a camp play that draws together the efforts, skills and talents of the entire camp. Over the course of each two-week session, the staff works with the children on developing an original play that is presented on stage before the entire camp, as well as to the children's parents, siblings and guests. In the months leading up to the camp, four individuals are charged with the responsibility of finding stories appropriate for children that they will transform into scripts and eventually direct. The choice of the stories is collectively debated, the scripts are discussed and amended, meetings are held with set designers, costumer makers, choreographers, musicians and actors who will be bringing the words on the page to life. It is a process that goes on for a number of weeks, but the end result is usually exciting.

Once the camp begins and the children arrive, the collaboration is put in motion. On the first day of each two-week session, the writer/director of the story tells the story from the stage to the children immediately following lunch. The children are invited to be in the play but their participation is voluntary. Children who are interested must commit to one rehearsal period each day over the two-week session. Staff members play the principle roles in the story, thus relieving small children of the responsibility of learning lines and projecting their voices in a large outdoor space. This practice also avoids the competition among children for featured roles and thereby prevents hurt or hostile feelings of those not selected. The children do play, however, supporting roles in the stories, appear in costumes and perform in dances that have been choreographed and practiced with the staff during the two weeks leading up to the presentation.

Like the stories told after lunch, the plays enacted on stage are based on wisdom tales taken from around the world that teach valuable lessons. The goal of each play is not only to entertain but also instruct. In *The End of Education*, Postman (1995) writes that the young minds of children need to be guided by such stories, that is, by a story "that tells of origins and envisions a future, a story that constructs ideals, prescribes rules of conduct, provides a source of authority, and, above all, gives a sense of continuity and purpose" (pp. 5–6).

After the play, parents are invited to stay, meet other parents, spend time with the children, picnic, and visit with the staff. In the art rooms, there is an exhibit of the work that the children have produced during the two-week session. There is also a "vaudeville show," that is, a camp talent show where children have the opportunity to tell jokes and perform songs, do acrobatics, magic tricks, and the like, on a smaller stage for their parents and other children. No prizes or awards are given in the vaudeville show or at the art exhibit: the incentive is the doing, the reward is sharing that moment with others. Huizinga (1938/1955) reminds us that play "is an activity connected with no material interest, and no profit can be gained from it" (p. 13).

Camp Liberty is very much a summer festival that returns for eight weeks every July and August. Perhaps the key to the camp's success is the fact that the yearly gathering of individuals of different ages and different backgrounds represents a culturally needed public celebration of the summer season. It is, as we said before, a "happening," an environmental work of art with many moving but interconnected pieces. Huizinga (1938/1955) was well aware of the importance of such celebrations and the creation of a pageant-like atmosphere:

> Ritual is thus in the main a matter of shows, representations, dramatic performances, imaginative actualizations of a vicarious nature. At the great seasonal festivals the community celebrates the grand happenings in the life of nature by staging sacred performances, which represent the change of seasons, the rising and setting of the constellations, the growth and ripening of crops, birth, life and death in man and beast. (p. 15)

Camps can function as something of a modern-day oasis, a respite from the tyranny of the electronic screens that surround us. Camp can be the counterweight at the other end of the digital seesaw.

Conclusion

Cat Stevens' song "Where Will the Children Play?" asks a seminal question that we shouldn't push aside too quickly. In the 50 years since he first asked it, the availability of time and suitable places for children to play has only been reduced. The rise of the digital revolution has exponentially compounded the problem for children who now spend hours upon hours entertaining themselves on screens and with mobile devices—especially during the summer months—and not absorbing the kinds of learning associated with actual face-to-face play. If the digital revolution is to be balanced in the lives of children, there needs to be sufficient weight at the other end of the cultural seesaw. Arts and recreation can do that.

Summer camp is the ultimate counterenvironment. Without the omnipresence of electronic media in their lives, children have the opportunity to experience life and other children in a way that is really quite different. It would be foolish not to acknowledge that much—much too much—is being left out of the socialization of children in the digital age. Small steps, like a place set aside that specializes in play and creativity, can have a huge impact on the summer of a child. There is no reason why this experiment cannot be tried elsewhere. Cultural art centers that teach children everything from gardening and cooking to music, dance and drama can be established within easy reach of all children.

The unfortunate reality of contemporary life, however, is that most children do not have safe neighborhoods in which to play and, as a consequence, are relegated to sit for hours on end in front of a television or computer screen. As we noted in Chapter Two, there are several consequences that are problematic with extensive digital use including the possibility of behavioral addiction, inability to concentrate or read deeply, physical atrophy and so on. Neighborhood or community youth centers with educational artists, trained in the use of recreational and crafts activities, are a civilizing requirement in the digital age.

Barring the existence of such centers, children are necessarily abandoned to televisions, cell phones and laptops. Like Zoraida, the little girl on the swing that we met at the beginning of this chapter, children just need a time, a place, and a little push.

References

Elkind, D. (2007). *The power of play: How spontaneous, imaginative activities lead to happier, healthier children*. Philadelphia, PA: Da Capo Press.

Graham, J. (2014). Narrative therapy for treating video game addiction. *International Journal of Mental Health and Addiction, 12*(6), 701–707.

Hanson, R. E. (2014). *Mass communication: Living in a media world.* Los Angeles, CA: Sage.

Huizinga, J. (1938/1955). *Homo ludens.* Boston, MA: Beacon Press.

Hussain, Z., & Griffiths, M. D. (2009, October). Excessive use of massively multi-player online role-playing games: A pilot study. *International Journal of Mental Health and Addiction,* 563–571. Retrieved from http://link.springer.com/article/10.1007%2Fs11469-009-9202-8#page-1

Landreth, J. E., & Landreth, H. F. (1974). Effects of music on physiological response. *Journal of Research in Music Education, 22,* 4–12.

Lule, J. (2014). *Understanding media and culture: An introduction to mass communication.* Washington, DC: Flat World Knowledge.

Magill, L. A. (1980). *The effects of live versus tape recorded music on hospitalized cancer patients* (Unpublished master's thesis). New York University.

Mumford, L. (1952). *Art and technics.* New York: Columbia University Press.

Mumford, L. (1961). *The city in history.* New York: Harcourt, Brace & World.

Pignatiello, M. F., Camp, C. J., & Rasar, L. (1986). Musical mood induction: An alternative to the Velten technique. *Journal of Abnormal Psychology, 95,* 295–297.

Postman, N. (1982). *The disappearance of childhood.* New York: Delacorte.

Postman, N. (1992). Seven ideas about media and culture. *The Speech Communication Annual, 6,* 7–18.

Postman, N. (1995). *The end of education: Redefining the value of school.* New York: Vintage.

Postman, N. (1999). *Building a bridge to the eighteenth century: How the past can improve our future.* New York: Alfred A. Knopf.

Race, K. (2016, July 13). Give kids' brains a break from screen time. *NY Times.* Retrieved from https://www.nytimes.com/roomfordebate/2016/07/12/pokemon-go-get-outta-here/give-kids-brains-a-break-from-screen-time

Rideout, V., Vandewater, E., & Wartella, E. (2003). *Zero to six: Electronic media in the lives of infants, toddlers, and preschoolers.* Menlo Park, CA: The Henry J. Kaiser Foundation.

Sanders, J. L., & Williams, R. J. (2016). Reliability and validity of the behavioral addiction measure for video gaming. *Cyber Psychology, Behavior and Social Networking, 19*(1), 43–48.

Singer, D. G., & Singer, J. L. (1990). *The house of make-believe: Children's play and the developing imagination.* Cambridge, MA: Harvard University Press.

Spintge, R. (1988). Music as physiotherapeutic and emotional means in medicine. *International Journal of Music, Dance and Art Therapy, 8,* 75–81.

Statista. (2018). *U.S. online gaming industry: Statistics & facts.* https://www.statista.com/topics/1551/online-gaming/

Sterin, J. C. (2012). *Mass media revolution.* New York: Allyn & Bacon.

Vandewater, E. A., Bickham, D. S., & Lee, J. H. (2006). Time well spent? Relating television use to children's free-time activities. *Pediatrics, 117*(2), 1–13.

Weinstein, A., & Lejoyeux, M. (2015). New developments on the neurobiological and pharmo-genetic mechanisms underlying internet and video game addiction. *American Journal on Addictions, 24*(2), 117–125.

Winn, M. (2002a). *The plug-in drug: Television, computers, and family life.* New York: Penguin.

Winn, M. (2002b). What television chases out of life. *American Educator, 26*(2), 40–45.

Epilogue

Children are the living messages

we send to a time we will not see.

Neil Postman[1]

We began this book by asking you to stop, look and notice how deeply absorbed people are in their digital devices. We will end it with the same request. Look around you. What do you see? This is the new normal. It is still somewhat visible to us because it is still somewhat new to us. Shortly it will become old hat and fade from view. Soon, we will experience the omnipresence of digital media and the behaviors they bring as the only environment possible. It will take on the guise of the "natural" and the status of the assumed.

Our students come to school very much connected and dependent upon digital media. No secret here. They spend more time with digital media than they do in any other activity including family, friends, study or sleep. The technophile, well-funded and well-heeled, wants us to ignore that which is right before our eyes. More technology, they argue, will solve the problems of more technology. The sales pitch is working a bit too well. We are now being pressured to transform our schools into technology centers and our children's summers into prolonged periods of online activity. Even during June, July and August, months when we use to expect youngsters to be outside playing with friends and learning games, many children are corralled in their homes watching screens or pushed into classes that instruct them in digital applications. Certainly, children need something more than this during their formative years.

Inventors and entrepreneurs are absolutely intoxicated by the possibilities of the digital revolution, but pedagogues and parents need to be a bit more cautious. What we have proposed in this book is not the elimination of digital media but the cultivation of a balance. The arts, conceptualized as inclusive, interpersonal and learning experiences, is a logical and effective place to begin. Call it a "counterenvironment," a "thermostatic mechanism," or a "seesaw," the educational use of the arts can help reinforce and extend oral and literate communication at a time when they are being routed by the onslaught of the digital.

We addressed our book to the general reader because we believed that the points we raise and the solutions we propose are ones that we all need to be discussing. Citizenship is not only about rights, it's also about responsibilities. We can't blame the corporations for their excursions into education—that's what they do. They see their chances and they take them. The rest of us, however, need to be more attentive and aware. Our duty is to question. A democracy can endure many things, but it cannot survive silence.

In writing this book, most especially we had the teacher and the teacher-to-be in mind because they are the ones who are in the classroom six hours a day, five days a week, ten months a year. Like them, we are also teachers. We've hailed them as creative people for we believe that imagination and critical reflection are the essence of education. A teacher's vocation—their calling—is to respond to the needs of his or her students and invent methods that will work. Digital media has the upper hand in the lives of children, but the arts used prudently as pedagogical methods in the classroom can help to balance and offset that influence.

Trying to counterbalance the impact of digital technology in the lives of children is perhaps a quixotic mission that many would ridicule as nostalgic and out of step with the inevitable. But the greatest folly of all, Miguel de Cervantes reminds us, is "to see life as it is and not as it should be." As parents, artists and teachers, don't we have the responsibility to step forward and make sure that we control our technologies and not the other way around? Who and what entities are we entrusting our children to? Yes, digital media are inevitable but the ways in which we incorporate them is not. Marshall McLuhan understood well that artists are always building arks "for facing the changes at hand." Neil Postman repeatedly asked schools to step up and confront the ecological imbalances of our technological society.

Is it mad to suggest measures that resist the excesses and disorientations of the digital revolution? Is it insane to courageously open our eyes to see that which is staring us dead in the face? Maybe. Or is it just a bit of foresight and good sense?

Twenty-three centuries ago, Plato asked his students "What is the right way of living?" And then, after an exchange with his students, the philosopher concluded, "Life must be lived as play, playing certain games, making sacrifices, singing and dancing, and then a man will be able to propitiate the gods, and defend himself against his enemies, and win in the contest" (*Laws*, vii., 803). Teaching should not be "a job" for us any more than making art should be a job for artists. It is our place to gather and hopefully reinvent a saner world. We must now take our stand before the ultimate contest of this time and place and, ironies of ironies, we will win it not with the use of force or the awesome wonders of technology, but through the power of the arts, reason and the creative pleasures of play.

Note

1. Neil Postman (1982), *The Disappearance of Childhood*, p. xi. New York: Delacorte.

Index

1984 32, 40, 51, 119, 120, 125, 134, 135
addiction 25, 26, 27, 35, 40, 41, 42, 43, 143, 157, 158, 159
agnosia 70
Airport game 105
Albrecht, Robert 49, 61, 85, 119, 121, 135
Altamira 100, 108
Alter 26, 27, 36, 39
amusia 70
aphasia 70
art 14, 31, 52, 53, 59, 60, 62, 72, 74, 77, 78, 81, 89, 90, 91, 96, 97, 99, 100, 101, 102, 103, 108, 109, 119, 125, 130, 149, 152, 153, 154, 156, 157, 163, 171
arts 2, 17, 32, 52, 63, 67, 68, 69, 71, 72, 73, 75, 77, 78, 81, 120, 134, 135, 157

Bauerlein, Mark 29, 32, 37, 40, 94, 112
Bettelheim, Bruno 96
Blacking, John
Blake, William 63, 80
Bolton, Gavin 119, 134

Boy Who Went Swimming 130, 131, 133
Brave New World 51
Bruner, Jerome 130, 134
Bumper Cars 106

Campbell, Joseph 34, 42, 98, 101, 112
Carr, Nicholas 29, 31, 32, 40
cellphones 11, 14, 27, 35, 36, 50, 93, 149
Change 3 activity 104
Che Che Kole 106
Children of the World 109
commercialization 143, 145
Common Sense Media 11, 12, 19, 25, 40
counterenvironment 3, 45–62, 68, 74, 77, 87, 111, 117, 120, 137, 138, 139, 157, 162
curriculum 9, 13, 15, 35, 38, 55, 56, 58, 60, 62, 67, 87, 92, 93, 94, 97, 99, 100, 102, 103, 104, 105, 106, 108, 110, 111, 112, 117, 118, 120, 134, 135, 138, 139

Dewey, John 117, 134
digital immigrants 24

digital media 2, 9, 10, 12, 13, 14, 17, 18, 21, 24, 25, 28, 34, 36, 37, 38, 58, 60, 68, 75, 79, 87, 91, 98, 106, 107, 110, 111, 137, 138, 139, 141, 146, 161, 162
Dolci, Danilo 3, 4
drama 3, 16, 18, 28, 67, 68, 69, 73, 74, 89, 96, 97, 108, 117, 118, 119, 120, 121, 122, 125, 126, 127, 129, 130, 134, 135, 145, 149, 150, 152, 157
Drama in Education vii, 3, 115
Dretzin, Rachel 31, 40, 79, 81

Edmiston, Brian xii, 119, 125, 135
educational arts 3, 9, 13, 17, 18
education-industrial complex 38
Eisenstein, Elizabeth ix, 55
Eisner, Elliot 76, 80, 81
electronic media 2, 8, 9, 10, 12, 15, 16, 17, 18, 23, 24, 32, 33, 35, 37, 40, 47, 52, 56, 60, 79, 88, 89, 90, 99, 110, 111, 138, 140, 141, 144, 145, 147, 155, 157
Everyone Has Stories activity 102

Facebook 1, 10, 11, 21, 24, 26, 27, 28, 29, 31, 36
Fahrenheit 451 51
Faust 23, 25, 39, 76
Frankenstein 50, 51, 90
Fulghum, Robert 88, 92, 110, 112

gaming disorder 25
Gardner, Howard 72, 73, 76, 81, 108, 112, 114
global village 10, 100
Greene, Maxine 68, 81
Guzzi, Ray 32

Hand, Samuel
Havelock, Eric ix
Heathcote, Dorothy 119, 134, 135
Hercules and the Wagon Driver 130, 131, 133
Herzog, Werner 28, 77, 81

Huizinga, Johan 34, 41, 96, 97, 113, 148, 149, 150, 151, 152, 153, 154, 156, 158

I'm Thinking of a Word 108

Jung, Carl 96, 98, 154

Kubrick, Stanley 49, 52, 54, 76

Langer, Susanne 68, 69, 81
Leakey, Richard 77, 81
literacy 3, 15, 19, 30, 54, 78, 79, 80, 85, 88, 115, 117
LuPone, Patti 27

McCaslin, Nellie xii, 118, 119, 135
McLuhan, Marshall 3, 7, 8, 9, 10, 13, 20, 21, 24, 42, 45, 61, 46, 47, 48, 49, 50, 51, 52, 53, 54, 56, 62, 77, 78, 87, 93, 111, 120, 133, 134, 148, 162
Mead, George Herbert 71, 81
media ecology 3, 8, 9, 13, 17, 18, 30, 47, 48, 49, 133, 139, 171
media environments vii, 3, 45
media literacy 9, 13, 15, 16, 17, 60, 114
Mithen, Steven 77
Morgan and Saxton 100, 119
multitasking 12, 28, 29, 41, 142
Mumford, Lewis 9, 77, 78, 81, 147, 149, 158
music, movement and dance 97, 105, 106, 107

neural circuitry 31

O'Neill, Cecily 118, 119, 120, 125, 135
Ong, Walter 55, 88, 89, 113
online gaming 16, 26, 27, 28, 143, 145, 158
Oprah 92
oral communication 88, 89
oral curriculum 3, 85, 87, 92, 94, 97, 99, 108
orality 88, 91, 110, 111, 113
Orwell, George 51, 76, 81

Paglia, Camille 53, 62, 77, 81
Paleolithic art 101

Piaget, Jean 96, 113
Pied Piper 126, 128
Plato 149, 163
Play 95, 97, 112, 113, 114, 139, 145, 150, 157
Poe, Edgar Allan 7, 19
Pop-up Puppet Theater 129, 130
pornography 33, 41, 43
Postman, Neil 1, 4, 8, 9, 13, 21, 23, 24, 25, 30, 32, 33, 42, 45, 46, 47, 48, 51, 54, 55, 56, 57, 58, 59, 60, 61, 62, 77, 78, 85, 112, 87, 91, 92, 93, 99, 100, 111, 113, 114, 115, 116, 117, 120, 133, 134, 135, 138, 140, 141, 143, 146, 148, 154, 156, 158, 161, 163, 162

Sales, Nancy 25, 27, 36, 42
school 20, 31, 37, 60, 94, 107
school-wide pageants 108
Seat on my Right 104
seesaw principle 3, 137, 138, 139
Shelley, Mary 50, 51
singing 106, 150
social media 8, 10, 25, 27, 92, 142
songs 73, 74, 75, 80, 86, 89, 90, 106, 107, 108, 140, 143, 146, 147, 150, 152, 153, 155, 156
Spolin, Viola 104, 114
STEM 80, 107
Sternberg, Robert 96, 99, 114
Storr, Anthony 70, 82

storytelling 97, 98, 99, 102, 103, 130, 154
Strate, Lance 8, 21, 30, 31, 42, 89, 114, 116, 135, 171
Swortzell, Lowell and Nancy xii

Tabone, Carmine 119, 121, 135
teaching 4, 13, 47, 55, 56, 57, 58, 62, 83, 112, 93, 113, 114, 135, 163
technophile 9, 12, 13, 14, 17, 18, 27, 30, 35, 38, 78, 161
television 1, 11, 12, 15, 16, 17, 19, 20, 21, 23, 24, 28, 29, 30, 33, 34, 39, 40, 43, 47, 48, 51, 56, 57, 58, 60, 78, 79, 90, 92, 95, 99, 104, 111, 121, 123, 124, 137, 138, 140, 141, 143, 144, 145, 146, 147, 148, 151, 154, 157, 158, 159
therapy 73, 81, 158
Tiger and Ox game 105
To Sir with Love 94
traditional children's games 34
transcendent narrative 58
Turkle, Sherry 36, 37, 43

video games 1, 12, 16, 17, 23, 24, 26, 40, 41, 42, 53, 78, 79, 137, 144, 146, 158, 159
Vygotsky, Lev 96, 97, 114

Ward, Winifred 118, 135
Weltsek, Gus xii
Who Started the Motion 105

Lance Strate
General Editor

This series is devoted to scholarship relating to media ecology, a field of inquiry defined as the study of media as environments. Within this field, the term "medium" can be defined broadly to refer to any human technology or technique, code or symbol system, invention or innovation, system or environment. Media ecology scholarship typically focuses on how technology, media, and symbolic form relate to communication, consciousness, and culture, past, present and future. This series is looking to publish research that furthers the formal development of media ecology as a field; that brings a media ecology approach to bear on specific topics of interest, including research and theoretical or philosophical investigations concerning the nature and effects of media or a specific medium; that includes studies of new and emerging technologies and the contemporary media environment as well as historical studies of media, technology, and modes and codes of communication; scholarship regarding technique and the technological society; scholarship on specific types of media and culture (e.g., oral and literate cultures, image, etc.), or of specific aspects of culture such as religion, politics, education, journalism, etc.; critical analyses of art and popular culture; and studies of how physical and symbolic environments function as media.

For additional information about this series or for the submission of manuscripts, please contact:
    Lance Strate, Series Editor | *strate@fordham.edu*
    Erika Hendrix, Acquisitions Editor | *erika.hendrix@plang.com*

To order other books in this series, please contact our Customer Service Department:
    peterlang@presswarehouse.com (within the U.S.)
    order@peterlang.com (outside the U.S.)

Or browse online by series:
    www.peterlang.com

CPSIA information can be obtained
at www.ICGtesting.com
Printed in the USA
BVHW042114120121
597696BV00017B/560